"My role in anti human trafficking in The Salvation Army means that I have told the story of The Maiden Tribute many times and know it well - or at least I thought I did until I read this book. The author's attention to detail, use of primary sources, and careful compilation of the facts gives the account real authenticity and the reader new insight into the horror of the exploitation and abuse of vulnerable girls and women in what might have been termed "very proper" Victorian England. In much the same way that Stead's nineteenth century account of women and girls being bought and sold into the sex trade kept the Gazette's readers impatient for the next day's instalment, I found myself propelled from chapter to chapter in anticipation of some new revelation. The question that must be asked is why is it that this account of lust, greed, and exploitation resulting in the brutalisation of innocent girls and women resonates so profoundly with the experience of those of us working with victims of human trafficking and modern day slavery today? My hope is that this compelling account of an extraordinary campaign will encourage many to once again join the battle to end this heinous crime against humanity once and for all."

MAJOR ANNE READ, ANTI-TRAFFICKING RESPONSE COORDINATOR, THE SALVATION ARMY

"Over a century later and the Eliza Armstrong Case is still relevant today. A story of what happens when individuals get a 'fire in their bellies' and as a result, the world is changed. As the author points out, there are still millions of 'Elizas' around the world and the fight still goes on. Thanks Cathy for relighting the fire in my head and soul again."

MAJOR ESTELLE BLAKE, ANTI-HUMAN TRAFFICKING COORDINATOR, THE SALVATION ARMY ITALY

"A real pleasure to read. A wonderfully honest retelling of a story that involves politics, law, intrigue, sex, scandal, and media coverage as well as a cast of compelling characters motivated by faith to change their world. The gripping story not only brings history to life but makes it impossible not to recognize parallels with our own society."

LT COLONEL EIRWEN PALLANT, THE SALVATION ARMY

**Other books by this author**

*William and Catherine: the love story of the Founders of The Salvation Army told through their letters*

*Life Lines*

# ARMSTRONG GIRL

## GIRL

## Cathy Le Feuvre

LION

Published by Lion Books
an imprint of
**Lion Hudson plc**
Wilkinson House, Jordan Hill Road,
Oxford OX2 8DR, England
www.lionhudson.com/lion

ISBN 978 0 7459 5699 2
e-ISBN 978 0 7459 6821 6

First edition 2015

A catalogue record for this book is available from the British Library

Printed and bound in the UK, May 2015, LH26

*Dedicated to all those who still work tirelessly to rescue and help those who find themselves the victims of human trafficking*

# CONTENTS

Chapter 1: Eliza in the Witness Box 9

Chapter 2: Sex and Victorian Society 15

Chapter 3: Rebecca Jarrett's Story 21

Chapter 4: Rebecca Meets The Salvation Army 29

Chapter 5: The Age of the Innocents 39

Chapter 6: Introducing William Thomas Stead 47

Chapter 7: Mr Stead, the Editor 55

Chapter 8: Getting the Girl 67

Chapter 9: The Maiden Tribute of Modern Babylon 79

Chapter 10: "A Child of 13 Bought for £5" 87

Chapter 11: An International Sensation 97

Chapter 12: "Filth and Obscenity" 109

Chapter 13: Getting Personal 121

Chapter 14: A Two-and-a-Half-Mile-Long Petition 129

Chapter 15: A Case of Abduction 139

Chapter 16: The Road to the Old Bailey 151

Chapter 17: On Trial 159

Chapter 18: Mother and Father in Court 165

Chapter 19: The Case for the Prosecution     177

Chapter 20: The Defence Begins     191

Chapter 21: Stead on the Stand     197

Chapter 22: The Defence Wraps Up     211

Chapter 23: Verdict     225

Chapter 24: Prison     233

**Epilogue**     247

**A Note from the Author**     257

**Endnotes**     261

**Bibliography**     279

# CHAPTER 1

# ELIZA IN THE WITNESS BOX

———

*I was 13 years old last April. Up to the beginning of June last I was living with my father, Charles, and mother, Elizabeth Armstrong, at 32, Charles Street, Lisson Grove. My eldest sister Elizabeth is 17; she was out at service. I have three little brothers, aged 11, 7, and 4. My father is a chimney-sweep. We had all been living at the same address for many years. I used to nurse and look after the youngest child, a baby. I attended at the Board School, and can read and write. I know Mrs. Broughton, who lived with her husband at No. 37 in the same street.[1]*

———

When Eliza Armstrong stepped tentatively into the witness box on an October morning in 1885 at England's most prominent court, it marked the beginning of a thirteen-day trial which would be followed closely by people at all levels of society, from royalty and government ministers and advisers at Westminster, to churches the length and breadth of England. The Old Bailey proceedings captured the imagination of those sitting comfortably in their aristocratic clubs and the parlours of the rising middle classes, right down to those on the poorest streets of the British capital where the majority of the population scraped a living however they could.

The high-profile trial was the culmination of a series of events which had obsessed Great Britain across the summer of 1885 and which had begun with a startling headline on a warm day early in July in one of the prominent daily London newspapers:

### Notice to our Readers: A Frank Warning
*The Pall Mall Gazette, 4 July 1885*

The articles published over the following week had exposed details of life in Victorian England which had outraged society and touched the conscience of the nation. The "Maiden Tribute of Modern Babylon" reports were salacious and scandalous for a society in which sex – the theme of the articles – was rarely spoken of. And the editorial gave fair warning of what lay ahead for its readers.

> *Therefore we say quite frankly to-day that all those who are squeamish, and all those who are prudish, and all those who prefer to live in a fool's paradise of imaginary innocence and purity, selfishly oblivious to the horrible realities which torment those whose lives are passed in the London Inferno, will do well not to read the Pall Mall Gazette of Monday and the three following days. The story of an actual pilgrimage into a real hell is not pleasant reading, and is not meant to be. It is, however, an authentic record of unimpeachable facts, "abominable, unutterable, and worse than fables yet have feigned or fear conceived". But it is true, and its publication is necessary.[2]*

The "pilgrimage into hell" which the readers of the *Pall Mall Gazette* were invited to join would include the tale of a child – called "Lily" – who the newspaper claimed had been purchased for the sex trade, a story that had eventually brought little Eliza to the Old Bailey where she faced a crowded courtroom.

The "Maiden Tribute Trial", as the case would later become commonly known, involved individuals from across the social spectrum starting with Eliza, a working class London girl who lived in what was then a rather run-down part of Central London – Marylebone.

The man presiding over proceedings at the Old Bailey was one of the leading judges of the day, the esteemed Mr Justice Henry Charles Lopes, and the prosecuting lawyer was none other than the Attorney General for England, Sir Richard Everard Webster, whose responsibilities included giving legal advice to Queen Victoria. Sir Richard led the case against an unlikely group of co-defendants.

There was the influential and self-assured editor of the *Pall Mall Gazette*, the often flamboyantly dressed William Thomas Stead (often known as W. T.), notorious for his outrageous campaigning journalism and the man behind the Maiden Tribute articles. Standing in the dock with him was Rebecca Jarrett, a haggard-looking reformed prostitute and brothel-keeper. In sharp contrast was the other female defendant – Mrs Elizabeth Combe, a refined Swiss national described as a "rich widow".[3]

Next in line was Sampson Jacques, a sometime private investigator, a tall and burly Greek man in his sixties. This mysterious individual, whose real name was "Mussabini", was variously described a "war correspondent"[4] and as a "freelance writer".[5] And finally, there was a gentleman in military-style uniform, William Bramwell Booth.

Bramwell, as he was known, was second-in-command of a new and growing Christian movement and the son of the founders of that organization, The Salvation Army. Standing upright in the dock, he held the large trumpet of a hearing aid to his ear. He had been hard of hearing since childhood, and without this he would have struggled to make sense of Eliza's evidence.

All eyes were turned on the child who was barely able to peer over the witness box into the room below as she began to tell her story.

—◆—

### Friday, 23 October, Central Criminal Court: Eliza Armstrong (Witness for the Prosecution)

*On the 2nd June a little girl told me someone wanted a servant and I went to Mrs. Broughton's house. Mrs. Broughton and the prisoner Jarrett, whom I had not seen before, were there. Mrs. Broughton asked me whether my mother would let me go out to service. I said I would go and ask my mother. I did so; my mother came up and went with me to Mrs. Broughton's.*

*Jarrett was still there, she asked my mother if she would let me go to service, mother asked her whereabouts she lived. I understood her to say Wimbledon. Mother asked why she could not get another girl where she lived? Jarrett said she could do so, but she thought a poor girl would like to go to a home where she lived...*

*Mother asked her what to do? She said to scrub and to clean oilcloth, because she could not kneel, and she would do the dusting and the other part of the work. I afterwards saw she was lame.*

*... The next day was the Derby Day. I saw my mother with Mrs. Broughton about 11 on the morning of Wednesday 3rd June. My mother told me something when she came back, which Mrs. Broughton had said to her, and I went with her to Mrs. Broughton's. Mrs. Jarrett was there, she asked mother if I had any nice clothes to go in, mother said I had not. Jarrett said she would buy me some, because her husband was a particular man. Jarrett told me to go home, wash myself, and get myself all ready, and I was to go along with her to buy some clothes.*

*... Afterwards I came back to Mrs. Broughton's. Mrs. Jarrett was there, and put on her things, and went with me to the boot-shop at the corner of Charles Street. Up to that time I had not heard what Jarrett's name was.*

*While going to the boot-shop she said I should like going into her service very much. She then took me into several shops, and bought various articles of clothing for me. She paid for them and brought them with her. We went back to Mrs. Broughton's, where I put on my new clothes. Nothing further was said by Jarrett, nothing was said about what my wages were to be. I went home for about an hour, and had dinner there. I had left Mrs. Jarrett trimming my new hat at Mrs. Broughton's, the other clothes I had got on.*

*When I went home to dinner I saw my mother. I don't remember whether I saw my father. Afterwards I went back to Mrs. Broughton's, at about 2 o'clock in the afternoon. My mother did not go with me. I saw Jarrett in the room, and she said she was going to start at 3 o'clock. I stayed there till 3, I had seen my mother at the door, and kissed her before I came away.*

*My mother said she would see me off. At 3 o'clock she was to meet me in Mrs. Broughton's room. I waited at Mrs. Broughton's about an hour, till 3 o'clock, when Mrs. Jarrett said it was time to go. I was then all dressed ready to start, with the hat on which Jarrett had trimmed. Jarrett, Mrs. Broughton, and I went out together. Nothing was said about mother not having come back.*

*When we started Mrs. Broughton and Jarrett went into a public-house. I waited outside. Jarrett and I got into an omnibus at the corner of Chapel Street... I said good-bye to Mrs. Broughton, we got out of the omnibus past the Marble Arch, and went to a house I know now as 16, Albany Street.*[6]

———

Although the prospect of standing in the imposing Old Bailey courtroom must have been daunting for the child, Eliza Armstrong gave her evidence simply, coaxed gently by the Attorney General to explain what had happened to her on Derby Day, 1885.

The details she outlined may have seemed inconsequentially mundane but they were the fundamental building blocks of the case. Eliza's removal from her home in Charles Street, Lisson Grove, in the Marylebone area of London, on 3 June was at the heart of the circumstances which led to the trial.

How had her departure from Charles Street come about? Did Eliza's parents know where the woman walking with a limp and a stick was taking their daughter? Apart from the fact that she appeared to be friendly with their neighbour, Mrs Nancy Broughton, what else did they know, or suspect, about the woman who suddenly appeared in their street seeking a young girl who might work for her?

The five defendants listening carefully to the evidence of the child on that first day of their trial all faced the same charge: "Unlawfully taking Eliza Armstrong, aged 13, out of the possession and against the will of her father" and other counts charging them for the taking of Eliza from the possession of the mother.[7]

In plain English, Stead, Booth, Jarrett, Jacques, and Combe were all charged with *abducting* Eliza Armstrong. For Eliza was, of course, "Lily" – the girl bought for the sex trade, whose story in the *Pall Mall Gazette*'s Maiden Tribute of Modern Babylon articles had so outraged the nation.

## CHAPTER 2

# SEX AND VICTORIAN SOCIETY

"From three o'clock in the afternoon it is impossible for any respectable woman to walk from the top of the Haymarket to Wellington Street, Strand." With these shocking words, just a handful of years before Eliza stepped up into the Old Bailey witness box, Howard Vincent, director of the Criminal Investigation Department at police headquarters at Scotland Yard had reported to a Committee of the House of Lords on the state of prostitution in London.[1]

The 1881 inquiry was the latest investigation into the sex trade in a society which was becoming increasingly obsessed with what some saw as the moral decline of the nation. Although there had always been prostitutes willing to sell sexual favours to those lining up to buy, by the mid to late nineteenth century in England there was a growing number of social campaigners who believed the sex trade had reached unacceptable levels and was undermining the very bedrock of their culture.

Formal reports to Parliament, official studies, and newspaper reports had down the years all served to fuel the concern of those worried not just about the women and girls who they believed were exploited in the sex trade, but also the spiritual and moral state of a nation which appeared to tolerate such "immoral" behaviour. A growing group of people, many of them motivated by their Christian faith, also believed the current laws relevant to the sex industry were both unfairly biased towards protecting those who used prostitutes and inadequate to safeguard the vulnerable women who were the sellers of sex. The debate around what was becoming known as "The Great Social Evil" was growing by the year.

Despite this increasing awareness, sex (particularly prostitution) was not generally spoken of in polite society, or even in impolite society in Victorian England, although you didn't have to dig very deep to find evidence of it. People perhaps preferred not to consider what the brightly dressed and rouge-cheeked girl on the corner of the street under the gaslight might have been up to, as she slightly lifted her skirt to momentarily reveal a flash of ankle to the young man on his way home from work. And in the upper class drawing rooms of Great Britain, some wives might have secretly wondered why their husbands sometimes returned home from their clubs later than usual with a whiff of cheap perfume about them. At a time when marriage was often undertaken for convenience rather than any notion of romantic love, wives remained silent. Sex within marriage may have produced children but it was not guaranteed to come with any expectation of enjoyment or even fidelity. Indeed, at some levels of society there was an understanding that men would inevitably get their pleasure outside the marital bed.

There were the courtesans of high society in their salons and fancy carriages in which they paraded in Hyde Park. They mixed, often quite publicly, with members of the aristocracy [2] and some even had royal patronage. The heir of Queen Victoria, later King Edward VII, loved the company of women, from the actresses Lillie Langtry and Sarah Bernhardt to several long-term mistresses, including society hostess Alice Keppel. His voracious sexual appetite made him a frequenter of high-class brothels, including the exclusive La Chabanais in Paris, and it was said that women threw themselves at him especially on his travels in Europe.[3]

At the other end of the sexual social spectrum there were brothels in gloomy backstreets where "street girls", and boys in some cases, made a living in rented rooms. For those who could not even afford that luxury, there were the many dark alleyways and corners of London. Here was the living of many a woman who, in the absence of regular well paid work in any other field, turned to the one asset they were sure of – their own bodies – and the knowledge that there were always men who would pay for them.

However, in summer 1885, when the *Pall Mall Gazette*'s Maiden Tribute of Modern Babylon articles claimed that the newspaper not only had *evidence* of the depths to which some of those involved in the sex trade were sinking, but also *proof* that some of the "girls" in the capital's brothels and sex establishments were little more than children, it lifted the lid on a world about which most people either remained largely ignorant, or preferred to ignore.

Despite, or maybe because of, the "frank warning" delivered to its readers on 4 July, the *Pall Mall Gazette*'s stories on the extent of the sex trade were a sensation. Editions of the newspaper were consumed in their hundreds of thousands across the United Kingdom and further afield, and in Parliament the articles reignited interest in this most contentious of issues.

For campaigners against the Great Social Evil, the Maiden Tribute of Modern Babylon was just what was required to awaken the world to reality. More importantly, it was intended for a specific purpose by its author William Thomas Stead, who had a long-time interest in exposing the exploitation of women.

In 1885, the age of consent – defined as "the age up to which it shall be an offence to have or attempt to have carnal knowledge of, or to indecently assault a girl"[4] was just thirteen. The limit had been raised from twelve in 1875 but Britain was still far behind many other European countries where the age of consent was much higher; in France at this time, for example, the age of consent stood at twenty-one.[5]

The age of consent was crucial to the debate around the Great Social Evil because although child prostitution was common and, indeed, informally accepted,[6] if not entirely condoned, there were those who felt differently. Many campaigners were both angered and disgusted by it and believed that if the age of consent were raised, a generation of young girls would be protected from being abducted, procured, or lured into the sex trade.

There was a general belief among some campaigners that most women would not choose a life as a street woman, prostitute, courtesan, or mistress but that wasn't entirely the case. There were certainly those in the sex trade for whom it was a choice, or at least an option through which they could make more money than in domestic service or other such menial employment.

There had been several attempts to calculate the numbers of full- and part-time prostitutes working the streets of London and of Great Britain but these had failed to bring about consensus, largely because they were often based on extrapolations of population numbers rather than firm evidence.

In 1857, the medical journal *The Lancet* estimated that one in sixty houses in London was a brothel, and one woman in every sixteen was a "whore",[7] which if correct would make the number of brothels 6,000 and the prostitute population 80,000 in the capital alone. However, in that same year the doctor and author, William Acton, claimed that the police believed there were 8,600 prostitutes in London. In 1870, in a second edition of his book, *Prostitution, Considered in its Moral, Social, and Sanitary Aspect, in London and other large cities and Garrison Towns, with Proposals for the Control and Prevention of Attendant Evils,* Acton quoted other possible figures. These ranged from 6,371 – the responses to a police survey presented to Parliament in 1839 – to an estimation by the Bishop of Exeter "of the numbers of women working the streets as reaching 80,000". Through his own calculations based on birth and marriage statistics and other facts and figures available to him, Acton believed that there were many more street women than even that estimated figure. He claimed that "219,000, or one in twelve, of the unmarried females in the country above the age of puberty have strayed from the path of virtue"[8] reflecting the view that many of those following this profession had *chosen* a life of impurity.

Whether or not that was the case for adults working in the sex trade, campaigners believed that children who found themselves caught up in the world of brothels were too young to make that sort of choice. They were victims, and the age of consent was part of the problem. Because of the low age of consent at that time – thirteen – sexual crimes against children were almost impossible to prosecute. When it came to children of no consequence, including working class girls like Eliza, the police had better things to do with their time than deal with the circumstances surrounding such a child's disappearance from home.

Even if the police had been concerned, they could not act against brothel owners because the power to investigate brothels lay in the hands of the local authorities.[9] However, those local magistrates and officials who had the right to check up on and even prosecute brothel owners had to use the police to investigate on their behalf. And even if proof was found against someone running a brothel, the only charge that could be made was one of "keeping a disorderly house", which protected the neighbours more than the girls who might have been the unwilling occupants.[10]

Campaigners in favour of raising the age of consent were becoming aware of the flow of young girls into the sex industry, from the evidence they saw on the street and stories they heard from those whom they spoke to when they were "rescued" from the brothels. But the extent of the problem and the size of the wider sex industry were still largely unknown.

That's where Mr Stead and his investigation leading to the Maiden Tribute of Modern Babylon articles came in. For some months, Stead, already well known for several successful journalistic campaigns, had been looking for a new cause to further raise the profile of his newspaper. This had coincided with a number of debates in Parliament which had failed to raise the age of consent, upon which the *Pall Mall Gazette* and other newspapers had reported and commented. Over the months running up to summer 1885, Stead had also been courted by several campaigners who wanted him to get involved in raising the profile on the sex industry with a view to shaming Parliament into reviewing the age of consent legislation.

Among those who contacted him was Bramwell Booth, aware that Salvation Army leaders, or "officers", were increasingly seeing vulnerable women and girls turn up at their shelters seeking help. Bramwell had been persuaded to approach Mr Stead by his mother, Catherine, and his young wife, Florence, who headed up The Salvation Army's women's work and had already related some very distressing stories to her husband.

Catherine Booth had become an advocate for street women as early as the mid-1860s. She had first visited the Midnight Movement for Fallen Women[11] when preaching in Bermondsey, and from that time help and "salvation" for this particular group had been high on her agenda. She was part of a loosely connected group who became increasingly determined to improve the lot of and provide protection for what they considered "fallen" women. In some quarters this was called the "Purity Movement" and central to it were not just the Booths, but others of their acquaintance, including Josephine Butler, the wife of George Butler, the Anglican Canon of Winchester. She too was a long-standing advocate of the rights of street women, a vehement opponent of laws which criminalized prostitutes, and a leading campaigner for raising the age of consent.

And it was ultimately as a result of the connections between Mrs Butler and the two Mrs Booths that Bramwell Booth, the second-in-command of The Salvation Army, and Rebecca Jarrett, one of its new converts, found themselves facing an abduction charge at the Old Bailey.

# CHAPTER 3

# REBECCA JARRETT'S STORY

*My father died and left my mother with 7 young children with no means to keep them. The eldest of them begged of my mother never to marry again, they would do what they could to help her, two of them got into Woolich dock yard [sic]. From there they went off on ships… My eldest sister was sent to Melbourne in Australia. We never heard of her again. I was the baby left. The two boys got lost in the ship, 2 sisters died with cholerie [sic] so I was only left with my mother. She had to keep her home on for me and herself. She had to work hard for her living. She sent me to a good private school but I was left a lot to myself. On Sunday my mother was at home it took her all morning to clean up and get her home clean and strait [sic], look after my clothes to see they were clean and tidy for me to go to school with the next day. She was very proud of my hair. Poor old mother.*

*I had very fair hair then, it took her some time to wash it and keep it clean and then if it was fine she take me to Cremorne Gardens if she had the money to spare. If not there was public house right facing Chelsea College. In that gardens was as much wrong going on as there was in Cremorne but they were the old pensioners and the women. It was little summer houses. Many a time I had to bring my poor mother home the worse for drink on Sunday night. I was only 8 or 10 years of age.*

*You wonder why so young I got in the way off [sic] an impure life, why I was brought up in it though clean but impure? That was why I left my home so early to begin my life of sin and degradation. At Cremorne I got my money, was well known...*[1]

Aged nearly eighty, Rebecca Jarrett looked back on her life and recalled the point at which she had started life as a sex worker. It was forty years since her trial at the Central Criminal Court in London – four decades during which she had led a virtuous life as a member of The Salvation Army. At the start of this "life-sketch", penned seven years before her death, Rebecca introduced her short memoir with these words: "This is written by my own self, not to boast of my disgusting life, no, but to show how good Jesus is to a poor, lost, degraded woman."[2]

The young Rebecca Jarrett was typical of the sort of girl who became part of the London street scene in the mid-1800s, from a poor background, with a mother who had turned to drink and had little income or even perhaps little inclination to work. But for the trial at the Old Bailey many years later when the world got to know about her, Rebecca's life and story would have remained as anonymous as those of the millions like her.

Rebecca had been born in Pimlico, near to the present day Victoria area of London, which was then "the borderland between some of London's very poor and very rich homes".[3] Some reports say her father was a rather well-to-do rope merchant who spoke out on "the drink",[4] but Rebecca claimed that he squandered his money on other women and her mother had to "work like a slave to keep me, her thirteenth child".[5] At some point when Rebecca, the youngest of their thirteen children, was a baby, Mr Jarrett disappeared. Rebecca believed that he died, which is probably what she was told by her mother, although he may have deserted the family, leaving Mrs Jarrett with seven or eight children still at home and requiring support. Up to that point, Rebecca's mother appears to have been a kind parent and a good housekeeper.[6]

When two of the three brothers at sea were drowned it would

have been not only a devastating personal loss, but also a financial one. The boys had allowed half their pay to be sent home to support their mother and siblings. Mrs Jarrett, it seems, found life increasingly hard to deal with and she took to drink. Ale and beer were readily available and especially popular because the water supplies were not to be trusted. Although the communal water pumps had been much improved since the 1850s, when a link was first proven between dirty water supplies and cholera, a disease that had already killed many millions of Londoners, the pumps were still not a guaranteed source of clean water. Watered-down beer would have been preferable for most and it appears that Mrs Jarrett increasingly used it. She also turned to "strong drink" and that required money.

No matter how much Mrs Jarett loved her youngest daughter, Rebecca would also have been considered an economic asset, especially as she grew into womanhood. So, before the child was thirteen, she was introduced to a life of promiscuity. The visits to the alehouse and the perpetual drinking sprees of her mother and her drinking buddies could now be financed.

Cremorne Gardens, in Chelsea, was one of the many "pleasure gardens" which existed across London. They were large gardens in the centre of the busy city, with what was described as "grand old trees" and plenty of amusements, including bands and even firework displays. For an entrance fee, which included a glass of wine or spirits, there was dancing to be had, and a good deal more. Although in the daytime these gardens might have presented themselves as innocent places for family gatherings,[7] Rebecca herself declared that Cremorne and places like them were known for what else was on offer and "respectable" men would avoid them.[8] It was a market place, and Rebecca and many thousands of young girls like her were bought and sold:

> *Cremorne Gardens were my ruin. My mother was often*
> *under the influence of drink, and she got me into the way*

*of looking for my share. Sometimes on Sunday nights the*
*gardens were closed at ten, and if you had seen our procession*
*coming home you would never think you were in a Christian*
*country. All that was in the beginning of my young life.*[9]

With the example of such a mother, Rebecca's own life soon also became a long round of public houses, drink, and sex with men of all ages. There was a brief glimmer of hope for a better future when her last remaining brother returned from the sea, got a job in the West End as a stoker, and was prepared to help support his mother and sister. However, when he learned what was going on at home, he challenged his mother, saying that the fifteen-year-old Rebecca's lifestyle would have to alter, otherwise he wouldn't allow her into the house. Not long afterwards, mother and daughter arrived home, drunk as usual, and Rebecca did, indeed, have the door slammed in her face. She slept in the yard that night and then set up her own home, undoubtedly paid for by some of her "customers".[10]

By the time she was sixteen, Rebecca was managing a house where men would bring girls for sex. In places like Cremorne Gardens, the owners of such houses would walk about and when they saw a man and a woman or girl together, would invite them back to the house for their "liaison". It was a lucrative business. Rebecca admitted in her memoir that she could charge what she liked once the men had used the room, threatening to tell their wives about their secret lives and effectively holding them to ransom.[11] Even if they never returned, there would be more clients the next day.

Apart from a couple of years when she moved to Derbyshire with a man with whom she lived until their child died, this was Rebecca Jarrett's life for over two decades. Well into her late thirties she was still a brothel-keeper and indulging in what she herself would later describe as a "gay" life... Her youth and charm had all but gone, her lifestyle showed in her features and demeanour, and she was no longer in demand. With the prospects of sex work drying up, she began to realize that she needed to find another way to make a living and, like many before her, she tried all sorts of menial tasks. One particular job in a high-class hotel favoured by aristocrats and royalty brought her into contact with another person who would feature prominently in the events of the summer of 1885.

---

### Thursday, 29 October, Central Criminal Court: Rebecca Jarrett (Witness for the Defence)

*In the year 1883 I was at work in the laundry at Claridge's Hotel; about May, I think it was... Mrs. Broughton was employed there during that time; she was employed in the wash-house and I was in the ironing room. I became acquainted with her... I became intimate with Mrs. Broughton at that time, I visited at her house, I went there on the Sunday when the work was finished; on the Sundays I have been round three times to tea there...*

*When I used to be in the laundry we used to go in the washhouse during our dinner-hour; we had young men employed there to look after the machinery. We used to carry on with a young man... It was on these occasions that it came out about my past life. I told her during the dinner-hours that I had been bad, and had kept a gay house. I mentioned Manchester to her, and Bristol, and I told her, through my health being so bad with my gay life, I had to give it up, and that was why I was trying to get on in the laundry...[12]*

---

Rebecca's time at Claridge's came to an end after three months due to her hip "coming to be bad" and she left with a month's meagre wages of £1.16s.6d.

After a six-week hospitalization at St Bartholomew's, she was sent to a "convalescent cottage" in Petersfield, Hampshire, in the south of England. On returning to London and with nowhere to stay, Rebecca turned to her friend from Claridge's, and Ann Broughton – nicknamed "Nancy" – offered hospitality. She stayed at the Broughtons' house, near to the home of the Armstrongs in Lisson Grove, at one point travelling to Margate on the Kent coast but subsequently returning to London and the Broughtons while she attended the nearby Marylebone Infirmary.

The Marylebone "hospital" was typical of the institutions of the day which catered for those who could not afford private doctors or health care. Victorian England was no place for the poor and ill. The only places available to the sick and impoverished were charity institutions or workhouse infirmaries, including Marylebone. The workhouses and the infirmaries were not designed to be attractive long-term residences, so Rebecca and many thousands like her, who required medical attention, would not have lingered long in "hospital". It was fortunate Rebecca had friends she could stay with nearby, and she also relied on private charities for handouts and help.

Through the Charity Organization Society, in April 1884, Rebecca was found employment in Chiswick, an area of West London. Within months she had to leave, owing to her continued failing health. By September of that year she had gone back to the streets to make ends meet, even though she could hardly stand up due to her bad hip. She was living with a man, a "Mr. Sullivan" who had been a commercial traveller but who, during their time together, lived off Rebecca's street earnings. She was ill and drinking heavily.

In November 1884, Rebecca made a decision which would ultimately alter her life.

*Well, you say, how came you to get mixed up with The Salvation Army? In those days if you were over twenty-five years of age no rescue home would take you in. Here I was, about thirty-six. I was too old to be reclaimed, besides I was almost dying through the drink. How could I give it up? It made me have a bit of a life; if you were not bright the men would not come again; they paid your rent and supported you. No, you must drink, if it finished you up.*

*At last I got taken out of London to Northampton, to see if the change would help me. It was no use, the doctor down there said so; I was given up; in fact, I gave myself up.[13]*

## Chapter 4

# REBECCA MEETS THE SALVATION ARMY

When Rebecca Jarrett arrived in the East Midlands town of Northampton she was far from well. She wasn't alone but travelled with a male friend. The company she was keeping may not have been entirely helpful in complying with the orders of her doctor, that she needed "rest and recuperation and a break from heavy consumption of alcohol".

On checking into their hotel, Rebecca spotted a notice that announced a meeting arranged by something called "The Salvation Army". They promised "great doings" by a "hallelujah clergyman", someone called the "Hallelujah Sweep" and "Great Firing by Great Guns".[1] Although there's no evidence that she had shown any interest in religion before, the poster intrigued her.

The "Hallelujah Sweep" in question was a certain Elijah Cadman, who was typical of the sort of characters which The Salvation Army was attracting to its ranks and who helped it to expand rapidly.

Cadman was an illiterate former drunkard who had been forced up the chimneys from the age of six and who, by the age of seventeen, reckoned he could "fight like a devil and drink like a fish".[2] Aged twenty-one, after heckling a street preacher in the town of Rugby, Cadman was converted to Christianity, learned to read and write, and then spent his spare time as a Methodist lay preacher. After meeting William and Catherine Booth, renowned preachers and evangelists who had just created their own Christian

Mission in London, the little man – he stood just five feet tall – was captivated by their enthusiasm and radical thinking. In 1876, he sold his chimney sweep business, travelled with his wife and children to London, and joined the Mission in Hackney, where he visited the slums by day and preached by night.

Although rough and ready, he became one of the leading lights of the Booths' Mission and crucial to its early development. Even before 1878, when William Booth, his aide-de-camp, George Scott Railton, and his eldest son, Bramwell Booth, decided to change the name of the Christian Mission to "The Salvation Army", Elijah Cadman had been among the first to begin using military terminology. He addressed his leader as "General" William Booth – short for "General Superintendent of The Christian Mission" – and referred to himself as Booth's "lieutenant". Cadman is also credited with the idea of The Salvation Army uniform. At the movement's first "War Congress" in August 1878, just months after its name was changed, Cadman announced, "I would like to wear a suit of clothes that would let everyone know I meant war to the teeth and salvation for the world." [3]

The Salvation Army which Rebecca Jarrett met that day in Northampton was, therefore, not the product of the Booths alone, but also people like Elijah Cadman. While it is not clear whether Rebecca actually heard the influential Cadman preach or if the announcement she saw outside her Northampton hotel was an old poster, the description of the "Hallelujah Sweep" and his "great doings" was enough to fascinate her, and so she found her way to the local Salvation Army meeting hall in an old prison building.[4]

There she would have found a congregation which mixed the poor and the rich, the educated and the illiterate; in its early years The Salvation Army attracted people from all levels of society. Although most of the first converts of the new Christian movement were working class, the Booths' message of "salvation through Jesus Christ" was for everyone. While William Booth often preached to the "common people", Catherine was invariably to be found addressing middle and even upper class audiences. The Salvation Army reflected this diversity as the "salvation" message got through not only to drunkards, thieves and ruffians, and street women and prostitutes like Rebecca, but also to those who, despite their education and even wealth, felt a lack of something spiritual.

Rebecca's friends at the hotel would have laughed if they'd known she intended to slip out that night to attend a peculiar religious gathering but she did just that, and the reception she found there astonished her. Hoping to remain inconspicuous, she took a seat at the back of the crowded hall, but in her large and rather flamboyant hat, and looking very unwell, she stood out. The leader of the meeting, Captain Susan Jones, made a mental note of the tall woman who had slipped into the gathering after proceedings had started.

The meeting hall was crammed full and it was hot and stuffy. As was normal in the early Salvation Army, the singing of hymns, choruses, and songs was enthusiastic and loud, as was the preaching and the "altar calls", when people were urged, in an atmosphere charged with emotion, to make their way to the front to kneel at the "penitent form" to give their lives to Jesus and be "saved" from their sins. At some point in all this, the frail woman in the large hat succumbed to the heat and fainted.

As Rebecca dropped to the floor, Captain Jones rushed the length of the room, along with some of the other Salvation Army "officers", urging the crowds to make space so the woman could breathe as she came round. As she bent over Rebecca, Captain Jones could see how ill she was and inquired as to where she was staying so that someone could see her safely back to her accommodation.

Rebecca declined. As she later wrote, "I did not want the man to see all those people with strange bonnets, some with tambourines in their hands, taking me to the hotel."[5] But the very next day, Captain Jones turned up on the doorstep, having done a little inquiring as to the tall woman's whereabouts. Rebecca had obviously been on her mind, and when she tracked her down she learned the truth about her circumstances and, more importantly, her very poor health.

Rebecca Jarrett's collapse at The Salvation Army meeting in Northampton had brought her into contact with one of the many colourful characters who inhabited the early Salvation Army and to whom Rebecca would have felt some affinity. Captain Susan Jones was the daughter of a rat-catcher. Her early life had been hard as she travelled the country with her father selling his rodent extermination services, which led to her nickname of "Hawker". She too had liked a drink or two herself in the past[6] and her harsh experiences of life on the road meant she hardly flinched at the sight of a debauched old prostitute. After her conversion to Christianity and her recruitment by The Salvation Army, the down-to-earth Susan Jones had already helped street women in two of her previous appointments – at Keighley in Yorkshire and in Warrington (then in Lancashire). She had even cared for girls in her own home when they expressed a desire to leave prostitution.[7]

So when Captain Jones met Rebecca at the Northampton hotel after her collapse at The Salvation Army meeting the previous evening, she recognized the woman was in desperate need of some loving care and attention. Much to Rebecca's astonishment, the Captain offered to take her home. Rebecca's male companion gladly accepted, perhaps relieved to no longer have the responsibility for such a decrepit and sickly woman. Captain Jones and the other Northampton Salvation Army "officers" arranged for Rebecca to visit a doctor, who thought that hospital was the only place for her. Her new Salvation Army friends had other ideas and took her back to their "quarters" – their own home – to be nursed and cared for.[8]

For Rebecca Jarrett, whose life to date had been largely one of abuse, corruption, and rough living, which had made her not just the exploited but also, on many occasions, the exploiter, these simple kindnesses were a revelation.

Captain Jones and other leaders across the country would have known that in London, where The Salvation Army's mission was most developed, ad hoc arrangements for helping vulnerable women had in recent months led to the creation of a "refuge" for street women. A "hostel" had been established in the East End, in Hanbury Street, in the same Whitechapel vicinity where the Booths had originally established their movement.

The opening of the Hanbury Street Refuge was a landmark moment for the young Salvation Army, because it effectively initiated the movement's official residential "social work" among the disadvantaged, part of the charitable work for which it is now renowned worldwide. As soon as it opened, Hanbury Street Refuge became home not only to girls and women from London but also from across the country. Salvation Army officers like Captain Susan Jones now had somewhere to refer the women who came to them seeking assistance to leave the sex trade and find a place of safety.

Florence Booth, young wife to The Salvation Army's Chief of Staff, Bramwell Booth, was in charge of the recently established outreach work among women. But these were early days for the mission and soon Florence and her team found themselves overwhelmed with the needs of the many women who came to them for help. Within months of opening, the Whitechapel Refuge was full to overflowing, and on 25 October 1884, The Salvation Army weekly newspaper, *The War Cry*, carried the following announcement on behalf of Florence Booth:

**SPECIAL NOTICE!**
*Captains must not send any cases to The Salvation Army Refuge for Women in Whitechapel without first ascertaining whether there will be room to receive them, or they will have to be sent back, which causes great inconvenience and disappointment to all concerned.*

**Write to Mrs Bramwell Booth**[9]

*The War Cry* was warning its readers, and its Captains, not to send girls there without warning. So would the Hanbury Street Refuge take Rebecca Jarrett? Most of the girls there were young and Captain Jones was concerned that Rebecca might be considered too old. But she was convinced that it was the best place for her, and she contacted Whitechapel. It didn't take long for the decision to come back. There was a place for the old brothel-keeper and not just a bed, but a welcome, as Rebecca later recalled in her memoir.

> *The Captain drove up to Hanbury Street Refuge,*
> *Whitechapel, a place where I had never been in my life*
> *before. It was certainly not the place that attracted me...*
> *But there I saw what for many years I had never seen.*
> *Everybody had shut the door against me. I was one of*
> *London's kept women, living a life of immorality, getting*
> *my living by it; but a lovely young mother with a red jersey*
> *on rushed up and kissed me and said "I have been waiting*
> *for you to come, dear". It was a poor little back kitchen, but*
> *its memory is very sacred to me. It was their welcome! The*
> *frozen-up heart got a bit of a crack.[10]*

Rebecca was in the care of a Mrs Cotterill and her staff and she couldn't have been in safer hands. Many years later when writing his memoirs, Bramwell Booth, by then second General of an international Salvation Army, would outline the role Mrs Cotterill had played in the development of the work among street women and the start of The Salvation Army's social work programmes.

> *From our earliest days as the Christian Mission, there*
> *came, occasionally, to our penitent form in Whitechapel,*
> *unfortunate girls who looked to us for some means of*
> *enabling them to throw off the fetters of their deadly calling.*
> *Here and there kind women-comrades would fix up these*
> *poor creatures for a night or two, but that was only a very*

*casual and uncertain method of dealing with the problem.*
*Presently, one motherly woman, a baker's wife, who had*
*already given up her front room to Magdalen, suggested to*
*me that if only she had more accommodation she could take*
*in these girls for a few days and look after them until they*
*were passed on to some employment.*[11]

The baker's wife was Elizabeth Cotterill, a member of the
Whitechapel mission and Salvation Army "corps", or mission
station. For some years she had been taking street girls home
when she found them, despite the fact that she had a husband and
six children already. On some nights, the family's little house at
the aptly named No. 1 Christian Street in the East End of London
also sheltered three or four "unfortunate young women".

In spring 1884, Mrs Cotterill, who had been praying that a larger
property might become available for her "girls", saw a house for
rent on nearby Hanbury Street. As she could not afford the rental,
she got in touch with Mr Bramwell Booth[12] and very soon the place
was acquired and opened as the first Salvation Army refuge.

Safely in the care of this Mrs Cotterill, Rebecca Jarrett was
soon also visited by Florence Booth who took her to the London
Hospital, where the orders were "ten weeks' bed rest". As Rebecca
lay sleeping, being cared for by these angels of mercy, she felt
loved – a whole new experience for her. She also received a visit
from the "Army Mother" – Mrs Catherine Booth herself – who,
like her daughter-in-law, made a great impression on her.

Florence was a quietly spoken and sincere young woman who
had lived a very sheltered life until she came into contact with
the Booths and The Salvation Army. The daughter of a doctor,
she had shown great academic potential and secretly harboured
an ambition to become a physician herself, but in the days when
female doctors were only just coming on to the scene, that
profession was not open to her. However, to celebrate passing
her final school exams, she visited a couple of aunts in London.

While there, she attended a meeting of The Salvation Army in Whitechapel, in the East End. She heard a woman preacher – Catherine Booth – and decided to "follow Christ" and learn more about this new "Army" of Christian believers.

Soon the young Florence Soper joined their ranks. By 1881, she had been promoted to the rank of "Lieutenant" and, as her schooling had included instruction in French, spent time in France helping the Booths' eldest daughter Catherine, also known as "Katie", launch The Salvation Army's work there.

Florence had become increasingly close to General and Mrs Booth and also to their eldest son. On 12 October 1882, aged not yet twenty-one and so requiring special permission from her at first reluctant father, "Captain" Florence Soper married Bramwell Booth. In a few short years, her life had changed dramatically and although she was becoming accustomed to dealing with a whole host of difficult issues and individuals, she admitted in later life that she found her early meetings with Rebecca Jarrett difficult.

The woman's appearance was a challenge to her faith, because "the marks of her dissolute life were very plain". Florence recoiled at first, but her impression, written many years later in a magazine called *Sunday Circle*, gives us a good idea of the image Rebecca Jarrett presented to the world at that time and undoubtedly to those gathered at the Old Bailey not more than a year later. Rebecca's face, Florence Booth wrote in March 1933, was "almost repulsive and showed plainly the ascendancy that alcohol had gained over her".[13]

It's likely that Rebecca was aware of the effect her appearance had on others, and this may have made her doubly grateful for the love she was being shown while resting and recuperating at the Hanbury Street Refuge. While being physically cared for, Rebecca Jarrett was also coming under the spiritual influence of The Salvation Army. When she had regained her strength and was on the mend, she went to lunch with the two Mrs Booths, Catherine and Florence, and it was there that she prayed for the very first time, expressing a desire to be "saved" from her sinful life.

But that wasn't the end of it. Rebecca, like so many before and after her, struggled to maintain the change in lifestyle and expectations that living a Christian life required. Not long after that lunch, Rebecca wrote to Florence Booth, saying that she couldn't keep up the new life. It was too hard. She admitted that she had made an appointment with a "former companion in evil" and would "go back to the old life".[14] Florence rushed over to Hanbury Street, and she and the other refuge officers spent a whole day trying to persuade Rebecca against going back to the streets.

"I made an earnest appeal to her, saying that if she left us she would be turning her back on God and Heaven and deliberately choosing sin and hell. Rebecca suddenly fell on her knees sobbing, prayed earnestly, and as I listened I realised the Saviour had received her afresh,"[15] Florence later recalled.

To help Rebecca Jarrett in her new life away from the streets and the only work she had ever known, arrangements were made for her to move away from London. What better than to place her in the care of someone who might help her to develop in her new spiritual life – a great friend to the Booths, Mrs Josephine Butler, who lived miles from the capital, in the ancient city of Winchester?

# CHAPTER 5

# THE AGE OF THE INNOCENTS

---

***Monday, 2 November, Central Criminal Court:***
***Josephine Butler (Witness for the Prosecution)***

*I am the wife of Canon Butler, of Winchester. I have a hospital there for the assistance of poor women who have been in trouble; it is called "The House of Rest".*

*I made the acquaintance of Rebecca Jarrett in January last. Mrs. Bramwell Booth introduced her to me. I had heard of her coming under the influence of the Salvation "Army" people at Northampton, some little time before. She was a patient in my hospital for some weeks; then I introduced her to mission work in our own town, and in Portsmouth, to carry out the mission work. She continued under my superintendence to work in that way until May, when she came to London, and after that she resumed; but up to May she worked continuously at mission work, and gave entire satisfaction to me, and conducted herself apparently well and zealously.*

*During the last week in May I had a communication from Mr. Stead, in consequence of which I spoke to Rebecca Jarrett to see whether she would go up to London, and told her what she had to do. She was unwilling to come, on account of her own feelings. She had lived on intimate terms with me as a friend and fellow-worker, and I communicated to her my intense desire to reform this system; and then I urged upon her that to make reparation*

*for her past life she should do what was required of her,*
*and she partook of my feelings in the matter.*[1]

———∽∾∽———

Josephine Butler, devout Christian, wife of a Church of England canon, was a well-known and passionate campaigner for the rights of prostitutes not to be criminalized by the law, and those who knew her well would not have been surprised that she was involved in the case which resulted in the Maiden Tribute trial, giving evidence on behalf of one of the defendants. She and Catherine Booth were both part of the Purity Movement, and for years Mrs Butler had been a prominent voice against something called the Contagious Diseases Acts, which she believed were unfairly biased against women in the sex trade.

The Acts had been first introduced in 1864 (with updates in 1866 and 1869) following a series of parliamentary reports into the levels of venereal disease in the armed forces. This legislation was designed to cut the levels of sexually transmitted diseases such as syphilis and gonorrhea. In order to reduce the number of women on the streets who might infect the men, the Acts allowed police officers to arrest prostitutes in some ports and army towns. The women were forced to submit to medical checks, and if found to be infected, could be confined in what was known as a Lock Hospital until cured.[2]

Campaigners such as Josephine Butler were furious about the inequalities of the law, which criminalized women while allowing men who were infected with venereal disease to avoid any consequences. She persuaded Catherine Booth of the need to campaign both to reform or even to repeal the Contagious Diseases Acts. However, she and her cohorts were not only interested in promoting the legal rights of women; they were also concerned for their physical and spiritual well-being. Accommodation and support for the likes of Rebecca Jarrett was established, including Mrs Butler's House of Rest in the south of England.

So close was the relationship between Mrs Butler and the Booths that when Rebecca needed somewhere safe to go, preferably outside London and away from all her old haunts, The Salvation Army turned to their friend in Winchester. Rebecca travelled south to live in the care of Mrs Butler, where she very soon got involved in helping other women who came to the House of Rest. But it wasn't enough for Mrs Butler, Catherine Booth, and the other Purity Movement campaigners to offer practical assistance to adult prostitutes like Rebecca. These campaigners were also focused on the numbers of young girls who, they were aware, formed a proportion of the sex industry in Great Britain, and particularly London.

The parliamentary reports on various aspects of the sex trade and prostitution across several decades had begun to expose not just the extent of prostitution in the British capital city, but also the ages of those involved. Indeed, twenty years before the 1881 Committee of the House of Lords when Howard Vincent of Scotland Yard reported streets crowded with prostitutes who openly solicited clients in broad daylight, there was evidence of the numbers of young girls working in the trade. In the early 1860s, a London Police Survey had calculated that there were 30,780 women working on the streets of the capital and more than 2,000 of them were under sixteen. In the year of the survey, London Hospital treated 2,700 children between the age of eleven and fourteen for venereal disease.[3]

Campaigners such as Catherine Booth condemned polite society "which winked at such cruel slavery" and allowed "the participants in such vice to escape with impunity".[4] Catherine and others like her maintained that most prostitutes had been "lured" or bullied or seduced into a life of prostitution; in their minds there was no doubt that a child could not choose such a life.

The close friendship and liaison between Mrs Butler and Catherine Booth meant that when Bramwell Booth himself began to hear some of the stories of girls who claimed they were forced into the sex trade, Mrs Butler was among those to whom he turned for advice.

Bramwell Booth had been involved in his parents' mission from boyhood. Born in 1856, just a year after his parents' marriage, as a young child he and his seven siblings had been encouraged to "give their hearts to Jesus" and spend their lives serving the Lord. Aged about fourteen, he had taken on his first responsibility, heading up the Christian Mission's "Food for the Millions" feeding and relief programme. From his earliest years, he had been destined to follow in his parents' footsteps and was the heir apparent of his father, General William Booth.

Bramwell's profound deafness was not seen as a hindrance and he was at the very centre of The Salvation Army. Indeed, it had been partly as a result of his initiative that the Christian Mission had been renamed. When reviewing the Christian Mission's 1878 Annual Report with his father, William, and his aide George Scott Railton, Bramwell had apparently objected to the fact that the Mission was referred to as "a Volunteer Army". He claimed that he was no "volunteer" but a "full timer" in the service of God. His father, William Booth, had leaned over the document, deleted the word "Volunteer", and written in its place the alternative description: "Salvation". The Salvation Army had been born.

By the mid-1880s Bramwell appeared older than his age, with an often serious look and a long, thick, dark beard covering a good deal of his face. He was invariably to be found wearing the navy blue military-style uniform, tight to the neck and with braid across the chest, which was the hallmark of his Salvation Army. He would often top this off with a peaked military cap and a voluminous cape as he made his way back and forth to the Central London offices and travelled across the country in the course of his increasing duties as second-in-command, or "Chief of the Staff" of the Army.

Bramwell's mother, Catherine, was confident that once he knew the extent of the problem concerning the girls "lured" into prostitution, her son would find a way to help put society right. And when his young wife, Florence, started telling him about some of the girls who were resident at the Hanbury Street Refuge, the pressure to do something was on. Bramwell knew Florence had been suffering from bouts of sleeplessness, but was unaware that what was keeping her awake at night were the intimate and distressing stories of some of the girls with whom she was working. Even though they were married, such intimate matters were not generally spoken of but eventually Florence had blurted out the reasons for her insomnia and, although he was at first embarrassed to hear the details, Bramwell listened as she poured out the pain she felt on behalf of the women who came to her for help. Bramwell required more evidence. He undertook his own investigations and had taken counsel not just from Mrs Butler, but also the 75-year-old Benjamin Scott, whose experience as the Chamberlain of the City of London confirmed some of his wife's stories.[5]

Bramwell's worst fears about what he, his parents, and other campaigners believed was the moral decline of his nation were confirmed one day when he arrived at work. Early that morning, a girl called Annie Swan had presented herself at the front door of The Salvation Army's new headquarters building in Queen Victoria Street, just south of St Paul's Cathedral, asking for refuge.[6] It was only when he spoke to Annie that Bramwell began to realize the extent of what could only be described as a "slave trade".

Bramwell's own memoirs contain Annie's story:

*The girl was brought to me, a decent, well-favoured girl of about seventeen, wearing a very beautiful red silk dress. She told me that she had come from the country to London in answer to an advertisement for a girl to help in the general work of a house, and had been received on arrival by the mistress who had answered the application. She soon found, however, that she had been entrapped into a brothel.*

*As the days went by her "mistress" urged her with increasing force to be a "lady" like the others in the house, gave her the red silk dress, and compelled her to visit a certain music-hall in her company. The girl resisted all importunities, but escape seemed to be impossible, and she did not know what to do or where to go. On the previous night a man had made himself very objectionable, whereupon she fled and barricaded herself in one of the kitchens, yielding neither to threats nor cajolery. After some time she heard the landlady say, "Leave her there till morning; she will come to her senses when she wants her breakfast."*

*Left alone, the girl remembered amid her alarm and agitation that in her own town she had attended some meetings of The Salvation Army, and that in her box was an old song-book, which bore on its cover the address of General Booth. He was surely the one person in the entire great city who would help her! It was four o'clock in the morning; everything was still in the house. She waited a while and then crept up to her room, found the little red-covered song-book, and slipped out. Inquiring her way of a policeman, she walked from Pimlico to Queen Victoria Street, and remained outside the door of Headquarters until it was opened.[7]*

Annie's claims might have at first appeared far-fetched but her story was quickly confirmed. Bramwell sent a man to the address from which the girl said she had escaped and although initially denying any knowledge of her, when The Salvation Army officer told them they had Annie and she was safe in their care, the residents admitted that she had been in the house and they released her box of belongings.

Annie's story and the other harrowing narratives which his wife had shared with him gave Bramwell many days of questions and anguish. He wondered where the police were in such circumstances and why this kind of offence was allowed to go on in the heart of civilized London. He wanted to change things, including wanting to increase the age of consent. It might not help people like Annie – but it would help girls younger than her.

## CHAPTER 6

# INTRODUCING WILLIAM THOMAS STEAD

The Booths were determined to raise the age of consent in order to protect girls from the Great Social Evil, but they knew they couldn't do it alone. And the man to whom Bramwell turned for help in order to stir the conscience of the nation and Parliament was someone they believed could achieve just that: William Thomas Stead.

As an up-and-coming newspaper editor, Stead was a man on a mission to make his mark on the world. But he was impatient. Not for him years of quiet endurance in a back office. Stead was determined to make a noise, and on a day in late spring 1885 when Bramwell Booth sought him out at his London offices, he realized he had discovered the perfect opportunity to do so.

Stead was unlike most of the London newspaper editors of the day. He spoke in an accent which indicated an upbringing in the north-east of England, and he was by all accounts rather brash. He eschewed the usual dark suits and tall black silk hats of gentlemen for lounge suits, invariably of brightly checked, garish tweed. A crumpled brown hat could often be found crushed on his head, and he was to be seen rushing from appointment to appointment with a well-used notebook and pencil in one hand and a battered old leather bag stuffed to overflowing with papers hanging from his other elbow.[1] Within a short time of arriving on the London scene he had gained a reputation for being "one of the worst dressed men in London".[2]

In July 1885, a London correspondent of the *North Eastern News* gave this description of the man who had recently masterminded the series of newspaper articles which had shocked society:

*The editor of the Pall Mall Gazette is somewhat under average height. He has a reddish beard, and his light-blue eyes give a singularly frank and youthful appearance to a face which would otherwise have an old and careworn look. His manner corresponds with his expression; it is frank and simple almost to childlikeness. He begins to talk about the subject uppermost in his mind almost before he has got well inside the room, and anyone who listens to him is at once convinced that he is saying exactly what he thinks.*[3]

Stead had been with the *Pall Mall Gazette* since 1880, and editor since 1883. The paper was based in offices in No. 2 Northumberland Street in London, which ran into the Strand at the south end of Trafalgar Square. In Stead's day, this area was not particularly fashionable. The down-at-heel accommodation – made up of a series of cramped rooms described as a bit of a "rabbit warren" with a rat-infested basement that housed the presses[4] – might not have been ideal, but it suited Stead because it was relatively close to Parliament and polite London society which provided many of the stories he fed to his growing readership.

Northumberland Street was a long way from William Stead's boyhood home, the mining village of Howdon, near Newcastle, on Tyneside, where he was raised in a large family, the son of a minister of the Congregationalist Church, a nonconformist, puritan, and conservative Christian denomination. The family's finances were tight, and the Stead children were initially educated at home, which proved to be no disadvantage. By the age of twelve, William had learned Latin, German, and French, as well as all the usual school subjects of reading, writing, and arithmetic.[5] Being raised in a devoutly Christian environment, he read the Bible daily.

William was always on the go, running rather than walking, and always full of ideas and enthusiasm, traits that would travel with him into adulthood. He enjoyed drawing, and writing stories. As a boy, he entered essay-writing competitions, all penned in beautiful copper-plate handwriting. He was an intent listener and early on developed a knack of being able to transcribe conversations he had had with other people, a skill which would serve him well in his later chosen career of journalism. As he grew older, his parents encouraged him to teach Sunday school and he became an excellent public speaker.[6]

In 1861, aged twelve, William was sent to Silcoates School, in Wakefield, Yorkshire, where he reportedly enjoyed life, despite the strict regime. Here he contributed articles and poems to the school magazine and, although he had been brought up to be a good Christian boy, at Silcoates he experienced what he described as a real "conversion" to the Christian faith, at a prayer meeting.[7] Years later, in a memoir of her father, his daughter Estelle presented William's account of that period in his life, which he wrote down in 1904 as he thought back to that time:

*The tradition of the school in the fifties had not been distinctly religious. All of us came from Christian homes, but, as a school, it was very much like other schools. About a month after I entered Silcoates, some of the lads started a prayer-meeting of their own in a summer-house in the garden. They asked me to join, and I went, more out of curiosity, and to oblige my chum, than for any other reason. There were about half-a-dozen of us, perhaps more, none of us over fourteen. We read a chapter in the Bible, and we prayed. No master was present, nor was there any attempt made on the part of the masters to encourage the prayer-meeting. One master, indeed, was frankly contemptuous. The majority of the boys had nothing to do with "the prayer-meeting fellows". One or two of us were under deep conviction of sin, and we talked among ourselves, and read the Bible and prayed.*

*Suddenly one day, after the prayer-meeting had been going on for a week or two, there seemed to be a sudden change in the atmosphere. How it came about no one ever knew. All that we did know was that there seemed to have descended from the sky, with the suddenness of a drenching summer shower, a spirit of intense earnest seeking after God for the forgiveness of sins and consecration to His service. The summer-house was crowded with boys. A deputation waited upon the Principal and told him what was happening. He was very sympathetic and helpful. Preparation class was dispensed with that night; all the evening the prayer-meeting was kept going. There was no singing, only Bible reading, a few words of exhortation, a confession of sin and asking for prayers, and ever and anon a joyful acknowledgment of an assurance of forgiveness. Those of us who could not find peace were taken out into the playground by their happier comrades, who laboured with them to accept Christ. How well to this very day do I remember the solemn hush of that memorable day and night in the course of which forty out of the fifty lads publicly confessed conversion.*[8]

For William, this was no passing childhood phase. He became a member of the Congregational Church in Wakefield – a denomination to which he would belong for the remainder of his life. His conversion during that heady time was real and would be one of the defining factors in his life, motivating much of what he did in the future, even those moments which others considered "scandalous".

Being from a nonconformist family which believed in a "personal" relationship with God through Jesus Christ, William's conversion would have been celebrated. His brilliant father, who it's said William tried to emulate throughout his life,[9] now had even higher expectations of the son who was named for him. William's mother, Isabella, had already been a tremendous influence on the boy, to whom she had passed a love of literature and art.[10] She was an early campaigner for the rights of women and one of the opponents of the government's controversial Contagious Diseases Acts and from his mother the young William took on the conviction that a man must always uphold the rights of the "fairer sex".[11]

Aged fourteen, with school days behind him, William moved to Newcastle to begin his working life as a clerk in a shipping office – Carr and Company in Broad Chare, the notoriously dark and rather dangerous Quayside district, where vagabonds lurked around most corners. On his daily journey from his lodgings to the Manors Railway Station and then a walk to his workplace he would have passed some of the worst streets in Newcastle, where girls plied their trade and beggars were numerous.[12]

Under the supervision of a genial and devout employer, Charles Septimus Smith, who was almost certainly a family friend as well as a great influence on William, the young clerk continued to learn diligence and charity. He earned four shillings a week but lived simply, keeping only three pence a week for himself: one of which he spent on an edition of Shakespeare and the second which he gave to charity, leaving just one penny for "pocket money".[13]

Stead was already displaying habits that would distinguish him as an adult, and it was an incident involving his generosity which led to his first ever published article for a local newspaper. In the Quayside district where he worked, paupers and beggars could often be found asking for a hand-out and there was one man who, particularly on payday, would appear to seek out the young clerk and ask for a penny or two. Touched by the man's need, William eventually gave him his overcoat, into the pocket of which he had tucked a small Bible. He also invited the man back to his lodgings for some food.

That night William received a lesson in the realities of life. The poor man to whom he gave his best overcoat did return to his lodgings. And he went away not just with food in his belly, but most of the young man's possessions. He stole everything he could lay his hands on and fled. The only thing he left behind was the Bible![14] William was furious, not just because an excellent con artist had duped him, but also because he felt that by stealing from him, the pauper had also deprived other more needy people of the benefit of his generosity.

There's no record of whether William reported the incident to the police, but he did write a letter to all the local newspapers in the north-east of England highlighting the need to avoid charitable giving at will. In the letter he suggested the setting up of an agency which would ensure that only people in "real need" were helped and which would weed out the cheats and rogues.[15] William even devised a name for this new organization – he called it a "Society for Organised Charity" or, using a word relating to the condition or activities of beggars, the "Mendicity Society".

When the editor of the recently established *Northern Echo* in the nearby town of Darlington received the young man's letter he was delighted, not just with its content but because it was beautifully handwritten, and it was published on 7 February 1870.[16] William was encouraged, and he wrote another letter. His subject this time was the slum properties in the area. This epistle was so impressive that the editor printed it as a leading article. Now William was inspired. He continued to write letters on similar subjects, and all were printed.

During the previous couple of years, Stead had already shown a great interest in journalism, following some of the latest national and international stories closely through the newspapers. He particularly liked the idea of educating the public through the reporting of news, as well as encouraging readers to action.[17] He admired the *Newcastle Daily Chronicle*, owned and edited by a local entrepreneur, Joseph Cowen, who had begun to introduce a more "personal" form of journalism imported from the United States of America.[18]

Stead was encouraged that a newspaper wanted to print his efforts in journalism and after he had had eighteen articles published, he decided to ask for some payment. There was no money for freelancers at the *Northern Echo*, but by now he had made quite a name for himself in the local newspaper world. When the editor unexpectedly resigned and no replacement could be found, the paper's owner, John Hyslop Bell, turned to the unknown contributor of the well-written letters who signed himself "W.T.S."[19]

It was 1871 and, at the age of just twenty-two, William Thomas Stead had not even stepped over the threshold of a newspaper office. Now he found himself the youngest newspaper editor in the country, in charge of a paper with a daily circulation of 10,000 copies. Instead of being intimidated as many a young man might have been, he embraced the opportunity. He had already realized that journalism was a great way to promote his many areas of interest, including his growing interest in international politics and his religiously motivated schemes and aspirations for the world. He was determined on a new type of journalism which would not just perpetuate the civic and political establishment of the day, but challenge and even lead the national agenda.

Through journalism, he believed, he could become a voice in a dark world that might speak out for the many thousands who had no voice. He saw the appointment as God-given, as he wrote in his diary at the time: "To be an editor!... to think, write and speak for thousands... It is the position of a viceroy... But... God calls... and now points... to the only true throne in England, the Editor's chair, and offers me the real sceptre... Am I not God's chosen... to be his soldier against wrong?"[20]

## CHAPTER 7

# MR STEAD, THE EDITOR

---

***Monday, 2 November, Central Criminal Court:
William Thomas Stead (the Prisoner). Examined by
Mr. H. Matthews, from a statement handed in by Stead.***

*I have been editor of the* Pall Mall Gazette *since the
midsummer of 1883… Since my connection with the press
I have constantly written in favour of the alteration of
the law for the protection of women, and I was cognisant
of the labours of the Committee of the House of Lords on
this subject, on the amendment of the Criminal Law, in
1883 and in 1884; I was aware of the various Bills for
the protection of women that passed the House of Lords,
and were in some way defeated in the House of Commons;
and I, as a public writer, discussed those measures as they
appeared from time to time, and constantly pressed for
their amendment in the sense of further protection being
given to women and girls.*

*Mr. Benjamin Scott was also very much interested in
this question; I may say his letter upon the subject of the
foreign traffic in English girls was one of the determining
causes which made me come to London from Darlington
in 1881, where I edited the Northern Echo for nine years.
One of the determining causes for my joining the London
press was in order that I might the more efficiently
advocate this cause.*

*Mr. Benjamin Scott had a committee of his
own, meeting on the subject in order to promote the*

*improvement of the law; and he communicated with me on the subject on the 23rd of May of this year, the day after the Criminal Law Amendment Bill was talked out in the Commons. I called on him on the subject of the failure of the Bill, the absolute sacrifice of it as I was told. Mr. Scott and I went together, and saw Mr. Bramwell Booth on that subject that afternoon. The subject of our conversation was the further protection for women and girls.*

*I had previously received communications from Booth on the subject and he, as well as Mr. Scott and myself, was interested in this subject. We discussed what best might be done in order to promote the cause I had at heart, with the view of getting facts. We did not know what could be done then, but what I did say was that before anything was done we ought to get to know the facts...*

*From Mr. Booth I learnt that there was such a person as Rebecca Jarrett. He wrote to Mrs. Butler at my request, and sent up Jarrett on Whit Monday. I went to Mr. John Morley, my predecessor on the Pall Mall Gazette, shortly after I left town, and I communicated with Lord Dalhousie, who was the Chairman of the Committee of the House of Lords – he had introduced the Criminal Law Amendment Bill into the House of Lords.*

*I first saw Jarrett on Whit Monday afternoon, the 25th May; she brought with her a letter of introduction from Mrs. Butler... I had a long conversation with Jarrett; about two hours I think. I questioned her very closely as to her past experience in the business of procuring girls. She gave me a considerable number of details of a very ghastly character. I told her that if all was true that she told me, she must prove it; it was too horrible to be believed merely upon the word of a person like her. She objected, and I insisted. I told her that if she was truly repentant she ought not to object to help us in this matter, or to help me… that she deserved, if what she said was true, to be hanged in this world and damned in the next, and the least she could do was to make what reparation she could for the crimes which she had confessed.*

*I think that argument had weight with her. I said that if she had procured girls for dissolute men she must procure some girls for me, as if I were a dissolute man. I said, "If what you say is true, there are girls who are in the market who are sold to brothel-keepers; if that is so, the best way to prove it is to go and buy in the market; will you go and buy for me one, two, or more girls who are in stock, and who would probably be sold?" I may have said, "who would be sold to someone else if you do not buy them".*

*She hesitated, and said she must ask Mrs. Butler – I had a long conversation, and I explained to her that, having bought the girls, instead of ruining them as they would be ruined in the ordinary course of business, we intended to rescue the girls, and then be able to use the facts of such purchase in such a way as to render all such purchases in future impossible or dangerous.*

*I pressed upon her the consideration that if she would do this thing she would be the means of saving far more girls than all those whom she admitted she had helped to ruin in the past.[1]*

———

When William Thomas Stead began giving evidence at his trial at the Old Bailey in November 1885, he gave the impression that he had long been interested in the righting of the cause of girls who were being sold into the sex trade. And by the time he came to writing The Maiden Tribute of Modern Babylon articles, he was not only wholeheartedly and publicly part of the campaign to highlight this evil but central to it. However, initially he had to be persuaded of the extent of the scandal before he would commit to becoming involved in helping to highlight the trade in girls, with the aim of persuading Parliament into quickly ensuring the passage of the Criminal Law Amendment Bill into law. Previously Stead had also been rather daunted by the task ahead, realizing that publication of the facts would break every taboo of society and media coverage, and that, given the history of attempts to get the law passed through Parliament, it stood little chance of success.[2]

Without Bramwell Booth his job would have been harder. As he explained to the court, it was Bramwell who facilitated the meeting with Rebecca Jarrett and he also gave Stead access to several young women who were able to provide first-hand accounts of their experiences, which left the editor shocked, as Bramwell later recounted in his memoirs:

> *When the interrogatories [sic] were ended and the girls had withdrawn, there was a pause, and I looked at Stead. He was evidently deeply moved by what he had heard. It had shaken his vehement nature, and presently his feelings found vent. Raising his fist, he brought it down on my table with a mighty bang, so that the very inkpots shivered, and he uttered one word, the word "DAMN!"*
>
> *This explosion over, I said "Yes, that is all very well, but it will not help us. The first thing to do is to get the facts in such a form that we can publish them." Stead agreed; we not only took counsel together, we prayed together, and then he went away.[3]*

The Booths and Stead were no strangers to each other. There is no doubt that with Stead's profile as a leading campaigning editor writing on the social issues of the day, among other things, the Booths would have heard of him. And Stead knew of the Booths. Growing up within the Christian community in the north-east of England, he must have become aware of William and Catherine

Booth, who ministered in the Methodist Church in Gateshead near Newcastle for a period prior to July 1861. He may have followed their progress after they left the safety of a denominational post to begin working as "freelance" evangelists across the country, and then onto London where they finally settled and established their Christian Mission.

Later he would write about the "arrival of The Salvation Army" to Darlington in 1879, an account which was later included in his daughter Estelle's *Personal & Spiritual Reminiscences* of her father. His report on his meeting with the early Salvation Army is a wonderful description of the organization with which he would later have so much contact. That first meeting also gave Stead great insight into the motivations of the people who had committed their lives to service in William and Catherine Booth's mission.

*At first respectable Darlington held aloof. Then the emissaries of respectability ventured down, in sheer curiosity, to see what was going on. They returned puzzled. Nothing was going on. No dancing, no extravagance, no tomfoolery, no sensationalism. The two girls, Captain Rose and Lieutenant Annie – one two-and-twenty, the other eighteen – conducted a religious service, not unlike an early Methodist meeting, with hearty responses, lively singing, and simple gospel addresses, brief and to the point. The penitent form and the after prayer-meeting, in which the lasses, going from seat to seat, personally addressed everyone who remained as to their spiritual welfare, were the only features in which it differed from an ordinary mission revival service. But the odd miraculous thing that bothered Darlington was the effect which it had. All the riff-raff of the town went to the Livingstone Hall, and many of them never returned the same men.*

*At last I went to see the girls who had turned Darlington upside down. I was amazed. I found two delicate girls – one hardly able to write a letter; the other not yet nineteen*

*– ministering to a crowded congregation which they had themselves collected out of the street, and building up an aggressive church-militant out of the human refuse which other churches regarded with blank despair. They had to provide for maintaining services regularly every week-night and nearly all Sunday, in the largest hall in the town; they had to raise funds to pay the rent, meet the gas bill, clean the hall, repair broken windows and broken forms, and provide themselves with food and lodging. And they did it. The town was suffering severely from a depression in the iron trade, and the regular churches could with difficulty meet their liabilities. But these girls raised a new cause out of the ground, in the poorest part of the town, and made it self-supporting by the coppers of their collection. Judged by the most material standard, this was a great result. In the first six months a thousand persons had been down to the penitent form and a corps or a church was formed of nearly two hundred members, each of whom was privileged to speak, to pray, to sing, to visit, to march in procession, to take a collection, or to do anything that wanted doing.[4]*

As someone determined to defy convention, Stead admired The Salvation Army's difference to other "churches". As a Christian he appears to have been impressed by their ability to attract congregations and bring a message to the "human refuse" who might not have felt welcome in the other churches. From what they knew of his reputation, the Booth family must have realized that W. T. Stead was also not averse to "rocking the boat" of respectable England.

Stead's campaigning journalism had begun almost immediately when he took up the editorship of the Darlington *Northern Echo*. The newspaper already had a good reputation for its reporting, but when Stead was appointed editor in 1871 he quickly took the content to a new level and within a couple of years the paper had become one of the most widely read journals not just in the north-east but further afield, with copies selling as far away as Edinburgh and London.[5]

Through his journalism, Stead began to articulate some of his personal agenda. He began to break some of the rules of "Society" editors. He published articles highlighting issues such as prostitution and the local Darlington brothels, referring in one leading article to "wealthy men, churchwardens and deacons, husbands and fathers, not only in the habit of frequenting houses of ill-fame but even acting as 'dealers in the very evil traffic'".[6]

He even used the pages of the Darlington *Northern Echo* to spotlight international issues. Stead had long been fascinated by Russian affairs, and at one point struck up a friendship with a Russian émigré called Olga Novikov, who gave herself the title "Her Excellency". Although Stead was by this time married and had fathered the first four of his six children, the editor still flirted with Madame Novikov. (This wasn't the first, and it certainly wasn't the last flirtation which Stead would have with women other than his wife. The long-suffering Emma would in due course withdraw marital rights and become cold towards her husband, not just because of his "affairs of the heart" but also as a result of outrage against some of his professional antics.)

Over the years since the Maiden Tribute trial, Stead's at times almost fanatical determination to throw light on the sex trade has been put down not just to his religious conviction. Some commentators have suggested that, perhaps, Stead was himself sexually repressed, resulting in an almost obsessive interest in the matter of sex. Some believe this crusading spirit came from his deep attachment to his mother and although self-control and religiosity kept him for the most part on the straight and narrow,[7] he is believed to have become Olga Novikov's lover, with liaisons arranged during trips south to London.[8]

Madame Novikov opened doors for the young Stead, however. She is thought to have been instrumental in helping to get him the post of deputy editor of the *Pall Mall Gazette* in the summer of 1880,[9] and he in turn often advocated on behalf of Russia in his columns. Early on he railed against the British government for its lack of action during the Bulgarian Atrocities of 1876. It was estimated that 8,000 men, women, and children were slaughtered in that country by Turkish irregulars responding to a nationalist uprising on the western boundaries of the Ottoman (Turkish) empire, but the British government was largely silent, wishing, Stead complained, to preserve a twenty-year diplomatic understanding with Turkey rather than tackle them about the atrocities.[10]

Stead was not afraid to upset the ruling parties of the day. In fact, he increasingly began to see it as his duty as a newspaper editor to do so. He gathered enemies, including Benjamin Disraeli, but also supporters such as William Gladstone – both Prime Ministers of the United Kingdom.[11]

By the time Stead reached the *Pall Mall Gazette*, he already had a reputation for outspoken reporting. When he arrived, the *PMG* was a rather Conservative paper intent on keeping a rich and powerful readership rather than being read by a wider population.[12] Politically, it was diametrically opposed to Stead's *Northern Echo* which was seen as Liberal. Yet when offered the post of *Pall Mall Gazette* deputy editor under the editor John Morley, Stead was persuaded to make the move to London and soon, despite some misgivings – he was being paid less than he'd hoped, for one thing – he agreed to take the position. Morley was mostly absent from his desk because he was writing a book and also had ambitions to sit in Parliament. Consequently, Stead quickly made his mark, not just on the content of the *Pall Mall Gazette*, but also on the style of writing, and even the layout.

British newspapers of the time were heavy on type and words, with few if any headlines and no images. There were news summaries and "Occasional Notes" in the *PMG* early into his tenure, but Stead expanded the news and introduced more gossipy elements into the Notes. He also persuaded the editor, and the newspaper's owner "Thompy" (Henry Yates) Thompson to introduce maps and diagrams. In addition, he broke up the long articles with crossheads or subheadings, a completely new innovation in English newspapers.[13]

Stead's inclusion of, for want of a better description, celebrity interviews and news, bold headlines, and campaigning journalism which took not just a political but often a religious and moral stance in line with its editor's personal agenda, left him with a legacy: today, he is often described as the world's first tabloid journalist.

Stead's first forays into spectacularly opinionated journalism came in 1883 after Morley decided to stand for election as MP for Newcastle, and gave up the editorship of the *Pall Mall Gazette*. Stead was, finally, in charge and could dictate the content and the message of the newspaper. His first major campaign as editor was a series of articles, run over a three-week period, which exposed the living conditions of London's poor.[14] Shortly after the articles ran, a Royal Commission was established to investigate the conditions under which many thousands of people were living, which Stead immediately claimed as a victory for the *Pall Mall Gazette*, and himself.[15]

Always seeking the next thrill, by New Year of 1884 Stead had moved on to even bigger subjects. His reputation for involving himself in foreign affairs had gone before him to the English capital. By the time he was in charge of a significant London newspaper, Stead's personal agenda included trying to influence government policy where he felt politicians were not taking action, and a crisis in the Sudan in north-east Africa gave him such an opportunity.

After invading Sudan in 1882, the British had control in the region but had come under attack from local insurgents, led by the Mahdi, a former slave trader who claimed to be the new messiah and whose aim was to rid his land of the British invaders.[16] The British army garrison at Khartoum was under siege, the whole area was considered unsafe for foreigners, and the British government, under the Prime Minister, Gladstone, was considering a wholesale withdrawal from the region, even though it would have left Khartoum vulnerable to being overrun by the Mahdi and his troops.

Initially the *Pall Mall Gazette* had called for this course of action while others in the country saw that withdrawal would be disastrous for the reputation of the British empire. By New Year 1883, however, Stead appears to have changed his mind, and his change of heart was reflected in the *PMG*'s leader columns which called for quick intervention.[17] The Mahdi must be stopped, Stead wrote. He and his "troops" were on the verge of taking over the whole of Sudan and then there was a danger that he would move on to Egypt which was historically, diplomatically, and geographically a crucial ally for Great Britain.[18]

Stead's new idea was that the government should send Khartoum a "hero" to save the day. The man he considered fit for the task was General Charles Gordon, a popular veteran army commander nicknamed "Chinese Gordon", who had gained notoriety about twenty years earlier when he had crushed another rebellion, in Taiping in China.[19] Gordon had had a distinguished military career, seeing action for the empire across the world, including Egypt and north and eastern Africa. He had also spent some time as Governor-General of the Sudan, where he had led initiatives against the slave trade. Now considered by some to be beyond his prime, he was back in England, but looking for his next opportunity.[20] Stead believed Gordon was the man to save Khartoum.

Through Reginald Brett,[21] a friend who knew General Gordon and who shared Stead's confidence in his ability to save the day, the editor made contact with Gordon, asking for an interview, a request which was promptly turned down. Gordon replied that he had "nothing to say". Undeterred, Stead immediately set out for Southampton, where he turned up on the doorstep of the house where General Gordon was staying with his sister. The door was answered by a slim, short man with bright eyes and a rather squeaky voice. Presuming this was the manservant, William Stead asked to see General Gordon.

"I AM General Gordon!" the man replied.[22]

Despite this inauspicious start to the meeting and the fact that General Gordon had not wished for the interview, the two men spent several hours together. Stead made no notes, but instead relied on his phenomenal memory when he wrote up the article, which was published on 9 January 1884 and entitled "Chinese Gordon on the Soudan" [sic]. This story was a sensation, although it was undoubtedly a mixture of Gordon's own views and those of the writer.[23]

Stead, as editor of the *PMG*, demanded that Gordon be sent to the Sudan immediately. The day after its appearance in the *Pall Mall Gazette*, the article was reprinted in other London newspapers and crowds in the streets were heard to chant "Gordon must go! Gordon must go!"[24] The pressure on the government and on Prime Minister Gladstone in particular, was immense. Imagine Stead's pride and pleasure at what he believed was *his* doing? He appeared to have forced the hand of government! He crowed about it in his next leader column, thanking the government for "tardily" obeying his instructions.[25]

Gordon was dispatched to the Sudan but he had only one other British officer for support on his journey and, when he reached Khartoum, could do little against the strength of the Mahdi's growing army. Despite using every trick in his military book to defeat the insurgents, Khartoum eventually fell in February 1885 when all Westerners, including General Gordon, were murdered. A small relief army, sent to help, arrived three days later.[26]

"TOO LATE!" was the headline in the *Pall Mall Gazette*. It was the first ever use in a British newspaper of a 24-point headline[27] and it shouted at readers across the road from the newsstands.

The government took the blame for the fiasco, although they tried to claim that Gordon had gone mad. On 9 June, the Liberal government led by Gladstone was defeated in a no-confidence vote, following intense criticism – not only of the fall of Khartoum but also their handling of ongoing violence in Ireland – and Robert Cecil, the Marquis of Salisbury, was invited to form a new Conservative government.[28] As for Stead, he seemed to quickly forget his part in the whole Sudan affair. At first he shifted the blame for the Khartoum fiasco and the death of a British hero onto others, and then promptly dropped the story altogether.[29]

Stead's friend "Reggie" Brett apparently once said of the editor: "Nothing has happened to Britain since 1880 which has not been influenced by the personality of this extraordinary fanatic, visionary and philanthropist."[30] Although that is an outrageous claim, it goes to show the high profile which Stead had already attained by the time he came to his next "big campaign" – the Maiden Tribute of Modern Babylon.

# CHAPTER 8

# GETTING THE GIRL

After its "Frank Warning" to readers on 4 July 1885 the *Pall Mall Gazette* had started publishing a series of articles entitled "The Maiden Tribute of Modern Babylon" on the following Monday, 6 July. The series ran across the week, with several articles each day.

The first article alerted readers to the "shuddering horror" which the Report of the Secret Commission undertaken by the *Pall Mall Gazette* would present, including the "awful picture of the crimes at present committed as it were under the very aegis of the law". At the start of the campaign, Stead, the sole author of all the articles, wrote that he believed once the evidence was given, there would be no doubt:

> … *that the House of Commons will find time to raise the age during which English girls are protected from inexpiable wrong.*
>
> *The evidence which we shall publish this week leaves no room for doubt – first, as to the reality of the crimes against which the Amendment Bill is directed, and, secondly, as to the efficacy of the protection extended by raising the age of consent. When the report is published, the case for the bill will be complete, and we do not believe that members on the eve of a general election will refuse to consider the bill protecting the daughters of the poor, which even the House of Lords has in three consecutive years declared to be imperatively necessary.*[1]

This was reference to the fact that over a period of years the House of Lords in the British Parliament passed a bill recommending that the age of consent be raised on three occasions.[2] On each occasion, the would-be law failed to make it through the House of Commons. The arguments against the raising of the age of consent were varied and even those wishing to see it raised disagreed on the age ceiling to be eventually put into place. Some wanted the age of consent raised to fifteen while others, including Bramwell Booth, were determined that it would be set at least at sixteen.

The debates in Parliament had seen vigorous arguments against raising the age of consent. Members of the House of Commons – all men at this stage – had repeatedly heard the argument that young women who appeared to be older than they were would exploit any new law to seduce and then blackmail rich old men.[3] Those who put forward such arguments appeared to be concerned to protect men who might be entrapped. However, those campaigning for the raising of the age of consent saw it as protection for young women who might be the victims of lascivious older men. When Bramwell Booth learned that, on the final day of Parliament before the 1885 Whitsun recess, yet another attempt to get the latest and third version of the Criminal Law Amendment Bill through the House of Commons had failed, having been "talked out" or filibustered, he decided action was required. Encouraged by his mother and with the reluctant agreement of his father – the General worried that his Army's association with such a campaign might compromise it[4] – Bramwell made contact with William Stead.

Meanwhile, Catherine Booth decided to apply to the highest authority in the land and wrote the first of a series of letters to Queen Victoria, imploring her to intervene. She wrote:

> *My heart has been filled with distress and apprehension on account of the rejection by the House of Commons of the Protection of Young Girls from the consequences of male*

> *profligacy… If I could only convey to your Majesty an idea of*
> *a tenth part of the suffering entailed on thousands of children*
> *of the poor by the present state of the law on the subject, I*
> *feel sure that your womanly feeling would be roused with*
> *indignation.*[5]

A reply came from a senior Lady-in-Waiting, the Dowager Duchess of Roxborough, who assured Mrs Booth that the Queen fully sympathized with her on the subject; she had spoken already to a lady closely connected with the government and Mrs Booth's letter would be forwarded to her.

A letter to Prime Minister Gladstone, imploring immediate action on the matter, was sent by Catherine that same day.

"I would entreat you to use your great influence in order to raise the age of responsibility for girls to seventeen and, further, that the Bill should confer power to search any premises where there is reasonable grounds to suspect that any girl under age is destined for immoral purposes," Mrs Booth wrote.

The government was at that time on the verge of a collapse and preoccupied with, among other things, the aftermath of the siege of Khartoum and the death of General Gordon. An answer quickly came back from the Prime Minister's private secretary dismissing Catherine's appeal. The letter said that "… the Government, by introducing the Bill, have shown their sense of the importance on the subject" but that, at a time like the present, Mr Gladstone could not commit to personally examining the subject about which Mrs Booth had written.[6]

Undeterred, there followed a series of public meetings at which Catherine spoke with great passion about the scandalous way in which the House of Commons had acted on this matter. She was never one to mince her words, as is shown from a report of part of her address to a gathering at The Salvation Army's Exeter Hall in London that spring:

*I read some paragraphs from reports of a debate in the
House of Commons which made me doubt my eyesight...
I did not think we were as low as this – that one Member
should suggest that the age of the innocents should be
reduced to ten and, Oh My God, pleaded that it was hard
for a man. Hard – for a man – having a charge like this
brought against him not to be able to plead the consent of a
child like that...*[7]

Against this background, Bramwell began to work with Stead,
who quickly decided that the only way to create a fuss big enough
to shame the British Parliament into immediately reviewing the
law was to present the facts of the sex trade, regardless of the
blushes and outrage which the content of the *Pall Mall Gazette*
would cause.

The resulting Maiden Tribute of Modern Babylon articles
were designed to shock. The pages of the *Gazette* in July 1885
were peppered with attention-grabbing subheadings: "The
Violations of Virgins", "The London Slave Market", "How Girls
are Bought and Ruined", "Strapping Girls Down", "A Child of
Thirteen Bought for £5". But the facts, however horrendous, were
insufficient. To ensure the success of their campaign, the Booths
and their Salvation Army, Mrs Butler and her supporters, and
W. T. Stead, needed absolute proof.

It was Stead who came up with an idea to *prove* that girls could
be bought and sold into the sex trade. Later, undoubtedly to try
to protect others who were implicated in his plan, he claimed it
was his inspiration alone and it was he who devised the plot to
buy a girl. However, there can be no doubt that others knew of
his motives and intentions, even if they weren't aware of the exact
details of his scheme.

Apart from proving that young girls were being bought and
sold for sex, another issue was taxing the campaigners at the time.
Benjamin Scott, the Chamberlain of the City of London, was also

chair of the London Committee for the Suppression of the Traffic in British Girls for the purposes of Continental Prostitution. He had given them information that girls could also be removed from the country without the knowledge of the authorities, and could end up in brothels anywhere in Europe where they were beyond reach. In Belgium, for instance, it was known that young women might be registered as prostitutes against their will and even put into the "state brothels".[8] So if, during the course of the plan to buy a child and put her into the sex trade, it could also be proved that she could be smuggled out of England, this would help to back up their claims of the international trade in children for immoral purposes.

The campaign needed financing, and there were people willing to underwrite the investigation by the *Pall Mall Gazette*. To acquire a child Stead would need someone who knew the sex trade and who had a reputation for procurement. It would be no good for Stead himself to start wandering the streets propositioning parents. He required someone who would be believable, and when Bramwell Booth introduced him to Rebecca Jarrett, he knew he had found the perfect individual. Rebecca, having so recently left the streets and being only a few months into her new Christian life and rehabilitation, was at first unwilling to participate in the scheme. But Mrs Butler and the Booths indicated to her that this would be a good way of making reparation for her previous life, so she agreed to work on behalf of the newspaper editor.

However, the "purchase" of a girl would not be a simple task, and Eliza wasn't the first target. Several young women were considered by Rebecca Jarrett before she was able to acquire the Armstrong Girl.

In October of that year William Stead would explain the details of the case to the Old Bailey, outlining how it was he was able to get the "proof" he required: a child would be purchased, which enabled him to tell the story of that girl, whom he called "Lily", in his Maiden Tribute articles.

—✺—

**Monday, 2 November: William Thomas Stead (the Prisoner). (Examined by Mr H. Matthews, from a statement handed in by Stead.)**

*Mrs. Butler and Mr. Scott had agreed to contribute to the expense of this inquiry, but as they never did contribute, perhaps I may explain how they did not. It was a guarantee fund in case the inquiry resulted in nothing, whereas I said if the inquiry results in facts which are publishable, of course the Pall Mall Gazette will pay the expense; I could ask the proprietors to pay the expense of the inquiry. I have no pecuniary interest in the Pall Mall Gazette, absolutely none; I get my salary.*

*The guarantee fund was to be 200l (200 pounds). I personally, out of my private means, undertaking to meet 100l., one-half of that; the other half was to be made up by the other guarantors, by Mr. Booth and Mrs. Butler, and subsequently Mr. Scott came in. I do not know whether Mr. Scott's was his personally or on behalf of the committee but as the inquiry resulted in matter [sic] which we did publish in the Pall Mall Gazette, the expense of the inquiry was borne by the proprietors – the inquiry cost about 400l. altogether.*

*Mr. Booth advanced altogether about 40l... He advanced it at various times; the first 10l. was on the Friday, the 29th of May. That which was sent down to Mrs. Jarrett at Winchester at my request – that was advanced for me – he knew what it was for. It was for the purchase of two girls, who were to be delivered at Waterloo Station next day, but they were not. And at various times he paid the expense of Eliza Armstrong going over to Paris, but I considered myself bound to recoup him for his expenses in this inquiry.*

*The reason I didn't advance the money out of my own pocket was that the person that went to Winchester was a member of the Salvation "Army", a young lady called Miss Peck, and she left from headquarters and went down. She called at the office. I would have advanced it, but Bramwell Booth had the money in his pocket at the time, and he handed Jarrett the money at my request. Jarrett left on the Tuesday and came back on the Wednesday. Miss Peck went down on the Friday with the money... I got a message from Jarrett through Miss Peck, and in consequence of that message I expected to receive two girls at the Waterloo Station on that Saturday. I went to Waterloo Station to receive two girls. I didn't find them.*

*On Thursday, the 28th of May, I received a letter from Mrs. Butler... Rebecca told me the same story that I had previously heard from Miss Peck to the effect that she had arranged for the delivery of two girls at Waterloo Station that day. Three were to be brought, out of which I was to select two. Mrs. Butler had previously told me that she would like to buy the third one, in order to save her from what appeared to be her inevitable fate.*

*Jarrett said they were to be brought by a brothel-keeper down Whitechapel way, and when they did not come she explained it on the ground that possibly a letter had miscarried, that she was not sure about the address, and there might have been some mistake.*

*I do not know whether I saw Jarrett again until the eve of the Derby Day, that is the Tuesday, the 2nd of June. I saw her at the house of a friend... Jarrett then told me of her failure to secure the girls down Whitechapel way, she had been to see the brothel-keeper, and asked how it was she had not delivered the children according to contract. She said that she had expected a letter from her confirming the bargain... The brothel-keeper promised on the following Monday to get her a little girl...*

*On Monday she had gone to get the girl, and paid
2l. down for a girl as half the purchase-money, and the
girl, hearing that Jarrett was going to take her into the
country, bolted, and got out of a cab where Jarrett was...*

*Jarrett also told me that she had found it more difficult
than she expected owing to her having been out of the
business, and that it was necessary for her to go and take
lodgings in some notorious street. That she had taken
them in Albany Street, in what she believed at the time she
took the lodgings to be a gay house, in the hope that the
landlady might put her in the way of buying the girls in
connection with the house, and ripening for seduction, as
you may say. Finding them first, and then buying them.
That she had found out that the house was not a gay house,
at least they denied that it was, but she then had suspicions.*

*At Albany Street she said she had to go back to her old
friends, which she was very reluctant to do, and although
she had gone so far, she would not carry the negotiations
further unless I would promise most solemnly not to expose
any of her old friends or acquaintances. I promised. I did
not wish, I told her, to expose individuals, I had no wish
to incriminate any person who helped her in bringing to
light the facts, that if her friends helped her to buy a girl
in stock, I would take care not to bring their names out.*

*She said she had been among her friends, and had
been to a woman whom she had described as a bad
woman living in a bad house, she had linked this woman
to help her and a little girl was offered her...*

*This little girl had a sister who was on the streets
getting her living, and who was in the house of this bad
woman when Jarrett visited it. She had hopes that she
would get this child the next day. She told me that the
sister... understood exactly what the girl was wanted for.
Its father was dead, its mother was far away, and this*

*elder sister was, she did not use the word "guardian", but
had charge of the child. That was in substance of what
Jarrett told me on the 2nd June. She told me that she had
to go back again next day if I was willing to give 5l. for
the child on condition she was pure. I said of course I
would buy the child if the child was for sale; and she had
my authority to go next day and buy the child...[9]*

—〜〜—

The child to be bought had to be scandalously young and there
had to be no doubt that the girl at the centre of the case was an
innocent, otherwise the impact of the story would be wasted. In
the event, the child with the older sister did not go with Rebecca.
Stead explained the circumstances during his trial, outlining how
it was that Eliza Armstrong eventually became the unwitting
"victim" of his journalistic plot.

—〜〜—

### Monday, 2 November: William Thomas Stead (the Prisoner) continued...

*I said I would go to Albany Street to tea and see the
child. I went next day to Albany Street in consequence
of that arrangement, about 5 o'clock I think. I found
Eliza Armstrong, Jarrett, and Miss Peck there. I first
had some conversation with Rebecca about the girl –
Eliza Armstrong – and Miss Peck went into the other
room. I had two conversations with Rebecca when Eliza
Armstrong was not present... Rebecca said, "This is not
the little girl that I expected to get, that little girl that
I told you about last night has another sister who is in
service, and this sister hearing of the intended destination
intervened". That was the substance. "This is another
little girl whose mother has got to know of the bargain
and suggested to the woman who was procuring her that*

her Eliza would do." She was a drunken woman, she told me; and then she said to Mrs. Broughton, "Won't our Eliza do?" and Mrs. Broughton said, "No; she is going to have another little girl," or "... to get a little girl".

I have got awfully mixed about the little girls, and more so since I came into Court – she might have said the other little girl. Jarrett said, when she went back, Mrs. Armstrong renewed her proposal and offered Eliza to Mrs. Broughton. I said to Jarrett, "Are you sure the mother knew what her child was wanted for?" Jarrett said, "Quite sure. I told her that she was wanted for a man, that she must be a pure girl." She told me she had asked Mrs. Broughton also whether Eliza was a pure girl, and Mrs. Broughton said something about Eliza messing about with boys in the street; romping about, I suppose, she meant. She had told Mrs. Broughton that if Eliza was in the habit of romping about with boys in the streets she might not be pure, and if she was not pure she would not serve her purpose, so she was particular in asking Mrs. Armstrong about her daughter being a pure girl.

Rebecca agreed to take her. She said she got new clothes for the child, and dressed her up in them – before that, before she went to bid the mother good-bye, she said that she had given Mrs. Armstrong a sovereign for her Eliza. I think Rebecca used the phrase, "a golden sovereign"; put it into her hand for her Eliza, and that she had given Mrs. Broughton 2l., and the rest had to be sent to her, "if the girl was proved to be pure". Rebecca added that it was a proof of the confidence which Mrs. Broughton had in her that she was willing to take the verdict of Rebecca's doctor, instead of having her examined by her own, as was the case when strangers were dealing.[10]

—∿∿—

Although it had taken a couple of days to secure the right child, Stead had his potential scoop. He had his "Lily". Now he required an attention-grabbing title which would give him the headlines he needed if the child's story was to shock the nation into action.

# CHAPTER 9

# THE MAIDEN TRIBUTE OF MODERN BABYLON

For his series of articles published in the *Pall Mall Gazette* in July 1885, Stead turned to a classical story that, he hoped, would be familiar to many of his readers. At the start of the first instalment of the story – which took up six pages of the paper on that first day of publication – Stead took time to explain why he had called his campaign "The Maiden Tribute of Modern Babylon".

—⁂—

*In ancient times, if we may believe the myths of Hellas, Athens, after a disastrous campaign, was compelled by her conqueror to send once every nine years a tribute to Crete of seven youths and seven maidens. The doomed fourteen, who were selected by lot amid the lamentations of the citizens, returned no more. The vessel that bore them to Crete unfurled black sails as the symbol of despair, and on arrival her passengers were flung into the famous Labyrinth of Daedalus, there to wander about blindly until such time as they were devoured by the Minotaur, a frightful monster, half man, half bull, the foul product of an unnatural lust... Twice at each ninth year the Athenians paid the maiden tribute to King Minos, lamenting sorely the dire necessity of bowing to his iron law...*

*And what happened to the victims – the young men and maidens – who were there interned, no one could surely tell. Some say that they were done to death; others that they lived in servile employments to old age. But in this alone do all the stories agree, that those who were once caught in the coils could never retrace their steps, so "inextricable" were the paths, so "blind" the footsteps, so "innumerable" the ways of wrong-doing...*

*The fact that the Athenians should have taken so bitterly to heart the paltry maiden tribute that once in nine years they had to pay to the Minotaur seems incredible, almost inconceivable. This very night in London, and every night, year in and year out, not seven maidens only, but many times seven, selected almost as much by chance as those who in the Athenian market-place drew lots as to which should be flung into the Cretan labyrinth, will be offered up as the Maiden Tribute of Modern Babylon.*

*Maidens they were when this morning dawned, but to-night their ruin will be accomplished, and to-morrow they will find themselves within the portals of the maze of London brotheldom. Within that labyrinth wander, like lost souls, the vast host of London prostitutes, whose numbers no man can compute, but who are probably not much below 50,000 strong. Many, no doubt, who venture but a little way within the maze make their escape. But multitudes are swept irresistibly on and on to be destroyed in due season, to give place to others, who also will share their doom.[1]*

At a time when the classics were still embedded in education, particularly for the rich and privileged, the story of the Minotaur and his Labyrinth would have been well known. But Stead cleverly wove the ancient story of despair, lust, and hopelessness together with the plight of the thousands of young women and girls who, he would claim as his series of articles unfolded, were the "victims" of a similarly corrupt system from which there appeared no escape.

Stead challenged his readers, making no excuses for the fact that he, a journalist, would print the horrific facts of life which his Secret Commission had uncovered. He also accused London and the "cultured" men of the world of being uncaring in the face of a national scandal.

> *... London's lust annually uses up many thousands of women, who are literally killed and made away with – living sacrifices slain in the service of vice. That may be inevitable, and with that I have nothing to do. But I do ask that those doomed to the house of evil fame shall not be trapped into it unwillingly, and that none shall be beguiled into the chamber of death before they are of an age to read the inscription above the portal: "All hope abandon ye who enter here."*
>
> *If the daughters of the people must be served up as dainty morsels to minister to the passions of the rich, let them at least attain an age when they can understand the nature of the sacrifice which they are asked to make. And if we must cast maidens – not seven, but seven times seven – nightly into the jaws of vice, let us at least see to it that they assent to their own immolation, and are not unwilling sacrifices procured by force and fraud.[2]*

On that first day of publication, he outlined much of the evidence his research and investigations had uncovered, and he gave his readers an insight into how the information was gathered, the people at the highest level of society who were approached for facts and advice, and the frustrations of the campaigners at the stalling of the Criminal Law Amendment Bill.

The "Secret Commission" which fuelled the Maiden Tribute of Modern Babylon articles had been, he said, a thorough examination of the "vice trade", particularly in London. He had interviewed many people, from those within the trade –

procuresses, brothel-keepersl and street women – to church societies helping "fallen women" and the newly created "London Society for the Prevention of Cruelty to Children". This organization, which would later become the National Society for the Prevention of Cruelty to Children (NSPCC) had been created just a year before, in 1884, but was already doing great work. As Stead himself wrote in an article on 9 July 1885, he had found it to be "an excellent society, not to be confounded with that half-moribund association the Society for the Protection of Women and Children".[3]

In this article, entitled "The Truth about our Secret Commission". Stead laid out the history of how the Commission had come about. After the Criminal Law Amendment Bill failed once again in the House of Commons, Stead told how the City Chamberlain, Benjamin Scott, the chairman of the London Committee for the Suppression of the Traffic in British Girls, had approached him to tell him of the plight of young women. It was Mr Scott, he said, who had made him aware of what he called "the Shoreham Case", the escape of a girl called Annie from a brothel in Pimlico who had made it to the headquarters of The Salvation Army. (This was Annie Swan, discovered on the steps of the Queen Victoria Street headquarters, whose story had so galvanized Bramwell Booth.)

It's interesting to note the slight variance in memory in this respect. Bramwell Booth later claimed that he was working with Mr Scott, Mrs Josephine Butler, and others at this time, but that it was he who shared with Mr Stead the story of "the facts of child enslavement and prostitution" which had come to The Salvation Army's attention, and that it was he who asked Stead to "give publicity to the business so that the Government should become aware of the pressure of public opinion".[4] Stead had another version, yet however he became aware of the story, he was quick to show his admiration of the movement which was already doing so much to help "fallen women" on the streets of the capital:

*The first step in the inquiry was to ascertain from the headquarters of the Salvation Army whether the story was correctly reported. This brought me into close communication with the chiefs of The Salvation Army, with whom I had previously been in communication on the subject, by whom this inquiry was welcomed with enthusiasm and assisted to the uttermost in every way by all its members from the Chief of the Staff down to the humblest private. And here let me state as a matter of simple justice to the Salvation Army that, so far as our inquiry necessitated operations of rescue, our Commission would have been almost helpless without the aid which was extended to us without stint at any hour of the day or the night, at any sacrifice of personal trouble or risk of personal danger, by the intrepid soldiers of that admirable organization. Nor does that by any means exhaust our indebtedness to the Army. In the elucidation of facts, in the investigation of obscure cases, in the furnishing at a moment's notice of men and women ready to do anything and go anywhere, the aid which we received from Mr. Bramwell Booth and his devoted comrades was simply incalculable, and far exceeding that rendered by all the other existing organizations put together.*

*After verifying the facts about the Shoreham case, and being assured of the hearty co-operation and loyal support of the London Committee for the Suppression of the Traffic in English Girls, of Mrs. Josephine Butler, whose vast experience was placed unreservedly at our disposal, and of the Salvation Army, the work of investigation was begun in earnest. The general idea was to waste no time on mere vice, to stick to the investigation of crime, and to bring up to date the evidence on the subjects dealt with by the Lords' Committee.*[5]

The Secret Commission, Stead wrote, was his initiative and the investigators were members of staff at the *Pall Mall Gazette* who were "instructed to elucidate facts altogether independently of the police". They had spoken to the Home Office and the Local Government Board but they received little help apart from access to some officials and statistics. Stead also told his readers about an early meeting with the Archbishop of Canterbury who he said kindly tried to dissuade him from getting involved in a risky affair which might end up with his death in a brothel, but nevertheless supported him. Similar expressions of support and counsel were received from the Bishop of London and the Roman Catholic Cardinal Archbishop of Westminster, from the Congregational Union, and other chaplains and well-wishers. Stead also reported how he had personal communication with many organizations and agencies that worked with and helped "rescue" children and families in particular.[6]

The members of the Secret Commission visited many locations in pursuit of the facts, including the "Lock Hospital" where women imprisoned under the Contagious Diseases Act were held, and the Rescue Home run by The Salvation Army and overseen by Mrs Bramwell Booth. Stead also revealed that he had spoken to many individuals involved in the sex trade, and even those who opposed the Criminal Law Amendment Act.

So, after such meticulous fact finding, albeit over a relatively short period, the very first article in the Maiden Tribute of Modern Babylon series was inevitably laden with details intended to shock. From the start there were details of the "pilgrimage into a real hell" which had been part of Stead's "Frank Warning" to readers just a couple of days before – a discussion on rape, references to "Virgins willing and unwilling", the "Confessions of a Brothel-Keeper", and the "London Slave Market" to which he had provided girls. Part of the edition of the *Pall Mall Gazette* centred on how the law "abetted the criminals" who procured girls for the brothels, and how the law as it stood was no protection. There were detailed facts about how girls were "bought and sold" in the East End of London, one story from a girl who had escaped, and some shocking details from inside some of the "secret chambers of accommodation houses" where, Stead claimed, girls were sometimes strapped down by their hands and feet to the bed, to allow men to have their pleasure.

Despite these grim revelations, the editor still managed to preface some of the early details of the Maiden Tribute with a note of optimism:

> *I have not yet lost faith in the heart and conscience of the English folk, the sturdy innate chivalry and right thinking of our common people; and although I am no vain dreamer of Utopias peopled solely by Sir Galahads and vestal virgins, I am not without hope that there may be some check placed upon this vast tribute of maidens, unwitting or unwilling, which is nightly levied in London by the vices of the rich upon the necessities of the poor.[7]*

And in his accompanying leading article on that day entitled "We bid you be of Hope" he continued that theme of a positive outcome for the case, while still using his editorial comment to pour scorn on those who allowed the trade in girls to continue.

> *… in dealing with this subject, the forces upon which we rely in dealing with other evils are almost all paralysed. The Home, the School, the Church, the Press are silent. The law is actually accessory to crime. Parents culpably neglect even to warn their children of the existence of dangers of which many learn the first time when they have become their prey. The Press, which reports verbatim all the scabrous details of the police courts, recoils in pious horror from the duty of shedding a flood of light upon these dark places, which indeed are full of the habitations of cruelty.[8]*

It was a damning indictment of society at large for allowing what Stead and the Purity Movement campaigners believed was the Great Social Evil of the day. But, as a religious man, Stead also wove into his writing references to Scripture and God and he served up one of his main criticisms for the church.

> *But the failure of the Churches is, perhaps, the most*
> *conspicuous and the most complete. Christ's mission was to*
> *restore man to a semblance of the divine. The Child-Prostitute*
> *of our day is the image into which, with the tacit acquiescence*
> *of those who call themselves by His name, men have moulded*
> *the form once fashioned in the likeness of God.*[9]

Alongside much moralizing and judgment on society, and lurid facts designed to ensure that readers of the *Pall Mall Gazette* would inevitably want to buy the next day's edition, that first article of 6 July 1885 also included the story which, ultimately, would see the editor and others face a trial at the Old Bailey.

That initial article, published on 6 July concluded with the story of "A Child of 13 Bought for £5", starting with how "a woman, an old hand in the work of procuration, entered a brothel in — st. M—, kept by an old acquaintance, and opened negotiations for the purchase of a maid."[10] This was the story of the girl Stead called "Lily" and it was the most shocking section of an already scandalous edition of the *Pall Mall Gazette*.

# CHAPTER 10

# "A CHILD OF 13 BOUGHT FOR £5"

*Lily was a little cockney child, one of those who by the thousand annually develop into the servants of the poorer middle-class. She had been at school, could read and write, and although her spelling was extraordinary, she was able to express herself with much force and decision. Her experience of the world was limited to the London quarter in which she had been born. With the exception of two school trips to Richmond and one to Epping Forest, she had never been in the country in her life, nor had she ever even seen the Thames excepting at Richmond. She was an industrious, warm-hearted little thing, a hardy English child, slightly coarse in texture, with dark black eyes, and short, sturdy figure. Her education was slight. She spelled write "right," for instance, and her grammar was very shaky. But she was a loving, affectionate child, whose kindly feeling for the drunken mother who sold her into nameless infamy was very touching to behold. In a little letter of hers which I once saw, plentifully garlanded with kisses, there was the following ill-spelled childish verse:*

*As I was in bed
Some little forths gave in my head.*

*I forth of one, I forth of two;
But first of all I forth of you.*[1]

So Stead described the child "Lily" who was at the centre of his first article in the Maiden Tribute of Modern Babylon series. This was the girl eventually picked out to be bought and the description of the innocent Lily was preceded by the outlining of how she and not another girl came to be taken from her home in June of that year.

> *The next day, Derby Day as it happened, was fixed for the delivery of this human chattel. But as luck would have it, another sister of the child who was to be made over to the procuress heard of the proposed sale. She was living respectably in a situation, and on hearing of the fate reserved for the little one she lost no time in persuading her dissolute sister to break off the bargain. When the woman came for her prey the bird had flown. Then came the chance of Lily's mother. The brothel-keeper sent for her, and offered her a sovereign for her daughter. The woman was poor, dissolute, and indifferent to everything but drink. The father, who was also a drunken man, was told his daughter was going to a situation. He received the news with indifference, without even inquiring where she was going to. The brothel-keeper having thus secured possession of the child, then sold her to the procuress in place of the child whose sister had rescued her from her destined doom for £5 – £3 paid down and the remaining £2 after her virginity had been professionally certified. The little girl, all unsuspecting the purpose for which she was destined, was told that she must go with this strange woman to a situation. The procuress, who was well up to her work, took her away, washed her, dressed her up neatly, and sent her to bid her parents good-bye. The mother was so drunk she hardly recognized her daughter. The father was hardly less indifferent. The child left her home, and was taken to the woman's lodging in A— street.*

*The first step had thus been taken. But it was necessary to have Lily's virginity confirmed – a difficult task, as the child was absolutely ignorant of the nature of the transaction which had transferred her from home to the keeping of this strange, but apparently kind-hearted woman...*

*... The poor child was full of delight at going to her new situation, and clung affectionately to the keeper who was taking her away – where, she knew not."[2]*

And in October the Old Bailey court heard the first-hand account direct from the girl – Eliza Armstrong.

―∿∿―

### Friday, 23 October 1885, Central Criminal Court: Eliza Armstrong (Witness)

*That was a private house... Jarrett and I went into a sitting-room. There was a young lady there who I had never seen before. Afterwards Mr. Stead came in. I did not know his name at the time, nor the name of the young lady. He asked me if I went to school. I said "Yes". He asked what school. I said "The Board School". He asked if I went to Sunday school, I replied "Yes, to Harrow Road Sunday School at 9 in the morning and in the afternoon, and to the Richmond Street Sunday School on Sunday nights". I went three times on Sundays. I had been attending the schools for four years, and I told him so. He asked whether I went to any of the treats there. I said "Yes, once to Epping Forest and twice to Richmond". He asked me if I wrote any grammar at the schools. I said "Yes"...*

*Mrs. Jarrett asked me to go into the other room. The young lady came with me. We all had tea together before I went out of the room... Mr. Stead went out then. Jarrett took me out and bought me some underclothing... I have pointed out all the shops to the inspector. I returned with her to Albany Street. When Jarrett, the young lady, and I were alone at Albany Street, Jarrett told me to put the things on, and I did so. I wrapped the old clothes up in a parcel...*

*Mrs. Jarrett was combing my hair, and said, "Shall I cut you a Piccadilly fringe?" I said my mother would not allow it. She did not cut it after I said that. After that, when we were ready to go out, Mrs. Jarrett and the young lady changed hats. I left the house with Mrs. Jarrett. The young lady came out with us. There was a Hansom's cab at the door, and I and Mrs. Jarrett got into it... the cab drove us to a house in Milton Street, Dorset Square. I think it was about 6 o'clock we started from Albany Street. The cab stopped at the house; Jarrett got out, paid the driver, and went into No. 3... It was a private house. Jarrett asked the servant who opened the door for "Madame".*

*I went into a room and saw Madame Mourey. She was French, because she could only speak English a little... Jarrett and Madame Mourey spoke together, I did not hear what they said. Madame Mourey took me into a little room. She pulled up my clothes; I was standing up; she put her hands in my private parts, touching the flesh; I tried to get away, and then she put her hands down. She had not said anything to me before doing this.*

*I went to the next room, the door of which was open, where Jarrett was. Madame came into the room as well. I said to Jarrett, "She is a dirty woman". Jarrett made no reply – she went out of the room with Madame, leaving me in the room for half an hour... Jarrett took me away from the house. I was still carrying the parcel of old things I had brought from Albany Street.*

*There was a four-wheeled cab waiting outside the house... Jarrett spoke to the cabman, and Jarrett and I got in, and were driven to Poland Street, Oxford Street.*

*We stopped opposite a ham and beef shop... Jarrett and I walked a little way towards Oxford Street. I saw two men. We went into a house in Poland Street next door to the ham and beef shop... The two men had gone into that house.*

*Jarrett and I went upstairs into a front bedroom. Mr. Jacques was one of the two men who were outside and who went in. I did not see who the other was then. I have no doubt of Jacques – I saw him again when I returned from France; I knew him then.*

*When I got into the bedroom the men came into the room. The men had something to drink in the next room. Jarrett also had something to drink in the same room as I was; the drink was something brown. She asked me if I would go to bed. I said I did not want to go to bed yet. Jarrett gave me a picture book, and said we would stay there that night, because she lived in a place a long way off, and it would take a very long time to get there. She did not say where we were to go in the morning.*

*Jarrett asked me again to go to bed, and I did so; I undressed and got into bed. Jarrett did not undress, she said she was waiting up for the young lady to come home. Afterwards Jarrett lay down outside the bed with her clothes on, by my side. She put a handkerchief up to my nose; I threw it away. She put it again to my nose, and said, "Give a good sniff up". I said I would not have it, and threw it away. Jarrett said it was scent; it had a nasty smell. I was still awake afterwards.*

*The door opened and someone came in. I could tell by the sound, I could not see because the curtains were round the bed. There was a lamp in the room. When the door opened Jarrett was off the bed and outside the curtains. She said, "She is all right," or something like that. I heard a man's voice, but I did not hear what was said. I screamed out, "There is a man in the room".*

*The man went away when I screamed out, and shut the door after him. Jarrett said, "What is the matter?" I said "There is a man in the room", Jarrett pulled up the curtains and said "There is no man in the room". I said "Because he is gone out". I saw there was no one in the room when the curtains were pulled up by Jarrett.*

*Jarrett left the room and returned in two or three minutes, saying "Get up and dress, there are too many men in this house". That was about 1 o'clock. We had been in the house an hour... I got up and dressed. She put her hat and jacket on, went out of the room and downstairs.*

*I saw nothing of the two men, Jacques and the other. We got into a cab which was waiting outside the house, and a man who I do not know got on the box seat. The cab drove to some house, where the man got off the box and went in. Jarrett and I waited at the door inside the cab for an hour. After that the man came out and said to Jarrett "You can sleep here to-night". Jarrett said "All right". We got out of the cab and went into the house... which is No. 27, Nottingham Place. I know it is the same house; it is a nicely furnished private house.*

*Jarrett and I went into a bedroom, undressed, and went to bed. She slept on a sofa; I on the bed... I went to sleep. I got up the next morning. I cannot say whether any one came into the room; no one came in while I was awake.*

*Next morning I got up to breakfast. While at breakfast Mrs. Combe, whom I then saw for the first time, and the young lady who had changed hats with Jarrett at Albany Street, came. Mrs. Combe asked me if I should like to go to a place along with her. I said "No".*

*Jarrett and Mrs. Combe went out of the room together, leaving me there. I was sitting crying when Jarrett and Mrs. Combe returned. Afterwards the young lady and Mr. Stead came in. Jarrett asked the young lady to go and* buy me a cloak. She did so. Meanwhile Mrs. Combe said she had a lot of little children and two sons, one was dead and one was in the Salvation "Army".

Mr. Stead said "The cab is all ready; let us go down now". I got into the cab with Jarrett, Mrs. Combe, and Mr. Stead. The young lady had not come back yet with the cloak. We went in the cab to some big railway station; I forget the name of it... we got to the station about 9 in the morning. The young lady was at the station with the cloak, and I put it on. I have it on now. At that time I had not been told where they were going to take me.

Jarrett, Mrs. Combe and I travelled in the train; Mr. Stead and the young lady seeing us off. We crossed the Channel and went to Paris. We got there about 6 in the evening... We went to the headquarters of the Salvation "Army" in Paris. I was employed in selling The War Cry in the streets of Paris. On June 5th Jarrett said she was going home to get her place ready for me to go there; that she would sleep there that night, and go to-morrow morning, and that Mrs. Combe would take me to a shop and buy me some more clothes...

I knew Miss Booth, the "Marshal", and Miss Green, the cook. Two or three days after I was in Paris I wrote to my mother. I put no address on it; I didn't know what to put. Mrs. Combe wrote a letter for me. She was there with me a week. The letter I wrote I addressed to my mother, 32, Charles Street, Lisson Grove, Marylebone, and gave it to the "Captain", a young lady, to post. I put no stamp on it, I did not get any answer. I also wrote to Mrs. Jarrett, whose name I heard as Mrs. Sullivan when at Paris. I did not know her name at all till I got to Paris.[3]

———

Eliza was encouraged to give her testimony by the prosecuting counsel, the Attorney General, Sir Richard Webster. As she explained her encounter with Madame Mourey – whose name was also sometimes written as Mourez – there must have been uncomfortable shuffles.

The Maiden Tribute articles had revealed that girls who were purchased for the brothels had to be proven to be "pure". Undefiled girls were highly regarded and could command a higher price for that first encounter. Indeed, occasionally young girls who had already been forced to have sex were later submitted to an intimate operation when their insides would be sewn back together so that they might be re-offered to clients as virgins.

These intimate examinations and procedures were usually the business of midwives who were also called upon to perform dangerous back-street abortions, which gave them a plentiful income. Madame Mourey was one such "midwife" who, for a fee, would check out a girl for a client. Like Eliza, the young person generally had no idea why a complete stranger would suddenly assault her.

Louise Mourey was not party to the Stead plot, but would have been selected by Rebecca Jarrett for the task of checking on Eliza's virginity, maybe because she wasn't quite as rough as others in her profession. Certainly there is no indication that Eliza was seriously harmed by the examination. The presence of Louise Mourey was crucial to the subterfuge which Stead and Rebecca were involved in. With proof that Eliza was "pure" she could be taken on to the brothel where, for all intents and purposes, she would be handed over to the man who had "ordered" her.

To ensure that the brothel-keeper in Poland Street believed that Rebecca Jarrett was indeed making a legitimate transaction with her charge, Eliza would need to be treated like any other innocent. Often, to ensure that they complied when first forced into sex, they would be drugged. And so Eliza was drugged before a man entered the room. Eliza's screams of fear would have been proof enough to the brothel-keeper that the hysterical child had been used for the purposes intended. Of course, the gentleman in question was Stead. The Poland Street brothel-keeper, who would have been paid for the use of the room, would not have known exactly what had transpired, but would have been confident that the transaction between Rebecca and her client had been fulfilled. All she heard were Eliza's screams.

By her own evidence to the court, Eliza was not defiled by the man in the room, although the "medical examination" was undoubtedly a physical assault. There were also no claims that the child suffered long-term effects, although others did state in the trial that Eliza wasn't completely happy. There was evidence that she was sometimes in tears when in France, and she must have certainly been very confused about what was happening to her.

That Eliza eventually ended up in France confirmed another of the Purity Movement campaigners' allegations: not only could a child be bought and then sold into an English brothel, but without the knowledge of her parents and the authorities, she might also be smuggled out of the country. For the likes of Benjamin Scott, one of the financiers behind the Maiden Tribute Secret Commission, this aspect of the case was vital.

Although Eliza, who ended up safe in the care of The Salvation Army across the English Channel, was certainly not a victim of a Continental sex transfer, the very fact that she had been taken to France without the knowledge of her parents had proved that a child could be secretly conveyed out of England, helping to validate Purity Movement's claims of an international trade in children for immoral purposes.

# CHAPTER 11

# AN INTERNATIONAL SENSATION

The *Pall Mall Gazette's* first instalment of its Maiden Tribute of Modern Babylon story, with its lurid descriptions of how young girls were lured into the sex industry and how one child in particular had been treated, had the effect which Stead had hoped for. By the following morning the offices of the *PMG* were mobbed. The crowds gathered outside No. 2 Northumberland Street included many hundreds of "newsboys" – independent newsvendors who made their living selling papers on the streets. They were desperate to get their hands on copies of the paper which had shocked its readers the previous day. As Stead put his feet up on his desk and lit a "smoke", as he often did when feeling satisfied with life, he would also be planning how he could get more copies of the *PMG* out to the public, and immediately.

Within days of the first article, rumour had it, copies of the paper were changing hands for up to twelve times their sale price of just one penny.[1] The daily circulation of the *Pall Mall Gazette* is said to have risen from around 12,000 copies to over a million over the course of the next few days. It ran out of ordinary paper for printing and for a while had to use coloured paper until extra newsprint was brought into London by special train to keep up with demand.[2] The old steam presses in its basement worked around the clock.

It wasn't just London and England and even the wider British Isles that wanted the story. Within days, the Maiden Tribute of

Modern Babylon proved an international sensation. Orders flooded in from abroad and, at great expense, words were telegraphed to New York so the American market had immediate access to the sensational scoop of the day.[3] On the Continent, the Maiden Tribute series caused uproar and embarrassment. In Brussels in Belgium, the Chief of Police was forced to resign as a result of the information in subsequent articles about the sale of girls for the Belgian sex trade.[4]

The articles were the talk of the town, read not just in the lounges of the London gentlemen's clubs but also in the street by people who might not normally buy a newspaper. It seemed that, in those first few weeks, everyone wanted to get their hands on the information which Stead's Secret Commission had uncovered. Some readers would have been concerned about the state of the nation and of the young women who seemed to be part of this modern slave trade, but many may have just been curious about the sexual content of the articles. Stead didn't pull his punches when it came to details.

On its second day, "The Maiden Tribute of Modern Babylon II: the Report of our Secret Commission" revealed the facts which the editor and his reporters had uncovered. It started where Day 1 had left off, with a reference to "Lily" and an explanation of why the age of consent was part of the problem when it came to helping young girls who found themselves victims of an unscrupulous trade. Here there was also a good dose of moral indignation from the editor, who did not hold back with sharing some personal views:

*The law at present almost specially marks out such children as the fair game of dissolute men. The moment a child is thirteen she is a woman in the eye of the law, with absolute right to dispose of her person to anyone who by force or fraud can bully or cajole her into parting with her virtue. It is the one thing in the whole world which, if once lost, can never be recovered, it is the most precious thing a woman ever has, but while the law forbids her absolutely to dispose of any other valuables until she is sixteen, it insists upon investing her with unfettered freedom to sell her person at thirteen. The law, indeed, seems specially framed in order to enable dissolute men to outrage these legal women of thirteen with impunity.[5]*

The taking of these young girls, Stead maintained, was rape, if not legally, then at least morally. He did admit that not all girls went unwillingly although he maintained they invariably didn't know what they were letting themselves in for.

*Now it is a fact which I have repeatedly verified that girls of thirteen, fourteen, and even fifteen, who profess themselves perfectly willing to be seduced, are absolutely and totally ignorant of the nature of the act to which they assent. I do not mean merely its remoter consequences and the extent to which their consent will prejudice the whole of their future life, but even the mere physical nature of the act to which they are legally competent to consent is unknown to them.[6]*

And who was to blame? Stead thought he had the answer and his high moral tone was firmly rooted in his perception of how Christian faith was also part of the problem.

### The Responsibility of the Mothers

*The ignorance of these girls is almost incredible. It is one of the greatest scandals of Protestant training that parents are allowed to keep their children in total ignorance of the simplest truths of physiology, without even a rudimentary conception of the nature of sexual morality. Catholic children are much better trained; and whatever may be*

*the case in other countries, the chastity of Catholic girls is
much greater than that of Protestants in the same social
strata. Owing to the soul and body destroying taciturnity
of Protestant mothers, girls often arrive at the age of legal
womanhood in total ignorance, and are turned loose
to contend with all the wiles of the procuress and the
temptations of the seducer without the most elementary
acquaintance with the laws of their own existence.
Experientia docet; but in this case the first experience is
too often that of violation. Even after the act has been
consummated, all that they know is that they got badly
hurt; but they think of it and speak of it exactly in the same
way as if it meant no more for them than the pulling out of
a tooth. Even more than the scandalous state of the law, the
culpable refusal of mothers to explain to their daughters the
realities and the dangers of their existence contributes to fill
the brothels of London.* [7]

The second day of the Maiden Tribute series was designed to
further scandalize an already outraged reader, with sections
entitled "Recruiting for the House of Evil Fame", "Unwilling
Recruits", and "Procuration in the West End". There were first-
hand accounts from a couple of working girls whom Stead and
his Secret Commission had spoken to, and also the "Story of an
Escape", the tale of Annie Swan, whose appearance at the door
of Salvation Army headquarters months before had helped to
initiate the whole Maiden Tribute campaign. Her story, then
related only to Bramwell Booth, was now shared with the world
as proof of how easily young women could be duped into a life
which they would not necessarily have chosen for themselves.

*My name is A––; I am seventeen years old. Last year,
about May, I was living with my grandparents who had
brought me up at Shoreham. They were poor people, and*

*as I had grown up they thought that it was well I should go to service. I saw an advertisement of a situation: "Wanted a girl to help in the general work of the house." My grandmother wrote about the situation, and as it seemed satisfactory, it was decided I should go. My mistress had to meet me at Victoria station and take me to my new home.*

*I arrived all safely, and at first I thought everything was going to be all right. Mrs. C-- was very kind, and let me go to bed at ten. After a time, however, I began to sea [sic] something was wrong. The ladies in the house used to drink very much and keep very late hours. Gentlemen were coming and going till three and four o'clock in the morning. I began to see that I was in a bad house. But when I mentioned it to my mother, who is living a gay life in London, she scolded me, and said she would give me a good hiding if I left my place. Where was I to go to? Besides, I thought I might be a servant in a bad house without being bad myself. By degrees Mrs. C. began to hint that I was too good to be a general servant; she would get another girl, and I might be a lady like the others. But the girl who had been there before me used to cry very much and tell me never to do as she had done. "Once I was as good as you, Annie, but now there is my baby, and what can I do?" and then she would cry bitterly. The other two girls, when they were sober, would warn me to beware and not come to such a life as theirs, and wish that they had never taken to the streets. And then they would drink again, and go and paint their faces and prepare to receive visitors. I used to be sent with money to buy drink for them, and many a time I wondered if I might run off and never come back. But I had to bring back either the money or the drink or be taken for a thief. And so I went on day after day.*

*One night Mrs. C. brought me a red silk dress and a new hat, and said she was going to take me out. She got into a cab* with me and took me to the Aquarium. There she walked me about and then brought me home again. This she did several times, never letting me get out of her sight, never allowing me to go out of doors except for drink and when she took me to the Aquarium. She became more pressing. She showed me a beautiful pink dress, and promised me that also if I would do as the others did. And when I would not, she called me a fool, and used awful language, and said what pleasure I was missing all from stupidity. Sometimes she would tell the gentlemen to take liberties with me, but I kept them at a distance. One night after I had come in with her from the Aquarium, a gentleman tried to catch hold of me as I was outside the bedroom. I ran as hard as I could downstairs. He came after me, but I got into the kitchen first, and there I barricaded the door with chairs and the table, so that he could not get in.

I was nearly distracted and did not know what to do, when I found in my box the back of an old hymn-book my grandfather had used. It had on it the address of General Booth, at the headquarters of the Salvation Army. I thought to myself Mr. Booth must be a good man or he would not have so many halls all over the country, and then I thought perhaps he will help me to get out of this horrible house, as I never knew what might happen any night. So I waited quietly all that night, never taking off my clothes. It was usually four o'clock before the house was quiet. As soon as they all seemed to be asleep, I waited till nearly six, and then I crept to the door, opened it, and stole softly away, not even daring to close the door. I only knew one address in all London – 101, Queen Victoria Street; where that was I did not know. I walked out blindly till I met a policeman, and he told me the right direction. I walked on and on; it was a long way; I was very tired. I had had no sleep all night, and I feared at any moment to be overtaken and brought back. My red silk dress was rather conspicuous, and I did *not know if, even after I got there, whether Mr. Booth would help me. But I felt sure he was a good man, and I walked on and on. The bad house was in Gloucester Street, Pimlico, and it was nearly half-past seven when I got to Queen Victoria Street. The headquarters were closed. I stood waiting outside, wondering if, after all, I might have to go back. At last someone came, and they took care of me, and sent me to their home, and then took me back to Shoreham, where I am now living.[8]*

With The Salvation Army confirming Annie's story and character, the Pall Mall Gazette and its editor were confident that hers was a legitimate account of the situation which many girls faced. And from the PMG the ultimate fate of Annie Swan was also revealed.

*The girl is now engaged to be married, and, so far as one could judge, seemed a thoroughly modest, respectable young woman. But for the accident of the hymn-book, there is little doubt that she would months ago have been a regular prostitute.[9]*

The future wasn't as rosy for all the young women who found themselves in Annie's position. Not all managed to escape and this was, according to Stead, partly because of the guile of the "procuresses". In a section entitled "An Interview with the Firm" the editor reported "a long conversation with Mesdames X. and Z." in which he discovered some of the secrets from inside the trade. This was a plain-spoken exposé of facts but Stead still couldn't resist making his own moral judgment as he reported his meeting with the two women:

*"I was told the other day," said I, by way of opening the conversation, "that the demand for maidenheads has rather fallen away of late, owing to the frauds of the procurers. The*

*market has been glutted with vamped-up virgins, of which
the supply is always in excess of the demand, and there are
fewer inquiries for the genuine article."*

*"That is not our experience," said the senior partner, a
remarkable woman, attractive by the force of her character
in spite of the ghastliness of her calling, compared to which
that of the common hangman is more honourable. "We
do not know anything about vamped virgins. Nor, with so
many genuine maids to be had for the taking, do I think
it worthwhile to manufacture virgins. I should say the
market was looking up and the demand increasing. Prices
may perhaps have fallen, but that is because our customers
give larger orders. For instance, Dr.—, one of my friends,
who used to take a maid a week at £10, now takes three a
fortnight at from £5, to £7 each."*

*"What!" I exclaimed; "do you actually supply one
gentleman with seventy fresh maids every year?"*

*"Certainly," said she; "and he would take a hundred
if we could get them. But he is so very particular. He will
not take a shop-girl, and he always must have a maid over
sixteen."[10]*

But simple reporting of facts was not enough for the editor of the
Pall Mall Gazette. Stead's appetite for the outrageous then kicked
in as he proceeded to explain to his readers how, as part of his
Secret Commission investigations, he had ordered five virgins,
thus indicating how the trade in humans was considered just like
any other business transaction.

*"Come," said I, in a vein of bravado, "what do you say
to delivering me five on Saturday next?" – it was then
Wednesday – "I want them to be retailed to my friends.
You are the wholesale firm, could you deliver me a parcel
of five maids, for me to distribute among my friends, after*

*having them duly certificated?" "Five," she said, "is a large
order, I could bring you three that I know of; but five! It is
difficult getting so many girls away at the same time from
their places. But we will try, although I have never before
delivered more than two, or at the most three, at one place.
It will look like a boarding-school going to the midwife..."*

*... And then and there an agreement was made that it
should be done. They were to deliver five at £5 a head all
round, commission included. But as I was buying wholesale
to sell again it was agreed that they would find the girls at a
commission of 20s. a head for each certificated virgin, and
deliver to me a written pledge, signed with the name and
address of each girl, consenting to come at two days' notice
to be seduced at any given place for a certain sum down.
I had to pay the doctor's fee for examination and make an
allowance for cabs, &c.[11]*

Then followed detailed descriptions of how the procuresses set
about preparing the delivery of girls who were virgo intacta –
virgins – and the certificates of authentication to that effect which
were subsequently issued to the purchasers. There were also
details of the prices being charged for the whole process.

*They had brought me altogether nine girls in ten days from
the receipt of the order, four of whom were certificated as
maids and five were rejected. I have now in my possession
the agreement for seduction of all the certificated maids
and of three of the uncertificated, of the virginity of whom
I have very little doubt. In all, I have agreements signed by
seven girls varying from fourteen to eighteen years of age,
who are ready to be seduced by any one when and where I
please, provided only that I give two days' notice, and pay
them altogether a sum not less than £24, nor more than
£29. Fees, expenses, &c., incurred in procuring these girls*

*cost, say, £10 or £15 more. Altogether I was in a position to retail virgins at £10 each, and make a handsome profit on the transaction," the Pall Mall Gazette editor reported.*[12]

For its readers, these revelations would have been enough to shock, but Stead went a step further, describing how the girls were "Delivered for Seduction". He reported conversations with some of the young women, most of whom he discovered were prepared to be seduced, even if it meant becoming pregnant. However one of the girls, according to Stead, hardly even knew what the word "seduced" meant but was still willing to go with a man because she was from a poverty-stricken background, needed the money and, over a period of months, had been groomed for the sex trade.

*"We are very poor," she said. "Mother does not know anything of this: she will think a lady friend of Miss Z.'s has given me the money; but she does need it so much." "But," I said, "it is only £2." "Yes," she said, "but I would not like to disappoint Miss Z., who was also to have £2." By questioning I found out that the artful procuress had for months past been actually advancing money to the poor girl and her mother when they were in distress, in order to get hold of her when the time came! She persisted that Miss Z. had been such a good friend of hers; she wanted to get her something. She would not disappoint her for anything.*

*"How much do you think she has given you first and last?" "About 10s. I should think, but she gave mother much more." "How much more?" "Perhaps 20s. would cover it." "That is to say, that for a year past Miss Z. has been giving you a shilling here and a shilling there; and why? Listen to me. She has already got £3 from me for you, and you will give her £2 – that is to say, she will make £5 out of you in return for 30s., and in the meantime she will have sold you to destruction." "Oh, but Miss Z. is so kind!"*

*Poor, trusting little thing, what damnable art the procuress must have used to attach her victim to her in this fashion! But the girl was quite incapable of forming any calculation as to the consequences of her own action. This will appear from the following conversation. "Now," said I, "if you are seduced you will get £2 for yourself; but you will lose your maidenhood; you will do wrong, your character will be gone, and you may have a baby which it will cost all your wages to keep. Now I will give you £1 if you will not be seduced; which will you have?"*

*"Please sir," she said, "I will be seduced." "And face the pain, and the wrong-doing, and the shame, and the possible ruin and ending your days on the streets, all for the difference of one pound?" "Yes, sir," and she burst into tears, "we are so poor." Could any proof be more conclusive as to the absolute inability of this girl of sixteen to form an estimate of the value of the only commodity with which the law considers her amply able to deal the day after she is thirteen?*[13]

Not everyone was pleased to have these facts out in the public domain, and the backlash against Stead and his Maiden Tribute articles began very soon after the first publication.

# CHAPTER 12

# "FILTH AND OBSCENITY"

As the old steam press at the *Pall Mall Gazette* turned out the first editions of its Maiden Tribute of Modern Babylon, WH Smith, the biggest chain of newsagents in the country, which had a monopoly on all the news stalls,[1] was among the first to respond.

The company refused to sell the *PMG*[2] so it was down to the independent newsboys who saw an opportunity to make a good deal of money, as we have seen. When General William Booth and Bramwell, whose part in the scandal would soon be known to the world, discovered that the *Gazette* had been banned from sale at railway bookstalls, they opened the doors of Salvation Army headquarters for sales. Groups of trainee Salvation Army officers – the "cadets" from the officers' training homes – also picked up supplies from headquarters and went out to sell them on the streets.[3]

High profile supporters also stepped up to help. It was said that the writer George Bernard Shaw, assisted by Mr Stead, helped to distribute some of the four hundred thousand free copies of the articles in the streets. Stead also saw to it that the church was made aware of the scandal he had uncovered, and he posted free copies of the paper to clergymen across the country.[4]

But others, who were opposed to changing the age of consent, were furious. There were those who believed that interference in the "private" lives of people was unacceptable. Other vested interests were concerned that a new law to raise the age of consent could destroy, or at least substantially curtail, lucrative businesses that hitherto had been allowed to continue without much intrusion.

There were those, including the MP for Whitehaven, George Cavendish-Bentinck, who had long opposed any new vice laws. He had taken the opportunity of a poorly attended House of Commons just before the late May Whitsun recess to "talk out"the bill, preventing its passage into law at its third attempt. On that occasion some reported that the fact that there were so few MPs present for the debate proved that the bill failed as a result of pure apathy.[5] One calculation said there were no more than twenty MPs present for that debate, although Cavendish-Bentinck lost an attempt to stop the debate on technical grounds. The House of Commons needed a quorum for a debate to go ahead and he argued that the numbers present failed to meet that. Other commentators believed that many in Parliament thought there was little point passing a new and substantial bill at that time because there was an election on the horizon. Gladstone's Liberal government was on the point of collapse,[6] and it would be better for a new government to bring the measures to the House.

Not everyone who had voted against the Criminal Law Amendment Bill over a period of years was against raising the age of consent and indeed, many MPs voiced deep concern about the need to protect vulnerable young women. But there were other aspects of the proposed new law which concerned them, namely the increase of police powers, which were incorporated into the bill.[7] But some may well have had other motives for consistently rejecting a law that would protect vulnerable young women from exploitation.

Whether he was an official part of the "brothels lobby" is not substantiated but George Cavendish-Bentinck may certainly have had some vested and personal reasons for obstructing the passing of a law which would strengthen the powers of the police and protected "innocents". He was a barrister as well as a politician and was first elected to Parliament in 1859 as the MP for Taunton in Somerset and subsequently elected the member for Whitehaven at the 1865 General Election. He served under

Prime Minister Disraeli as Parliamentary Secretary to the Board of Trade (1874–75) and as Judge Advocate General from 1875 to 1880,[8] and was responsible for the court martial process within the British armed forces.[9] In 1875 he had been appointed to the Privy Council, the formal body of advisers to the monarch.

But there may have been another side to Cavendish-Bentinck. A few years after the Maiden Tribute trial, Bentinck was among those named in another legal inquiry which followed the discovery by police of a homosexual male brothel in Cleveland Street in Fitzrovia in London. The "Cleveland Street scandal" resulted in several trials of a number of men accused of breaking Section 11 of the Criminal Law Amendment Act 1885, which had outlawed all homosexual acts between men, and procurement or attempted procurement of such acts.[10]

Several members of the aristocracy were named in the course of the trial and the newspapers also hinted at the involvement of others. The final defence witness, a male prostitute called John Saul, had in a police interview spoken of a George Cavendish-Bentinck who he claimed "frequently visited the home and had to do with boys". That reference does not appear in any other police or court reports and certainly didn't surface in any press coverage of the case.[11]

In early July 1885, Cavendish-Bentinck tabled a question in Parliament to the Home Secretary drawing attention to the "objectionable subjects" being circulated by the *Pall Mall Gazette*. He questioned whether there existed any means of "subjecting the authors and publishers of these objectionable publications to criminal proceedings".[12]

This last ditch attempt to discredit the *Pall Mall Gazette* and its editor might well have been initiated because Bentinck was concerned what more might come out in the Maiden Tribute articles. As part of his inquiry, William Stead interviewed a number of individuals including the MP for Whitehaven, as he wrote in "The Truth about our Secret Commission" published on 9 July.

*As an instance of the thoroughness with which this inquiry*
*was conducted, I may say that in the execution of my duty I*
*even interviewed Mr. Cavendish-Bentinck. To avoid exciting*
*undue expectations, I may say it was disappointing.[13]*

Stead had also reported that his Secret Commission had taken statements from people within the sex trade, including a certain "Mrs Jeffries", with whom Cavendish-Bentinck was widely believed to be connected.

The interview with Mrs Jeffries, as part of the *Pall Mall Gazette*'s Secret Commission, and the reference to her in the articles would have rung a loud bell with the newspaper's readers. Mary Jeffries was a renowned high-class former prostitute and, by the 1880s, a woman in her seventies, still one of the prominent madams. A procuress in London, she ran one of the few brothels which catered almost exclusively to the elite.[14] Her business operated from a row of interconnected terraced cottages in Chelsea, a quiet and respectable residential area and the unlikeliest of places to find a house of ill repute.[15]

Mrs Jeffries was the epitome of discretion, which kept her customers happy, among whom were prominent businessmen, high-ranking army officers, politicians, including at least one member of the House of Lords, and even aristocrats.[16] It was claimed that Mrs Jeffries' brothel specialized in "perversions" including sadomasochistic practices like whipping and bondage.[17] The girls she employed were the "crème de la crème" of sex workers – young, attractive, beautifully dressed. For their time Mrs Jeffries could be paid up to £5 a session – a very large sum of money in 1885. There were even suggestions that Mrs Jeffries may have operated a white slave house along the River Thames, near Kew, from where women and girls were abducted and smuggled to foreign countries.[18]

The perverse practices at Mrs Jeffries' and other brothels were covered by The Maiden Tribute articles and shocked polite society, even though, theoretically they were already partly in the public domain.

Mrs Josephine Butler had for many years been appalled by the activities of the likes of Mrs Jeffries, and had been determined to bring the plight of young girls ensnared into the sex trade to public attention. One of her campaigning partners was a Quaker called Alfred Dyer who in 1879 had visited Brussels to investigate claims that British girls were being kept as sex slaves in state licensed brothels. This had received some press coverage and, as a result, Dyer and Mrs Butler had created the "London Committee for the Suppression of the Traffic in British Girls for the purposes of Continental Prostitution", of which, as we have seen, Sir Benjamin Scott, was chair.

The 1881 House of Lords Committee to investigate juvenile prostitution had followed such revelations,[19] but by 1884 the Criminal Law Amendment Bill was still stalled. In that year the London Committee, which was persisting with its evidence gathering, obtained evidence about the activities of Mrs Jeffries but the Metropolitan Police would not prosecute. Thanks to a former Met Police inspector, who resigned from the force as a result, more evidence was amassed and the London Committee brought a private prosecution against Mrs Jeffries in March 1885.[20] They dubbed her "the Empress of Vice" but the only charge which the Committee could bring against her was for keeping a "bawdy house", a prosecution under the Disorderly Houses Act of 1751.

Sir Benjamin, Alfred Dyer, Mrs Butler, and the others on the London Committee had great hopes for the trial and the resulting publicity, which was expected to include evidence from a former housemaid who would testify that she had witnessed one thirteen-year-old girl being whipped and then raped by a customer.[21] But the court case, on 5 May 1885, turned out to be farcical because the trial judge appeared to be as concerned with preventing any witnesses from revealing the names of Mrs Jeffries' high profile clients as with proving the charge against her.[22] Her lawyer advised her to plead guilty, and by doing so, evidence in the case remained undisclosed and Mrs Jeffries avoided prison in favour of a fine, albeit a rather hefty one of £200. Despite the nature of the trial, the old madam had left the courthouse covered almost in glory, with a "guard of honour" formed by some of her young "employees", the very girls and escorts whom she was said to exploit.

All this had infuriated the Purity Movement campaigners and for them it had been proof positive that there were people in positions of power prepared to protect the interests of others at the very top of society. [23]

Now though, Mrs Jefferies was speaking through the pages of the *Pall Mall Gazette*. Stead's interview with Mrs Jeffries was a stroke of genius because it gave the editor and his reporters access to many sordid details. But it seems Mrs Jeffries, no matter the nature of her disclosures, managed to work her charms on Stead. He described this "much maligned lady" in almost glowing terms:

> ...[She had been] good enough to accord one of the ablest and most indefatigable of my staff two interviews of several hours' duration, in the course of which she shed a flood of light upon the profession of which she has been for many years the acknowledged chief. So far as our inquiry goes Mrs. Jeffries kept her business on as respectable a footing as that ghastly calling permits. Compared with other keepers (concerning whom Mrs. Jeffries was very communicative), the houses of accommodation which she is said to have kept for --, and which, according to her own story, were frequented by personages who would take precedence of either, were well conducted, and it was the irony of destiny that they should have been singled out for prosecution while so many others so much worse were allowed to flourish untouched. [24]

How the *Gazette* readers felt about the notorious Mary Jeffries being described by its editor as a "much maligned lady" is not known, but many may well have seen her as evil personified. At the time, some believed she was at the centre of the "brothels lobby" which had kept the Criminal Law Amendment Bill from the statute books for so long and indeed that the main opponent of the law, George Cavendish-Bentinck MP, was in her pay.[25]

By early July, even as he tabled questions to the Home Secretary and asked whether the authors of the Maiden Tribute articles could be prosecuted for the publication of obscene material, Cavendish-Bentinck must have known that, finally, he faced a powerful adversary. Stead was on the crest of a wave of popularity and faced his critics head on. Although his articles were denounced by some for their content, Stead believed his was a just cause which demanded the use of the strongest possible language. How else could the world know the state of affairs of the underworld of British society? How else might he and the campaigners for the Criminal Law Amendment Act get what they wanted, if he did not present the "truth" to the world, and to those in authority?

Stead was confident of his own invincibility. Writing on 13 July 1865, the week after the Maiden Tribute articles first appeared, he addressed his "censors" and those whom he had implicated as villains in the columns of the *Pall Mall Gazette*. He had earlier castigated the church for their lack of action in helping to protect the girls at risk among them, but now he reported an overwhelmingly positive response to the Maiden Tribute series from that sector.

*In thousands of places of worship throughout the metropolis, places which have no raison d'etre if they do not inculcate morality and defend virtue, pious men stood up to instruct and advise their fellows upon matters of morality and of religion. Among the number were Bishops and Deans and Archdeacons and Vicars, and all the sturdy*

*Nonconformist preachers who represent the traditions
of Puritan austerity and Puritan intolerance of vice. We
appealed to them for their verdict, and what has been the
result? We are simply overwhelmed this morning with
reports from hundreds of churches and chapels, but, so far
as we have been able to examine the correspondence, there
has not been one single word raised in protest against our
action.*[26]

In the same breath, Stead turned on "the forces of wickedness in
high places" which he said were bombarding him and his paper
with criticism. And he taunted his detractors with the news of the
great support he and his *Pall Mall Gazette* were receiving.

*We are accused of flooding London with filth and
obscenity. Messrs. W. H. Smith & Son do their best to
suppress our sale, the Prince of Wales stops his paper, and
Mr. Cavendish-Bentinck, posing in the name of outraged
morality, plaintively clamours for our summary extinction.
But upon our side there stand arrayed with hardly any
exception all the best and purest and noblest men and
women in London. Whether they are philanthropists,
or moralists, or religious men, we are borne up and
encouraged by the enthusiastic support of all that is sound,
and pure, and healthy in society and in the nation.*[27]

Bramwell Booth later remembered those July days:

*The sensation was all the more tremendous because the Pall
Mall Gazette had a high reputation for exactitude. It was a
paper of tone and privilege, much patronised by clubmen.
The hot waves of public feeling quickly swelled and lapped
up to the doors of the House of Commons.*[28]

In between the failure of the Criminal Law Amendment Bill at Whitsun 1885 and the publication of the *Gazette* articles, there had been a change of government. Barely a couple of weeks after Cavendish-Bentinck had filibustered the Bill, William Gladstone's Liberal government had lost a vote of no confidence. There was now a new Conservative administration and a new Prime Minister, Robert Cecil, Marquis of Salisbury.[29] He would only be in the post for a few months, before Gladstone took office again in January 1886.

His tenure would be also be short-lived and in July 1886 the Marquis of Salisbury would move back in.[30] All this uncertainty would provide an opportunity for the campaigners to fight to raise the age of consent.

Where previously there had been no thought of resurrecting the doomed Criminal Law Amendment Bill by the new Salisbury government – Salisbury's new Chancellor of the Exchequer and Leader of the House of Commons Sir Michael Hicks-Beach had not originally included it in their plans for the rest of the parliamentary session – suddenly interest was shown once again at the highest level. Years later, Bramwell Booth remembered this change of heart:

*On the very day of the publication of the first of the articles, Lord Salisbury's new Ministry had met Parliament. Sir Michael Hicks-Beach, in his programme for the remainder of the session, had made no reference to the Criminal Law Amendment Bill, which had been left in the air – and, being House of Commons air, none too healthy a medium in which to be suspended. Nor did the ex-Ministers opposite protest against the omission. But a day or two later, evidently prompted by the state of feeling outside, the Home Secretary, Sir Richard Cross, proposed to resume the interrupted debate, on a promise of co-operation from Sir William Harcourt.[31]*

When articles began appearing, Cavendish-Bentinck wasn't the only voice against the *Pall Mall Gazette*. Another MP wanted to discredit Stead and his newspaper further and so claimed in Parliament that the *Pall Mall Gazette* had raised its wholesale price by 25 per cent.[32] This, if widely believed, would have suggested the articles were just a stunt to make money and that Stead wasn't really interested at all in the greater good. He, of course, vehemently denied this allegation in the paper the following day.

The political fuss created by Cavendish-Bentinck and his cohorts almost worked. By the Tuesday evening, after just two days of publication, the newly appointed Home Secretary Sir Richard Cross sent for Stead and requested that he stop publishing the articles.[33] Not only did Stead refuse to do so, he urged Sir Richard not to be intimidated by the claims being made on the floor of the House, but instead to back the newspaper. He went so far as to give the Home Secretary some advice on what he should do next, suggesting that he could "say in the House of Commons that the *Pall Mall Gazette* has covered itself with everlasting glory".

When that request was refused, Mr Stead suggested the Home Secretary should instead "say that the *Pall Mall Gazette* has committed an abominable outrage on the public morals and that you have instructed the Law Officers of the Crown to prosecute me at once".

Cross also declined to follow that course of action or to be goaded by Stead, although there is some evidence in closed Home Office files, written by the Lord Chancellor of the time, which indicates that the government did consider prosecuting the *Pall Mall Gazette* at this point but decided not to lest it be seen as "shielding the depravity of the rich at the expense of the poor".[34]

But was it a coincidence that, after that meeting with Stead, the Tory government, with the promise of support from the opposition party of the day, the Liberals, announced that it would support the Criminal Law Amendment Act? The Home Secretary, although he had categorically told Stead that he would not endorse the actions of the *Pall Mall Gazette* on the floor of the House, on Wednesday 8 July opened the debate on the revived Criminal Law Amendment Bill and stood to address his fellow parliamentarians, saying "This is a question that has stirred England from one end to the other... There is nothing that the English are so determined to maintain as the purity of their households."[35]

It was a clear warning that, this time around, the Cavendish-Bentincks of the world would not be able to destroy the Bill or delay its progress into law.

# CHAPTER 13

# GETTING PERSONAL

When the Criminal Law Amendment Bill debate opened in Parliament, rather than toning down the content, the *Pall Mall Gazette* grew progressively more scandalous as the week progressed. The day after Stead was called to the interview with the Home Secretary and the debate in Parliament commenced, the articles became more personal. There must have been individuals for whom this now had the potential to ruin them and their reputation.

Under the title "The Maiden Tribute of Modern Babylon III: the Report of our Secret Commission" Stead wrote:

*Here in London, moving about clad as respectably in broad cloth and fine linen as any bishop, with no foul shape or semblance of brute beast to mark him off from the rest of his fellows, is Dr,---, now retired from his profession and free to devote his fortune and his leisure to the ruin of maids. This is the "gentleman" whose quantum of virgins from his procuresses is three per fortnight – all girls who have not previously been seduced.*

*But his devastating passion sinks into insignificance compared with that of Mr. ---, another wealthy man, whose whole life is dedicated to the gratification of lust. During my investigations in the subterranean realm I was constantly coming across his name. This procuress was getting girls for ---, that woman was beating up maids for ---, this girl was waiting for ---, that house was a noted place of – – –'s. I ran across his traces so constantly that I began to make inquiries in the upper world of this redoubtable personage. I soon obtained confirmation of the evidence I had gathered at first hand below as to the reality of the existence of this modern Minotaur, this English Tiberius, whose Caprece is in London.*

*It is no part of my commission to hold up individuals to popular execration, and the name and address of this creature will not appear in these columns. But the fact that he exists ought to be put on record, if only as a striking illustration of the extent to which it is possible for a wealthy man to ruin not merely hundreds but thousands of poor women. It is actually Mr. – – –'s boast that he has ruined 3,000 women in his time. He never has anything to do with girls regularly on the streets, but pays liberally for actresses, shop-girls, and the like. Exercise, recreation; everything is subordinated to the supreme end of his life. He has paid his victims, no doubt never gives a girl less than £5 but it is a question whether the lavish outlay of £3,000 to £5,000 on purchasing the assent of girls to their own dishonour is not a frightful aggravation of the wrong which he has been for some mysterious purpose permitted to inflict on his Kind.[1]*

There was no holding Stead back. On Thursday 9 July 1885, he directly addressed his opponents, including those who had tried to suppress the sale of the *Pall Mall Gazette* that week, in a leading article entitled "To Our Friends the Enemy". This time there were names:

*We owe our humble and heartfelt thanks to the City Solicitor, or rather to those unnamed and as yet unknown persons who instigated him yesterday to attempt to suppress the sale of the Pall Mall Gazette in the City of London.*
*After Mr. Cavendish-Bentinck, he has probably*

*contributed the most to break down the conspiracy of
silence which our contemporaries are maintaining, and
which we are quite willing they should maintain until they
have been fairly shamed into facing the truth. There is
something peculiarly characteristic in the mode in which
this unexpected attack was delivered.*

*The City Solicitor sent us no notice that any exception
was taken by the City authorities to the contents or the
Pall Mall Gazette. The first intimation we received was
in the shape of an incredible rumour that the City police
were seizing the paper in all directions and running in the
boys who sold it. At first we refused to believe a story so
contrary to the best traditions of English life. Police seizures
of offending journals are common enough in Vienna, but in
London such a high-handed outrage on the freedom of the
Press seemed impossible. So we dismissed the story as the
invention of ingenious youths, anxious to sell for sixpence as
a "suppressed" journal a paper which they had just bought
at the usual trade rate of ninepence the dozen.*

*Soon afterwards, however, the eleven boys who had
been "had up before the Lord Mayor", and dismissed
on undertaking not to sell any more copies in the City,
arrived at Northumberland Street for a fresh supply.
Then we received the report of the case from our ordinary
correspondent, when we were reluctantly compelled to
recognise the fact that the liberty of the Press had been
outraged in the very citadel of freedom...* [2]

Stead's claim that this was a deliberate attempt to squash the
freedom of the press would have been a novel although not entirely
unprecedented concept in 1880s London. Like his practice of
campaigning journalism, his use of big headlines, his interviews
with "celebrities" which often made the news, Stead's modern
approach to press freedom of speech was groundbreaking. As

"the world's first tabloid journalist", Stead was paving a way for the journalism of the future.

And it also appeared he was determined on a course of action which would see him propelled into even more controversy. A couple of evenings earlier, as we have seen, he had suggested, in private, to the Home Secretary that if his government was that unhappy with the *Pall Mall Gazette*, one option would be to prosecute the paper and its editor. Now he taunted his opponents in public:

> *It was rather mean, no doubt, not to give us notice of any intention to act, otherwise we might have been legally represented when the newsboys appeared before the Lord Mayor. But it is the nature of those whose weapon is the gag to be somewhat unscrupulous in its application, and we do not complain at this fresh demonstration of the nature of the evil with which we have to contend. That was a blow beneath the belt which was all very well for the first attack, but in future we hope that the City Solicitor will fight fair. Next time, instead of waging war against boys in the street, let him take proceedings against the responsible parties. In other words, we ask the City Solicitor to proceed, not against the poor lads who, as the Lord Mayor told him, are in a very minor degree responsible parties, but against ourselves.*
>
> *We are sick of this perpetual harrying of the poor, and leaving the well-to-do alone. If we have published anything that can by any reasonable construction be declared to be obscene, prosecute us, not the lads in the street. We emphatically deny that we have published a single line which deserves that censure. We are no advocates of obscenity. Some of those who are now using the cant cry of decency as a cloak for immorality may perhaps discover before we have done that we are more keen to secure the suppression of obscene literature and the punishment of those who produce it than they may altogether relish. That,*

*however, is by the way. What we have to say, as plainly as the English language will enable us to say it, is that if the City Solicitor or his backers feel it their duty to stand up in public court and declare that the Pall Mall Gazette is an obscene publication they are cowards and worse if they do not take proceeding against the paper. Either we are guilty or we are innocent. If we are guilty, it is we who deserve to be punished. If we are innocent, no man, whether the City Solicitor or any one else, has a right to slander us in public, without being compelled to make good his words.*[3]

Did Stead really believe that he would be prosecuted? Or was this just journalistic bravado? Perhaps he did assume that, even if there could be a case proved against his newspaper, he would have enough public support to prevent prosecution. The *PMG*, he said, had received an enormous number of letters and correspondence that week. Those who agreed with the paper had all signed their letters, while the critics had mostly written anonymously.[4] In print he thanked those supporters, including one "working silversmith" who, having heard that a prosecution might be likely, had even offered bail for the huge amount of £1,000.

For those determined to silence the *Pall Mall Gazette*, Stead was provocative in his challenge. He was not scared of what was to come and was prepared to stand by all he had written:

*Let there be no mistake about this matter. We challenge prosecution. We court inquiry. We have most reluctantly been driven to adopt the only mode – that of publicity – for arousing men to a sense of the horrors which are going on at this very moment. But having adopted this mode the more publicity we have the better. We are prepared, if we are driven to it, to prove our statements, and prove them to the hilt, although in order to do so it may be necessary to subpoena as witnesses all those who are alluded to in our inquiries, either in proof of our bona fides or as to the truth of our statements, from the Archbishop of Canterbury to Mrs. Jeffries, and from the Prince of Wales down to the Minotaur of London. One thing we will not do. We will not break faith with those who have trusted us, by giving us confidential information, which if admitted by them in court would lead to their imprisonment. But when all these are excluded, whom we are bound to shield from being punished for the service they have rendered in revealing the secrets of their prison-house, there will remain amply sufficient witnesses who are prepared to swear to the absolute truth of our ghastly and horrible narrative.*

*We are prepared to put every member of our Secret Commission in the witness-box, and support their testimony by a vast array of witnesses drawn from every rank, class, and condition of men...*[5]

It was stirring stuff from the eloquent Stead, who had done his groundwork. Before publication he had ensured that influential people, including the Archbishop of Canterbury, were aware of his "Secret Commission" and what he intended to print. This had resulted in support for the Criminal Law Amendment Bill from the Church of England and even the Upper House of the Convocation of Bishops[6] and could, potentially, be used as a defence in court.

Stead may have had confidence in his own invincibility and the belief that others would jump, if necessary, to his aid. Indeed, at his Old Bailey trial that October, Stead requested that the Archbishop of Canterbury Edward Benson and other key individuals – including the two Home Secretaries Sir William Harcourt and Sir Richard Cross, other high ranking politicians and even the philanthropist Dr Thomas Barnardo – be called to give evidence on his behalf, a request which was denied by the trial judge.

In July 1885, with his Maiden Tribute articles causing shock and scandal around the world, feeling secure in the knowledge that his articles had brought the Criminal Law Amendment Bill back to Parliament, and confident of high-level support, Stead may well have believed he was beyond the law.

# CHAPTER 14

# A TWO-AND-A-HALF-MILE-LONG PETITION

For Bramwell Booth and his parents and their Salvation Army, this was an extraordinary time.

Barely seven years previously, when The Christian Mission changed its name to The Salvation Army, it had received a great many legal, physical, and spiritual attacks, being assaulted on the streets by, among others, groups calling themselves names like "The Skeleton Army". These were usually hoodlums invariably rounded up by those, including publicans, who feared the Army's insistence on temperance would damage business. There had even been questions in parliament about the legitimacy of The Salvation Army, but now the group's leaders were being courted by the government and parliamentarians at the highest level.

The Criminal Law Amendment Bill was progressing well in the Commons, supported on this fourth attempt by personnel at the very top of government. The Home Secretary, Sir Richard Cross, officially reintroduced it.[1] In his address to the House, he endorsed the Bill's immediate passage into law, claiming that it was a measure that he had no doubt was "absolutely necessary". He was supported by the Attorney General, Sir Richard Webster, who would soon be leading the prosecution against those who had, in part, made this happen. However, on that day the Attorney General summed his feelings up by saying "Almost everyone who has spoken has agreed that there is a crying evil to be remedied."[2]

There was cross-party support for the measure – among those in favour of the Bill's resurrection was Sir Richard Cross's predecessor, Sir William Harcourt, lawyer, journalist, and Liberal Member of Parliament, who had been a Home Secretary under Gladstone. When the Liberals returned to government in 1886, Harcourt would be appointed Chancellor of the Exchequer, a position he was to hold several times in the following decade. He was known as "Gladstone's deputy" and would later also become Leader of the Opposition in a subsequent Parliament.[3]

With such friends and advocates, Stead and the leaders of The Salvation Army were moving in influential circles. Bramwell Booth and Stead, and "one or two other propagandists" as Bramwell described them later in his memoirs,[4] were even called upon to advise on how the measures being debated in Parliament might be strengthened.

But still, at this stage there was no indication that the Criminal Law Amendment Bill was guaranteed an easy passage through Parliament. Bramwell and his parents decided that if the age of consent was to be raised to protect the sort of children who had been proved to be at risk of an evil and decadent British underbelly of society, as claimed by the *Pall Mall Gazette* articles, something more than mere conversation with people in high places might be required.

That's where The Salvation Army's growing popularity and spread across the nation came in. While there were already the beginnings of dialogue with politicians at the highest level and the parliamentary debate was getting underway, the Booths decided to open another front in the war to see the age of consent raised. Up and down the country, public meetings were hastily arranged to focus on the sex trade, and the need for the Criminal Law Amendment Bill to be swiftly brought into law.

There was a rally for ladies only in a hall in Piccadilly in Central London on 13 July at which Catherine Booth was the main speaker. She spoke with passion about her horror at the "moral obtuseness" of those people in Parliament who could "pass such a law as that which lowered the age of the protection of the female child to 13". She questioned why in law a child could not legally dispose of her property or money until she attained the age of twenty-one but the legislature "gave her power to dispose of her virtue when she was too young to know the value of it, indeed to know what it meant".[5] This gathering was followed on the next day by a similar rally, where Mrs Booth and Josephine Butler put their case to a mixed audience.[6]

General William Booth had been ambivalent about the involvement of his wife and eldest son in the Maiden Tribute affair and was not entirely happy with the way in which Stead had conducted himself. Now, however, he threw himself into the campaign, travelling to the north of England for an impromptu lecture tour aimed at promoting the cause of the Bill.[7] He even defended the Army's relationship with Stead, saying that he was "a man with whom we are in the association of strong friendship".[8]

Mass meetings were organized in London, Manchester, Leeds, Sheffield, Newcastle-upon-Tyne, Portsmouth and other key locations,[9] and William Booth, his family and his organization shrugged off the criticism that was beginning to come their way. Many, especially those who knew relatively little about The Salvation Army, wondered why such "religious" people were involved in "this business" and General Booth was quick to answer the critics:

> *That for which God has peculiarly raised us up is to rid the poor of their miseries, to go to the drunkard, to the harlots, to the thieves and to the wretched people everywhere, wherever we can find them. Not only to those who are wretched and sinful but to those who are the most wretched and the most sinful.[10]*

On 3 June Catherine had written to Queen Victoria requesting her to get involved in ensuring the Criminal Law Amendment Bill would be reintroduced to Parliament. A senior lady-in-waiting, the Dowager Duchess of Roxburgh, had replied on the monarch's behalf, informing her that while Her Majesty fully sympathized with Mrs Booth on the subject, and had spoken to another lady closely connected with the government[11] she could do nothing more public.

With the series of meetings now underway, on 14 July Catherine Booth wrote again to the Queen:

> *Your Majesty will be aware that since your last*
> *communication to me, some heart-rending disclosures have*
> *been made about the painful subject on which I ventured*
> *to address you… it would be a great encouragement to*
> *thousands of those engaged in this struggle if your Majesty*
> *would at this juncture graciously send us a word of sympathy*
> *and encouragement to be read at our mass meetings in*
> *different parts of the kingdom.*

This time, the response from Queen Victoria came via the Dowager Marchioness of Ely:

> *The Queen feels very deeply on the subject… but her Majesty*
> *has been advised that it would not be desirable for the Queen*
> *to express any opinion upon a matter which forms at present*
> *the object of measures before Parliament.*[12]

Catherine Booth wasn't best pleased with the response and replied to the Queen via Lady Ely, suggesting that in her opinion this was not a "political question", and indicating that she would be referring to the Queen in her future addresses to the mass gatherings.

> *All I wish to be allowed to convey to the people of England
> is that Your Majesty is fully in abhorrence of the iniquities
> referred to… I am proposing therefore to read the note which
> Her Majesty has been pleased to send me by your Grace at a
> meeting of 5,000 on Monday night in London, and also at
> a large meeting in Yorkshire unless you have reason to believe
> that Her Majesty would have objection to such a course.[13]*

And so the letter from Queen Victoria in Lady Ely's hand, or
parts of it, was read out at several London meetings, and in Leeds,
Sheffield, Manchester, and Newcastle-upon-Tyne, where speakers
also included Bramwell and Florence, Stead, Mrs Josephine
Butler, and other supporters of the Booths and their cause.[14]

Apart from her royal correspondence, Catherine Booth had
communicated directly with the Prime Minister's office. Her
original June note to Prime Minister Gladstone, asking him to
exert any influence he had to ensure the "age of responsibility of
girls" would be raised to seventeen, had been given short shrift.
Now Gladstone's government had been ousted in favour of Lord
Salisbury and his Conservatives, and in July a letter was fired off
to the new Prime Minister containing a similar request.[15]

General William Booth, having cast aside his misgivings on
the Maiden Tribute affair, now shrugged off criticism that the
Army should not get involved in politics. He was forthright in his
responses to his critics:

> *We want our lawmakers to make just laws… I said to a
> friend who is mixed up with politics, "I think the time is
> come when you politicians ought to have another party
> – a party based on morality… Whatever differences of
> opinion there may be with regards to the special forms of
> government there can be no difference of opinion with good
> men that a good government ought to be the father of its
> people and the protector of their children.[16]*

But even all this was insufficient for the Booths. Mass meetings were one thing. To really grab the attention of Parliament and ensure that they could do nothing but immediately pass the Bill and protect young girls from what The Salvation Army maintained was a life of sin and degradation, abuse and exploitation, as identified by the recent *Pall Mall Gazette* articles, even more was required.

The answer was a national petition, which would demand legislation for the protection of children and would need to be raised immediately, while the Maiden Tribute articles were still fresh in the public mind and while talks were ongoing at a high level between Mr Stead, Bramwell Booth, and members of the government. A national petition was needed to gather as many signatures in as short a time as possible, while Catherine and William Booth were touring the country bringing the issue to the attention of "ordinary" people.

Over the course of a frantic few weeks in July 1885, The Salvation Army swung into action. A petition to government was drawn up which was placed for signatures in every Salvation Army hall, or meeting place, in the country. On 18 July, a "Special Notice" in the Salvation Army weekly newspaper, *The War Cry,* announced the petition. All officers and "soldiers" were asked to sign it and to "obtain as large a number of signatures as possible".[17] In less than three weeks, 393,000 names were gathered. Thousands more came in just too late to be included before the petition was due to be presented to Parliament in London.[18]

The petition had four key demands. The signatories wanted the "age of responsibility" for young girls to be raised to eighteen. This was a year older even than Catherine Booth had recently requested of two Prime Ministers. They also requested that the "procuration of young people for seduction or immoral purposes" be made a criminal offence with severe penalties attached. The new legislation being demanded would give magistrates the right to search any property if there was reason to believe it contained underaged girls detained against their will. And finally, those signing the petition wanted "equality of women and men before the law" in respect of solicitation. It was currently illegal for women to "solicit a man to immorality" and the new law should make it criminal for a man to "solicit a woman to immorality".[19]

The petition papers were gathered in just over a fortnight. When they were joined together in a long roll of paper, the resulting document was two and half miles long.

At Westminster, partly in response to the public outcry following the publication of the *Pall Mall Gazette* articles, the turnaround on the Criminal Law Amendment Bill had been rapid. Much of the opposition to the bill was swept aside when it was debated in the House of Commons. Even George Cavendish-Bentinck MP, who had long opposed any new vice laws, barely spoke in the debates. The passage of the bill into law seemed inevitable, but The Salvation Army wanted to be sure of a positive outcome, and behind the scenes work progressed on how and when to deliver the huge petition to Parliament. Because it had to be presented to the House by an MP, Professor James Stuart, the representative for Hackney, was approached and he agreed to make the presentation.

William Booth knew the value of publicity, and the delivery of the petition was an opportunity not to be missed. On 30 July, a spectacular public display was planned and huge crowds gathered along the way as the document was paraded through the streets of London on a horse-drawn vehicle. The wagon carrying the two-and-a-half-mile-long roll of paper was pulled by four grey horses and accompanied up to Whitehall by a fifty-piece brass band, and 150 "cadets" or trainee Salvation Army officers from the Clapham Training Home. Also in the procession were 300 female members or "soldiers" of The Salvation Army, resplendent in their navy blue uniforms and marching in time to the music.[20]

General William Booth desperately wanted to be able to take the petition right up to the doors of Parliament with his mighty procession following, but because Parliament was "in session", parades, bands, and banners were not allowed within the precincts of the House. Instead, once the procession reached nearby Whitehall, the huge roll of paper bearing the nearly 400,000 signatures of those supporting a change in law was placed on the shoulders of eight Salvation Army officers. They were permitted to take the huge petition onto the floor of the House of Commons where, as it was too big to fit into the pouch at the back of the Speaker's chair – the usual resting place for petitions during debates – the great roll of paper was deposited on the floor of the Chamber, in full view of a packed House of Commons,[21] the evidence of what The Salvation Army believed was the will of the people.

After just one week in committee for scrutiny, and following easy passage through the House of Lords, the Home Secretary again put the motion to the House of Commons and the bill was passed into law on 14 August 1885, by 179 votes to 71.[22] The Criminal Law Amendment Act 1885 raised the age of consent in Great Britain to sixteen – the age at which it still stands – and a year higher than the House of Lords had proposed.

The law effectively outlawed brothels, but the section which would have given magistrates the power to search premises where illegal activity was suspected was not included. The achievement of the Purity Movement campaigners put into place a law which not only served to protect vulnerable young people, but also changed the lives of many individuals for more than a century. The campaign to raise the age of consent was heralded as a magnificent success by all involved.

Stead claimed a central role in the change of heart at Westminster, although there's evidence that the Prime Minister, Lord Salisbury, was as much influenced by the findings of an inquiry by the Mansion House Group, which had investigated the claims made in the Maiden Tribute of Modern Babylon articles. The group included the great philanthropist, politician, and social reformer Lord Shaftesbury, the Roman Catholic Archbishop of Westminster Cardinal Henry Manning, and the Archbishop of Canterbury Edward Benson.[23]

The Salvation Army was delighted by the result of the petition and the public intervention by their troops on behalf of those less fortunate. The day after the law was passed, General Booth wrote a letter to all "The Soldiers of The Salvation Army throughout the World", via *The War Cry* newspaper, in which he expressed his thoughts about their achievements:

> *The Bill is only an instalment of the true measure of justice due to women, still it is a very substantial one. And if it is worked widely and perseveringly it will prove the beginning of the end of a vast mountain of vile iniquity that now exalts its proud head to the heavens.*[24]

A week after the law was passed a thanksgiving service was held at The Salvation Army's Exeter Hall meeting place in the Strand in London where many hundreds turned out to hear General Booth speak. But in his delight at the outcome for his Army, General Booth seemed to barely recognize the role of others in the success of the campaign.[25] As he wrote in that 15 August *War Cry* article:

> *Anyhow, while we thank God for the success He has given to the first effort of The Salvation Army to improve the laws of the nation, and pray that God may use this measure to put an end to at least some of the infamous iniquities that have been exposed, we must proceed with the adoption of such measures as seem likely to make the law productive of the largest amount of blessing to those in whose interest it has been passed.*[26]

The Booths and their Salvation Army had become much better known that summer of 1885 and the interest in them would only increase as the months progressed. Because, although the Purity Movement campaigners had won a battle, in ensuring the passage of the Criminal Law Amendment Act, there were those who remained infuriated by the outcome and the antics of William Stead.

Furthermore, there were individuals closer to the case who were also now appearing, who could be manipulated by those in authority and who wanted to see Stead have his comeuppance.

# CHAPTER 15

# A CASE OF ABDUCTION

While the Maiden Tribute of Modern Babylon articles were shocking the world and beginning to stir the consciousness of the British Parliament, on the poor streets of London the story of "Lily" was impacting on one family. The *Pall Mall Gazette* series soon began to register with the residents of Charles Street in Lisson Grove in Marylebone and within a few days of the first publication, Elizabeth Armstrong and her chimney sweep husband, Charles, had been made aware of the contents of the articles.

Since Eliza's departure from home on Derby Day a month previously, the only news her parents had received was in a letter to Mrs Broughton from Mrs Sullivan, reporting that Eliza was well. At first the Armstrongs had been either not concerned much about their daughter's welfare, or they were genuinely satisfied that she was safe and happy.

The *PMG* articles, however, activated the gossip-mongers in Charles Street, and although Mrs Armstrong would have sworn blind that Eliza had "gone into service", doubts began to surface in the minds of the neighbours and Eliza's own parents. The articles in the *Pall Mall Gazette* didn't name Eliza, but there were clues to the child's identity. "Lily's" school outings to Epping Forest and Richmond were mentioned, trips which Eliza had made and enjoyed. The "sale" of Lily seemed to have happened on Derby Day – 3 June – the same day Eliza had left home.

If Mrs Armstrong was concerned that "Lily" might in fact be her own Eliza, to make matters worse the girl's mother had been described as "a drunkard woman". As, on the night of Eliza's departure, Mrs Armstrong had, after being hit by her husband, got blinding drunk and been arrested, this seemed to indicate that they were one and the same woman.[1]

The neighbours may well have known, or at least suspected Mrs Broughton's reputation as a procuress, and the article had stated that money had changed hands during the "sale" of Lily. Gossip on the street corner quickly turned to open accusations – that Elizabeth Armstrong had knowingly sold her daughter, and that Mrs Broughton had pocketed a commission for the "introduction".[2] Elizabeth denied the accusations but she was concerned enough to go before the local Marylebone magistrate to seek help, saying that she had let her daughter go into service and now didn't know where she was.

The magistrate was unsympathetic, given that Mrs Armstrong had apparently let her thirteen-year-old child go away with a stranger a whole month earlier, and this was the first concern she had expressed. But he did order a police inquiry into the matter.

A Police Inspector Borner questioned Mrs Armstrong and Mrs Broughton, then travelled to Winchester, to the address on the letter received a short while previously. He found "Hope Cottage", a home for "fallen women", locked up. Rebecca Jarrett (the "Mrs Sullivan" of Derby Day who had taken Eliza) apparently ran the place but was away, in Jersey in the Channel Islands. Inspector Borner was told to speak to Rebecca's mentor, Josephine Butler, wife of the Reverend George Butler, Canon of Winchester.[3]

Mrs Butler did not trust the police, as they hadn't been very co-operative, when asked, to investigate the crimes against women and children that her London Committee and other inquiries had uncovered. She admitted she knew something of Mr Stead's "Secret Commission" but would tell him little else, and referred him rather reluctantly to Mr Bramwell Booth of The Salvation Army.

The following week Inspector Borner interviewed Bramwell Booth at The Salvation Army's headquarters in Queen Victoria Street. Mr Booth admitted he knew of the case of Eliza, and said that although he didn't know exactly where she was, he was assured that she *was* in service with a lady. He offered to get the address and to send it on to a friend of his – the Assistant Commissioner of Police. Inspector Borner seemed happy with the conclusion that Eliza had come to no harm, and he in turn reported back to Mrs Armstrong that her daughter was safe and there was no use pursuing the matter further.[4]

Mrs Armstrong, sticking to her claims that she had been unaware of the real fate of her daughter when she let her leave home on Derby Day, still made no official complaint and no claim that she suspected that the "Lily" of the *Pall Mall Gazette* was her daughter, Eliza. Any concern the Armstrongs might have had would have remained private but for the keen ears and eyes of a newspaper reporter who had been at Marylebone magistrates' court, covering another story on the day Mrs Armstrong appeared before the "beak" to report her concern about Eliza.

On Sunday 12 July a publication called *Lloyd's Weekly Newspaper* reported the hearing under the heading "A Mother Seeking a Lost Child". While there was no mention of the previous week's *Pall Mall Gazette* series, *Lloyd's* – which was known for its exposure of scandals and must have considered itself a great rival of the *PMG* – had sent a reporter to Charles Street, who had interviewed Mrs Armstrong and Mrs Broughton.[5]

Elizabeth Armstrong, perhaps persuaded by the attention in the press, now decided to pursue the matter further. There's no indication that she thought there was any financial gain to be had in doing so, but there's no doubt local gossip-mongers were making life for her and her family a misery. Her evidence in court later that year indicated this was the case. If nothing else, she wanted to clear her name with the neighbours.

Towards the end of July she reapplied to the local magistrate to try to get more information about the whereabouts of her daughter because The Salvation Army had still not sent her the information she required. Inspector Borner revisited Mr

Booth at Salvation Army headquarters, and was told that Eliza's circumstances had changed, and that the child was now staying with friends of his in France. Bramwell admitted that he had been doing some of his own investigations and come to the conclusion that to send Eliza back home to Charles Street would not be in her best interests, and that it would be better for her to remain in a safe, Christian environment.[6]

However, the Inspector was not happy with this turn of events and returned with Mrs Armstrong. Apparently the mother was so delighted to hear that Eliza was safe and still "pure" that she clapped and burst into tears.[7] It was during this interview with Bramwell Booth that she was reported as admitting that she had suspected that the "Lily" of the *Pall Mall Gazette* was her own Eliza. She insisted, in the presence of the police officer, that her daughter be returned to her to prove that she had not sold her into captivity. An address for Eliza in Loriol in Southern France was produced, and it was agreed that the Armstrongs would discuss the matter and let The Salvation Army know when they wanted Eliza to leave her current situation.[8]

By now *Lloyd's Weekly Newspaper* had discovered the connection between Eliza's disappearance and The Salvation Army and they took up the parents' cause. A reporter by the name of Hales escorted, and undoubtedly paid for, Mrs Armstrong's trip to Winchester,[9] where they discovered "Mrs Sullivan's" true identity and former occupation as a brothel-keeper and notorious former London procuress. Although Rebecca had reformed and was now working to rescue other girls from a life of vice, the newspaper still slammed into her reputation and that of the "Salvationists" and campaigners who were her friends, casting doubt on whether taking a child from its mother and deliberately "concealing" her whereabouts was a "religious act".[10]

*Lloyd's* was on to a great story. On 16 August, just two days after the Criminal Law Amendment Act had been passed in Parliament and received with great crowing by the editor of the *Pall Mall Gazette* and the General of The Salvation Army, *Lloyd's* ran another article which revealed that, despite a month having gone by since Mrs Armstrong's appeal to the Marylebone magistrate, she and her husband still didn't know where Eliza was. Now the spotlight was on The Salvation Army and its reputation was in jeopardy. Bramwell Booth issued a statement saying that Eliza Armstrong had been entrusted to their care to "save her from the demoralising surroundings in which she was placed" but that they still awaited confirmation of the Armstrongs' wishes.[11]

The *Lloyd's* article had the desired effect. George Cavendish-Bentinck once again took up the "brothels lobby" in the House of Commons, publicly asking the Home Secretary if he had seen the article and what he was going to do about it. Another MP rose and demanded to know whether the "decoying of a child under fourteen" was not a felony.[12]

Support for the Armstrongs was growing. Mr Edward Thomas of the London Female and Preventative Institute, who had also just happened to be in the magistrates' court in Marylebone on the same day as Mrs Armstrong first appeared, had also taken up their cause. He put out appeals for funds to help them in their case, and a big demonstration was planned in Hyde Park.[13]

Stead, meanwhile, sat back in his offices in Northumberland Street and watched this all unfold around him. Since the writing of the Maiden Tribute articles, which had made all sorts of outrageous claims, including the wrong assumption that Mrs Broughton was herself a brothel-keeper, he had done a little more investigating and may have started to feel vulnerable, concerned that some of the "facts" within his articles and his intention in writing them, could be challenged.[14] He would certainly have been aware of the growing and organized opposition against him, when only a few weeks earlier he had been applauded for his courageous journalism. But perhaps most frustrating for a man intent on making a name for himself was that the police had not come to him for confirmation of any of the facts of the case. It appeared there had been no direct mention of his *Pall Mall Gazette*, or of what he considered to be his groundbreaking Secret Commission and shocking series of articles in any of the subsequent publicity around the case.

Meanwhile, The Salvation Army *had* come in for attack and the General of the organization, William Booth, had already defended his people at a public meeting where he had denied the "allegations" against his band of missioners. Mrs Butler too had jumped to the defence of Rebecca Jarett and The Salvation Army. On her return from a trip abroad, she was horrified to discover how the matter appeared to have escalated out of control. She wrote to her local Winchester newspaper with a strong rebuttal of the criticisms of her friends.

Then, on 21 August, during an address to a Conference on the Protection of Girls in the St James' Hall in London, where he was due to call for the setting up of a "London Vigilance Society", William Stead also spoke out publicly for the first time on the whole affair. When a heckler at the back of the hall shouted out the single word "Armstrong!" the editor reacted strongly, with a dramatic announcement.[15]

Stead claimed that *he* and he alone, had been responsible for "taking Lizzie Armstrong away from her mother's house".[16] He maintained that the mother knew the child was headed for a brothel, and that Eliza had gone, very briefly, to such an establishment, but that no harm had come to her and that then he had put her in the safe hands of his friends in The Salvation Army. He insisted that the Salvationists had nothing to do with the child's removal from her home or her transportation to the brothel.[17]

Stead's pronouncement was just what his opponents had been waiting for. Since General Booth had publicly defended his Salvation Army in the case a week before, the *Pall Mall Gazette*'s rivals, including *Lloyd's Weekly Newspaper*, had been trying to substantiate the rumour which was now going about the city that the central theme of the Maiden Tribute articles, the buying and selling of the girl "Lily", had all been based not on a real situation but had been manufactured by Stead himself. And there was growing concern that the child Eliza was being kept away from her parents by The Salvation Army.

That weekend, Eliza was swiftly returned to England and reunited with her mother at Mr Stead's house in Wimbledon, although the editor was not there for the tearful reunion. Formal statements were taken back at Scotland Yard, the headquarters of the Metropolitan Police in London, and the child was, eventually, returned home.[18] Although it was certainly disappointing for Stead and the Booths that she was being returned to what they might have considered to be an inappropriate place in the slums of London,[19] the parents, at last, had their legal rights and their daughter restored.

General William Booth, whose main priority was his Salvation Army, now publicly took a step back from the debate that was raging around him and his organization. Even though his son and his missioners in England and in France had been central to the care of Eliza, and even though one might have expected William Booth to support those who had brought the plight of such as her to public attention, no one from The Salvation Army attended a rally in Hyde Park to support the *Pall Mall Gazette* and its editor. Did Stead feel abandoned by those he had considered to be friends? Or was he pragmatic enough to understand the extremely difficult position in which The Salvation Army found itself?

The editor was certainly prepared to take all the blame for the case himself. He had previously taunted Parliament and other authorities to arrest him on the basis of the sexual and shockingly "obscene" content of his Maiden Tribute articles, so he must have been prepared for what was to come. The legal case against those who had taken Eliza was almost ready. The Armstrongs, undoubtedly encouraged by others, had by now petitioned the Treasury Solicitor to take up the case for the abduction of their daughter.[20] Writs were issued for the arrest of Rebecca

Jarrett, William Stead, Bramwell Booth, and other accomplices. On 2 September a warrant was issued for the arrest of Rebecca Jarrett. Stead, who had just arrived in Switzerland for a holiday, immediately wired back to his office:

> Grindelwald, Wednesday night, September 2
>
> The arrest of Rebecca Jarrett is of a piece with the City Solicitor's prosecution of the newsboys. I alone am responsible. Rebecca Jarrett was only my unwilling agent. I am returning by the first express to claim the sole responsibility for the alleged abduction, and to demand, if condemned, the sole punishment. Meanwhile I am delighted at the opportunity thus afforded me of publicly vindicating the proceedings of the Secret Commission.[21]

Stead returned at once to England.

A week later there was a preliminary court hearing at Bow Street Magistrates' Court where evidence was heard to decide if there was enough to take Jarrett to trial at a higher court. By that time others had been added to the case. Stead himself was also charged, along with Bramwell Booth and Sampson Jacques. Mrs Elizabeth Combe, who had accompanied Eliza on her journey to The Salvation Army in France, was also charged, as was Louise Mourey, the "midwife" who had examined Eliza prior to her being taken to the brothel on Derby Day.[22] The charge was the abduction of a child. For Mourey, Stead, and some of the others involved in the intimate physical examination of Eliza Armstrong, there was a secondary charge of "technical assault".[23]

What just a few weeks previously had been a triumph of righteous journalism for Stead and the other campaigners in favour of raising the Age of Consent, was now turned on its head. The crowds who had so recently flocked to buy the *Pall Mall Gazette* and to hear the leaders of The Salvation Army and others extol the virtues of the Maiden Tribute campaign, now bayed for the blood of the accused at Bow Street Magistrates' Court. As the *Pall Mall Gazette* itself reported in a special supplement on 3 October the interest in the case was phenomenal.

*Early on Monday morning, the 7th of September, the day appointed for the first hearing of the case, a large crowd had assembled in Bow-street to catch a glimpse of any one who was to take a part in the trial. By half-past ten the large court was what an impartial critic would call "filled to its utmost capacity". No such thing. If there is one room in the world which has elastic properties it is a police-court on the day of an important trial. They came, and still they came, counsel and counsels' clerks, solicitors and solicitors' clerks, artists, reporters, and messengers forming the legitimate members of the audience to whom every one gives way by right. What may be termed in distinction the illegitimate crowd unfortunately comes too, and pushes and bribes its way in, until the whole is a mass of human beings wedged in almost inextricably. Seats were always found for a number of ladies interested in the case, among them being, Mrs. Josephine Butler, Mrs. Stead, and Mrs. Bramwell Booth, who formed one group. And this scene was repeated day after day while the trial lasted. Always the same crowd, inside and without, and always the formidable array of counsel.[24]*

For Stead's long-time enemies, who detested his brash, interfering, and outrageous journalistic tactics, this must have been a moment to raise a glass to victory in the smoke-filled libraries of the London gentlemen's clubs. Even some of his friends, including radical thinkers and parliamentarians who had helped to distribute the *Gazette* and to pass the Bill just a month earlier, distanced themselves.

The Maiden Tribute articles had, of course, received a mixed reception. Stead had been sent many messages of support and thanks for his exposure of this evil and the breaking of "the conspiracy of shameful silence which has so long oppressed our hearts". The Church of England and people of influence had officially supported him across the nation, but when the *Lloyd's Weekly Newspaper*, followed by other newspapers including the *St James's Gazette*, began to cast doubt on the whole case and the motives of the *PMG* editor, many began to reconsider their endorsement.[25] Indeed, forty years later the writer George Bernard Shaw, who had handed out free copies of the *Gazette* with Stead, told the editor's biographer that, following the revelation that the case of Eliza Armstrong was a "put up job" and that Stead himself had created the situation, "nobody ever trusted him".[26]

Things weren't much easier for The Salvation Army, which was lambasted for being central to the scandal, despite General Booth's attempts to distance himself from Stead.

In his opening statement at Bow Street Magistrates' Court, Stead had taken pains to try to exonerate Bramwell Booth and The Salvation Army. They had only accepted responsibility for Eliza Armstrong, he said, *after* they had received assurances that Rebecca Jarrett had bought her for "immoral purposes". They had been convinced that only by helping to take her away from the situation at home would she be rescued from a life of evil.[27]

The truth was, even if Bramwell Booth had been unaware of the exact details of Eliza's removal from home, as he claimed later in court, and even if The Salvation Army's only role in the case was the care of a child who they believed was in danger of being led into an immoral life if she returned home, the organization had played a central role in the affair. Mr Stead's glowing acknowledgment of their help in the matter, reported in the Maiden Tribute series, had proved that. The Salvation Army was implicated and not just because one of their "members", Rebecca Jarrett, had been persuaded to be part of Stead's plot. Others in The Salvation Army had taken the child "Lily" out of the country without parental permission. Although the whole organization wasn't on trial, it might have felt like that in the minds of its founders and the Booth family.

The Salvation Army were certainly not loved by all even though the outward opposition had died down in recent years, and this was an opportunity for their detractors to once again voice their concern. The *Freethinker* monthly journal, which had been set up in 1881 as the voice of atheists, humanists, and secularists, had been a constant opponent. As the case against The Salvation Army's second-in-command began, the journal's founder and editor G. W. Foote took the opportunity to voice his opinion that the Maiden Tribute affair would mean the end of the Army's aspirations.

> *However the Armstrong Case terminates, it is bound to do (William) Booth a great deal of harm. The public opened its eyes wide at his cadging of twenty thousand pounds on the strength of the "revelations" and now it begins to see what a mischievous and dangerous organisation the Salvation Army really is, with its thousands of ignorant fanatics under the despotic control of an unscrupulous, self-seeking chief whose policy seems inspired by Simon Peter, Barnum and Fagin... We believe this trial will be a dreadful, and perhaps a death blow to the Salvation Army. Like other pious adventurers, Booth will languish and perish from the disease of being found out.*[28]

How wrong the *Freethinker* was, but nevertheless the reputation of all of those facing trial for the abduction of Eliza Armstrong was at serious risk, as was their freedom.

## CHAPTER 16

# THE ROAD TO THE OLD BAILEY

*Rookwood Road,*
*Stamford Hill,*
*London, N.*
*Sunday Sept. 13, '85.*

*My Dearest Love,*

*We have had an anxious day, altho' I should not be anxious myself, but that it is Bramwell who I fear will worry about things. Still I believe that if they are committed to-morrow, which we all expect, he will feel much better. Rebecca [Jarrett] is all right they say, and has consented to some evidence coming out which blacks her.*

*The cross-examination on Saturday showed up Mrs. Broughton as a very low, bad woman. But Ranger and all think they are certain to commit. Whether the matter ever comes to a real trial or not, very doubtful in the estimation of Russell and others. They think that the Government has felt so bespattered with these Revelations that they have felt compelled to discredit them before the world, consequently they have fallen upon this case.*

*Perhaps they may never push the thing to the extremity of a trial; if they do, nothing very much can possibly come of a conviction if any Jury can be got together that will say "Guilty".*

> *My opinion is that any way the Army cannot suffer very much. We shall have after the trial, whichever way it may go, a splendid text for an appeal to the Country. If they convict, we can show up the injustice of the thing – if they acquit, we can show the infamy and groundlessness of the prosecution. If B[ramwell] goes to prison, they will make a martyr of him, and this alone will make him a heap of new friends and bind the Army and him more closely together and make thousands burn to go to prison too.*
>
> *Only one thing can hurt us, our own fears and worries; in other words, OUR OWN UNBELIEF...*
>
> *Have faith in God, Lucy has written across her breast. Oh, let us have it written across our hearts, and act it out...*
>
> **(William Booth)**[1]

The Bow Street Magistrates' hearing, which had begun on 7 September and which would determine whether Bramwell Booth, Stead, Jarrett, Combe, Jacques, and Mourey would face a trial at the Central Criminal Court, the Old Bailey, was nearing its conclusion.

As they had throughout the hearing, and as they would for the duration of the subsequent Old Bailey trial, the Booth family had been out in force, supporting Bramwell from the gallery. The presence of the uniformed contingent would have been quite a sight not just for the crowds with whom they mingled, but also for the press and the court officials. And one Booth sister – young Lucy – was openly demonstrating her faith, not just in her big brother, but also in the Almighty, through the inspiring words which she had written, perhaps pinned on to her chest.

Catherine Booth was out of town on a preaching tour, so it was through her husband's letters that she was able to keep in touch with the proceedings at Bow and the advice that William was receiving from, among others, The Salvation Army's solicitor, Dr Washington Ranger.

That William Booth was concerned about his eldest son is obvious but his correspondence shows that he was rather less sympathetic to the others in the court. He didn't even show much compassion for the poor Rebecca Jarrett, one of his own "soldiers" who, much against her better judgment and while still vulnerable, had been persuaded by others, including his son, to get involved. The hearings at Bow Street ran for five days and as Bramwell Booth would write much later in life, they attracted great crowds every day which made life very uncomfortable for the defendants.

> *Every blackguard in London must have assembled in Bow Street while the case was before the magistrate. From every foul den in the metropolis the people had come to gloat on the discomfiture of these modern Galahads. I was mobbed more than once, dragged out of a cab, and maltreated, and only rescued with difficulty by a police inspector, who drove the crowd right and left.[2]*

The use of a Black Maria police vehicle saved the defendants from serious injury at the hands of the mob, but it could not protect them from the shakes of the head and the silent derision from many of the "righteous and respectable people" who also gathered.

> *They were agreed as to the evil, were, in fact, horrified that such things could be in their midst, but, with here and there an exception, they strongly disapproved our methods of meeting it.[3]*

These words in Bramwell's autobiography seem to indicate that he might have known more of the whole Stead plot than he indicated at the time. Whatever the case, he truly believed that he had done no wrong.

Stead also went into the Bow Street proceedings sure of his ground. In the run up to his court appearance, however, he had prepared for the worst – a hefty legal bill – and had launched a

"Defence Fund" which he later claimed raised £6,000, equivalent to around half a million in modern currency.[4] However, he decided not to employ a legal team or even a barrister, preferring to defend himself at both the Magistrates' Court and the subsequent Old Bailey hearing.

Whether due to madness or excessive pride, Stead turned down the offer of help from a legal team being put together by Bramwell Booth – the eminent Sir Charles Russell, a Queen's Counsel and an eminent Irish lawyer, and the future Home Secretary, Henry Matthews QC.[5] Stead appeared convinced that the world would understand his motives when he stood in court.

Other newspapers, in covering the Bow Street magistrate's hearing, had much to report and to mock, and they were quick to point out what they considered to be Stead's arrogance. On 9 September Stead, reading a prepared statement, launched into a detailed justification of his behaviour and actions. A *Lloyd's Weekly Newspaper* reporter described the proceedings in court as "ludicrous in the extreme".[6] While the others in the dock had offered answers to questions in the usual manner, Stead's statement was more or less a moral justification for his actions. The magistrate, Mr James Vaughan,[7] cut him off and demanded to see a copy of his statement before allowing the editor to continue, but the moment had left Stead at a disadvantage.

In summing up at the end of the hearing the magistrate was scathing in his condemnation of those in the dock before him, but particularly of Stead. He said that, no matter how "praiseworthy" his motives, he believed the editor of the *Pall Mall Gazette* to have been seeking "self-glorification". He concluded that Stead had probably committed a number of statutory offences while putting together his "materials for the concoction of that deplorable and nauseous article" and he had no hesitation but to conclude that there was enough evidence to try the case. He referred Stead and the others upwards, for trial before the Central Criminal Court.[8] At first, Mr Vaughan was minded to keep all the defendants in custody until the main trial, but was persuaded to offer bail, which was set at £100 each – a huge sum of money at the time.[9]

At the beginning of the hearing, the roads outside Bow Street were blocked with crowds of people. *Lloyd's Weekly News* estimated a crowd of 2,000 on one day, many of them of "the roughest type".[10] But by the time the hearing was over, interest in the case was already on the wane and the numbers in the streets had dwindled. The thousands had, according to Stead's own *Pall Mall Gazette*, been "reduced to a few scores, and this handful was quiet and sympathetic". The *Gazette* put this down to better crowd control by the police and the fact that the public had realized that "the real nature of the prosecution" was political in nature and had, as such, lost interest.[11]

Although public interest appeared to have waned, with a trial at the Old Bailey on the horizon General William Booth, who had at first been keen to ensure that The Salvation Army's troops did all they could to reinforce the innocence of the Chief of the Staff, now realized the necessity of prudence.

Further on in the letter to his wife written on Sunday 13 September, William Booth urged caution in her public addresses over the forthcoming days:

> *You must be careful – there's some sort of a threat to bring an action for libel and damages against all concerned for asserting that Mrs. Armstrong sold her child. Now there are a lot of scoundrels who would find money for anything to get at our throats, so we must be careful. I hate this litigation. The time it consumes is awful. I can't make out why it should be so. But it goes to the heart direct.[12]*

At first General Booth had written that he planned a counter-demonstration and suggested that a card could be sold, which could also be sent to the Queen, Cabinet ministers, bishops, and more. But, even before he had time to post the letter, his right hand man, George Scott Railton, had advised him to change tactics. There was a scribbled postscript to the letter.

*P.S. Since writing the above I have had a talk with Railton about expressions of sympathy with the Chief in meetings, and about explanations of the matter altogether; and he argues with a good deal of force that anything like votes of sympathy of Soldiers or anybody else with Superior Officers is unwise and prejudicial to discipline. He thinks that explanations are beneath us; but would advocate the pushing forward of our Rescue Work, the showing up of what we are doing in this direction, bringing out the case, and then remarking that this is the sort of thing for which they are attacking our Chief of the Staff.*

*There is something in all this. Anyway it does not seem dignified for an Army meeting to sympathise with the Army. The proper thing to do is to get up a great Defence Committee outside of us and let them speak.*

*I am sure the best answer we can make to the whole affair is to go on with our own work, keep our heads up, and keep on with the song of victory.*

*The lasses went past here this morning from Tottenham, singing "Victory". They had had a quiet meeting, sold 200 War Cries, and had a collection of 15s in the open air. To be explaining yourself until the trial is over Railton thinks is humiliating.*

*Consider the matter carefully, and God give you wisdom.*
*W.B.* [13]

Stead could be forgiven for feeling abandoned, but despite the wave of feeling against him and the growing chasm between himself and the leader of The Salvation Army, his impending prosecution in one of the highest courts in the land was potentially embarrassing for the government. The court case was based around a campaign which had so recently galvanized them into a quick turnaround on the Criminal Law Amendment Act, and it also resulted in a large volume of correspondence to the Home Office in his defence. The letters, which were chiefly from supporters of the Purity Movement, questioned why the man who had disclosed the vice of the London underworld and even "caused the law to be changed" was now on trial, while "the guilty men were still walking free".[14]

These were embarrassing questions for the government and there was potentially more to come. Even as the Bow Street hearings proceeded and as he awaited trial at the Old Bailey, Stead, it appeared, was planning new revelations in the *Pall Mall Gazette*, a series on English girls in foreign brothels.[15] He had already contracted a German detective to undertake an investigation and when a rival newspaper, the *St James Gazette*, was made aware of the plan, they exposed Stead's next steps in his war against vice.[16]

In the end Stead did not proceed with the series – perhaps in losing the surprise element he considered it not worth his while. But he might also have been aware that there had been a flurry of correspondence between high ranking parliamentarians and government departments – including a letter from the former Lord Chancellor, Lord Hallsbury, to the Home Secretary – requesting clarification on the regulations on obscenity and questions on whether the government had any rights to prevent the series from being published. The result was that a Home Office official had ordered the Metropolitan Police Criminal Investigation Department (CID) to keep a close eye on the *Pall Mall Gazette* and any future plans for scandalous stories.[17]

With his trial now set at the Old Bailey, Stead had other things on his mind, as he prepared for his court appearance, and perhaps girded his loins for the inevitability of a period of imprisonment, should he be found guilty. The stage was set. Stead, Booth, Jarrett,

Combe, and Jacques would appear before a judge and jury at the Central Criminal Court in London, the Old Bailey, in about a month's time. The trial date was set for Friday, 23 October 1885.

# CHAPTER 17

# ON TRIAL

The Central Criminal Court of England and Wales, otherwise known as the "Old Bailey", has for centuries been London's prominent criminal court. It is known not just for the cases which have been heard within its courtrooms, but also the statue of the figure of Justice which stands atop the imposing building, situated to the north-east of St Paul's Cathedral in the City of London.

Criminal cases from within the City were the first to be heard there, usually in rooms hired in the vicinity, or even in nearby Newgate prison, which had been in use since the twelfth century. Very poor conditions in this most notorious of penitentiaries required the building of a new courthouse which led to the completion of the Old Bailey in 1785. It was nicknamed after the street it stands in – Old Bailey – which runs between the ancient Newgate Street to the north, and Ludgate Street to the south, and it soon became a place not just of trials and sentencing, but also of the hanging of those sentenced to death.

A second courtroom was added in 1824 and a decade later the Central Criminal Court's jurisdiction was extended by an Act of Parliament. No longer were cases only from the City of London and the adjoining Middlesex region to be heard at the Old Bailey. From 1834 the Central Criminal Court also heard trials involving crimes, including treasons, felonies, and misdemeanours[1] not just from the City of London but also from Essex, Surrey, Kent, and those allegedly committed on British ships on the "high seas".[2]

It was to this court that William Stead, Bramwell Booth, Rebecca Jarrett, Elizabeth Combe, and Sampson Jacques came on the first day of trial to be formally charged as the official court records show.

The indictment against them was as follows: "Unlawfully taking Eliza Armstrong, aged 13, out of the possession and against the will of her father." In addition the court records simply say there were "*Other Counts* charging the taking from the possession of the mother".[3]

On the first couple of days – Friday and Saturday 23 and 24 October – the hearing was in the "New Court". By the Monday it had transferred to the "Old Court" room, where it remained until the conclusion of the case nine days later. The Judge for the trial was Mr Justice Henry Charles Lopes, QC and a former Member of Parliament who, after sitting as a Justice of the Common Pleas Division of the High Court of Justice, was by 1885 a Lord Justice of Appeal. He had been knighted in 1876 and in 1885 was sworn into the Privy Council – the formal body of advisers to Her Majesty Queen Victoria.[4]

This was an important case for the Crown, both because of the great publicity which had preceded the case, and the enormous public and parliamentary interest which had been shown in the matters which lay at its heart. So the prosecution was to be led by the Attorney General for England, Sir Richard Everard Webster, who had only recently helped push the Criminal Law Amendment Act through Parliament.[5] In his prosecuting team he had Harry Bodkin Poland, a junior Treasury Counsel and already also an adviser to the Home Office,[6] as well as a Mr R. S. Wright.

But it wasn't just the prosecution that boasted legal representatives of the highest order. As we have seen, defending Rebecca Jarrett was Charles Russell QC, assisted by Charles Matthews. Mrs Combe was defended by a Mr Sutherst, and Sampson Jacques' team was led by Mr Henry Matthews QC, who in the following year would be returned to Parliament as Conservative member for Birmingham East and would be immediately appointed as Home Secretary.[7] He was assisted by Mr F. H. Lewis. Stead decided, as he had done at the Bow Street Magistrates' preliminary hearing, to defend himself. Bramwell

Booth had a trio of defenders – a Mr Waddy, QC, Mr Horne Payne, and a Mr R. F. Colam.

Although he had suffered profound hearing loss from childhood, Bramwell Booth was used to appearing in public and speaking at large religious gatherings. However, the Old Bailey "stage" was a very different prospect. While reassured by those around him that God and the Right were on his side, there was undoubtedly a great deal of pressure on the man in the uniform standing in the dock. In later life Bramwell would recall the Old Bailey where he described the atmosphere inside and outside the court as intense:

> At times during the hearing the Court was very subdued, the common hush almost suggesting a religious solemnity; at other times there was outburst and clamour. The public excitement could not be kept away from the precincts of the law.[8]

Bramwell Booth, Stead, and their co-defendants were not being treated like common criminals. All told, the court staff were amiable and even friendly, even if not sympathetic to the prisoners,[9] as Bramwell recalled:

> I am bound to say that on the whole we were personally treated with consideration. The robing room was given up to us, and we lunched together. Everything that could be unpleasant was dispensed with, except the necessary formality of locking us up for a few minutes in the cells each morning before we entered the dock. I had the "condemned" cell, by the way, not, I am sure, because of its associations, but because it happened to be the most commodious in the Old Bailey. The warders were very civil, the police quite nice, and all the time we were sustained by a current of friendliness, if not of sympathy, even on the part of some who were against us.[10]

Whatever the benign and even friendly nature of life behind the scenes at the Old Bailey, the courtroom itself was formal as the proceedings unfolded. The case would ultimately result in two trials.

In the first, Stead, Bramwell Booth, and the others were charged with being "concerned" in the abduction of Eliza Armstrong from "the care of her father". This charge was brought under sections 56, 24, and 25 of the 1861 Offences against the Person Act – Section 56 specifically stated that it was a *felony* to abduct a girl under fourteen. But right at the start of the first trial, the Attorney General and lead prosecutor announced an alteration to the charge. Instead of Section 56, the defendants would be prosecuted under Section 55 – which made it a *misdemeanour* to "abduct an unmarried girl under sixteen",[11] and which carried lighter sentences.

Sir Richard Webster explained this in his opening speech, but first he made an impassioned plea to the jury:

—∾∾∾—

*It will be my duty, gentlemen of the jury, on behalf of the Crown, to lay an outline of the facts of this case before you, as simply as I possibly can, in order to enable you to follow the evidence which will afterwards be given by the various witnesses. I will make one preliminary observation only, and that is to ask you to dismiss from your minds anything that you may have heard or read about this case; because no one can doubt that the question involved has been much discussed on both sides in the public press and elsewhere. I am sure I shall have the concurrence of my lord, when I urge the jury to try this case only upon the evidence which may be given in the witness-box.[12]*

—∾∾∾—

Given the publicity which had raged around the case the Attorney General had an almost impossible task on his hands: to appoint and instruct an impartial jury. And, if Bramwell Booth's later memoirs are to be believed, it wasn't only the jury who might have been biased in the case:

*Mr Justice Lopes, who behaved with great civility to me, personally, was against us from the beginning. His view was evidently that we were all guilty. He showed himself particularly hostile at first, but weakened considerably...*[13]

The second trial would involve just Stead, Jarrett, and Jacques who were charged with "aiding and abetting an indecent assault" on Eliza Armstrong. Madame Louise Mourey was separately charged with this offence.

First in the witness box on 23 October was Eliza Armstrong. The child, described as pretty with long black hair, was allowed to tell her story (under the guidance of the prosecuting counsel) from the moment she first came into contact with Rebecca Jarrett and Mrs Broughton on 2 June. She took the jury through that first encounter, on to her evening in the brothel in Poland Street, and her departure and stay in France with The Salvation Army. Most of what she said had already been in the *Pall Mall Gazette* so there were no surprises.[14]

The cross-examinations by the various defence lawyers, and Stead, were quiet affairs. All those involved obviously wished to bring as little anguish as possible to the child, and the questioning was careful and encouraging rather than aggressive. During the cross-examination there were opportunities to ascertain whether she felt she had been damaged by the whole experience. The overall impression left was that she did not believe so, even though she had been the victim of an assault when Madame Mourey had examined her to determine her purity.

Under questioning from Mr Charles Russell, representing Rebecca Jarrett, Eliza said, "Except what the French lady did in Milton Street, nothing was done to distress or vex me – the handkerchief put to my nose annoyed me, but it had no effect on me – I pushed it away."[15]

And so, after four hours of testimony Eliza left the witness box, to be replaced by her mother, Elizabeth.

## CHAPTER 18

# MOTHER AND FATHER IN COURT

As Elizabeth Armstrong stepped up into the witness box, she would have been aware that her evidence was crucial to the case against the defendants facing her across the courtroom. It was she who had, according to the allegations in the *Pall Mall Gazette*, allowed her child to be taken from Lisson Grove in the knowledge that she was destined for a brothel. Mrs Armstrong was determined to prove her innocence, even though she was not the one on trial.

—∿∿—

*Friday, 23 October, Central Criminal Court:*
*Elizabeth Armstrong (Witness for the Prosecution)*

*I am the wife of Charles Armstrong, and live at 32, Charles Street, Lisson Grove. My husband is a chimney-sweeper. I have six children, three boys and three girls. The eldest girl is seventeen; Eliza, the next, was thirteen last April; the baby is two years old... My eldest daughter was in service but left on account of her eyesight; she had been at work at the same place three or four months till Easter, when she stopped in the house. The boys went to a board school in Stephen Street. Eliza used to go to school, but latterly used to look after the baby while I was at work as a laundress. Eliza used to do a bit of work for Mrs. Hayden, of Spring Street, but she did not have enough to keep her in work altogether. Eliza washed and scrubbed there.*

*It was Wednesday, June 3, Derby day, that Eliza left home with Mrs. Jarrett. I remember the previous day;*

*Eliza came and said something to me. I then went to Mrs.*
*Broughton's with Eliza, and I saw Mrs. Jarrett there. I did*
*not know her name then, I did not learn it on that day. I*
*never asked her name, I thought Mrs. Broughton knew it,*
*and that Mrs. Broughton knew all about her, she gave me*
*such a good recommendation of the woman.*[1]

*⁓*

Mrs Armstrong's evidence was at first calm and matter-of-fact.
She relayed the story which had already been published in the
columns of the *Lloyd's Weekly Newspaper*[2] about how Eliza had
come to leave her care and how Rebecca Jarrett, who she thought
was called "Mrs Sullivan", had appeared to be caring, buying new
clothes for her child.

She appeared reasonable, and was adamant that she had not
received money for her daughter and did not know she was
intended for the sex trade. Even under cross-examination from
Rebecca Jarrett and Bramwell Booth's defence counsels, she
remained composed, although holes were beginning to appear in
her evidence.

*⁓*

### Saturday, 24 October, Central Criminal Court: Elizabeth Armstrong (Witness for the Prosecution) cross-examined by Mr Russell

*... Mrs. Sullivan or Jarrett... asked if Eliza was a "pure"*
*girl, and I said yes. I am quite sure that Jarrett asked if*
*Eliza was a pure girl. It was a lie if I said "Never" when*
*you asked me in the police-court. She did not mention*
*boys in the street, she asked if Eliza was a pure girl, and I*
*asked her what she meant. I do not know I am sure why I*
*told a lie; I must have forgotten.*

*I do not drink much. I know the Marquis of Anglesea. I*
*do not go to a public-house in Kendal Street; I never make*

*a practice of going to public-houses; if I sent for a drop of
beer I sent to the public-house for it, sent the children. I
used to send Eliza to the public-house if I wanted a drop
of beer. I never allowed my children to come to a public-
house; if I went out marketing on Saturday night, all
my children were in bed. Eliza has gone for my beer, but
never danced about in a public-house. They would not
allow boys and girls to dance in their back parlours. It is
certainly not true that she danced in a public-house; it
would be rather a peculiar place to dance in...[3]*

⸻

But then Stead rose.

As he was defending himself, it was vital that he portray Eliza's
mother in a poor light. He had claimed that the mother of the
girl "Lily" in the Maiden Tribute articles was a drunkard. It was
important for him to break Mrs Armstrong and enable the jury
to see that she was not such an innocent as she appeared, or as his
rival newspapers had seemed to suggest.

Stead questioned her vigorously about why she had not
been more concerned about where her daughter had gone, and
queried the timing of events. Mrs Armstrong grew more defiant
and louder as she tried to negate the line of questioning about
her motives, the sequence of events, and the money that changed
hands. She quickly got confused and ended up in floods of tears.[4]

⸻

**Saturday, 24 October, Central Criminal Court:
Elizabeth Armstrong (Witness for the Prosecution)
cross-examined by Mr Stead**

*... on the Wednesday afternoon I did not go to Mrs.
Broughton to ask her to lend me sixpence; I did not want
sixpence – I will tell you what I did say; the baby was
crying while Mrs. Jarrett was talking to me, I said "Lend*

*me a penny to buy something for the baby, for I cannot
hear what this person is saying"; she said "Yes, I will,"
and put her hand in her pocket and pulled out a shilling,
not six-pence. If Mrs. Broughton says I came to her to
borrow sixpence, that is untrue. I asked her for a penny,
not for sixpence; I got a shilling. I bought a comb, and
a pair of socks for the baby. I paid sixpence for the comb,
fivepence-three farthings for the socks, and I got drunk on
the farthing. They said I got drunk with the shilling, but
I could not get very drunk with that. I do not mean that
I spent a farthing in drink, or any portion of the money;
I bought a comb, which the child took away with her. I
did buy some drink that night – my husband gave me
the money, but not to get drunk on. I am not going to tell
you if it was my housekeeping money. I took a glass after
my husband struck me. I got money from my husband
at night, when he came home. He gave me money before
he asked for Eliza – it was for housekeeping – I did not
go and get drunk on it; I am not a person that goes out
drinking, I can assure you, although I have got that
character from you and other people.[5]*

—∿∿—

Although it was quite common for people seeking servants to
make private transactions with the parents of poor children who
might be looking for a way into service, Stead was determined, if
he could not extract an admission that she knew the purpose for
which Eliza was destined, at least to leave the impression with the
jury that Mrs Armstrong could not be trusted to tell the whole
truth if it did not suit her. There was confusion over whether she
took money, and whether she thought or knew that Mrs Broughton
received money for the "purchase" of her daughter. Under Stead's
cross-examination, her previously calm persona crumpled. She
became more and more muddled as she admitted previous lies.

The fact that it was on record that Mrs Armstrong had been arrested for drunkenness on the night of Eliza's departure seemed to throw her increasingly contradictory evidence into question.

———⟋⟍⟋⟍———

*I was locked up by the police for being drunk and disorderly, and that is not the first time, once was ten years ago – altogether I have been locked up three times. It is not true that I have been locked up and fined for using obscene language in the street. I do not use obscene language, but I was fined for it all the same, and I paid my fine.*[6]

———⟋⟍⟋⟍———

Elizabeth Armstrong's evidence, especially under cross-examination by Stead, descended into a chaotic mixture, as she tried to defend herself.[7] Stead picked away at other bits of her evidence. When had she first suspected the "Lily" of the articles was her Eliza? Why had she not got in touch with him directly to confirm her suspicions? Was she influenced in her beliefs and actions by others, including the campaigner Mr Edward Thomas, who had been helping to sponsor the Armstrong's case?

———⟋⟍⟋⟍———

*I read this article which has just been read over, on the 9th of July. With the exception of two trips to Richmond and one to Epping Forest, my child has never been in the country in her life. I identified my daughter by that passage. I knew about the school trips when I went to the Magistrate at Marylebone – the Magistrate never asked me about that. I have mentioned them since. Mr. Thomas has not put them into my mind since; I have not seen Mr. Thomas, the police did not. I have heard from you about the school trips to-day for the first time. The connection*

*between my daughter and the school treats came into
my mind then, although I did not mention it then. When
asked how many things led me to identify "Lily" with
Eliza at the police-court it was in my mind, and I did not
tell you. There are not other things in my mind I have not
told you. The fact that another girl had been asked to go
with Jarrett before my daughter was taken led me to think
this story had a connection with me. I had thought of that
coincidence before – those things have been spoken of to-
day here; not at the police-court. It has been found out
since. I found it out. It is found out now.*

*I do not know if it was in my mind when I was at
the police-court; I have been too much worried over this.
When I went to Mrs. Broughton to tell her of what a
shock I had got I did not read the article over to her... I
never said anything to her – I never mentioned any of the
circumstances in the article to her which led me to believe
she was a wicked woman... I did not speak angrily to her,
I spoke friendly to her. I did not think at the time that that
woman had been taking my child away for an infamous
purpose. I thought she let her go kindly at the time, and
then afterwards it turned out otherwise. I don't know what
to think. I did not when I went to Mrs. Broughton's accuse
her of having got 5l. – I did not ask Mrs. Broughton if she
had got 4l. or 5l. – it would indeed have relieved my mind
very much if I had thought it was not my daughter...*[8]

---

And so it went on. Finally, after four hours of examination, cross-examination, and re-examination,[9] Eliza's mother was allowed to leave the witness box. She would be called to clarify her evidence later in the trial, but on this first outing the judge and jury might undoubtedly have been left with the impression that Eliza's mother was neither a good mother nor a great witness for the Crown.[10]

Nor was her reputation enhanced when, as part of the prosecution case a day or two later, Eliza's father, who had been strangely silent to date, took the stand. Charles Armstrong, a self-employed chimney-sweep, had previously spent twenty-one years in the "militia" where, he told the court, he had attained the rank of full corporal and was of good character, before being discharged for "weak eyes". In court he was described, by the *Lloyd's Weekly Newspaper*, as being "a respectable-looking man… of somewhat spare figure and upright bearing".[11] But from the start, his evidence, like that of his wife, was also confusing, and it began with when he had last seen the thirteen-year-old Eliza before she disappeared from home.

---

### Tuesday, 27 October, Central Criminal Court: Charles Armstrong (Witness for the Prosecution)

*I was not at home when my daughter went away. It was on a Tuesday I think, Tuesday or Wednesday between 11 and 12 o'clock. I was not at home at breakfast time, I did not come home before 11 o'clock.*

*I had breakfast with my daughter Eliza. That morning I had some words with my wife – she wanted to go to a funeral, and I said she should not, and she said she would, and of course we had a few words, and I struck her, and I was sorry afterwards that I had done it… Then I went out again to work.*

*I got back again between seven and eight… I saw my wife upstairs. I was going to work, and I said, "Where's Eliza?" She says, "She is gone to service," and I says, "What?" She said, "She is gone to service; she is gone to Croydon.. I understood it was Croydon. She says, "Mrs. Broughton has recommended her; a young woman, a lady, a fellow-servant at one time; she was very well off, and got married to a commercial traveller."*

*I said, "Why didn't you stop until I came home, and ask
my leave?" and we had a few more words. I struck her, and
she went out, and I went and washed myself. I struck her
again the same night for letting my child go away without
my lief [sic]… Later in the evening I heard my wife was
locked up, and I went and got her bailed out quick. I went
to the landlord of the public-house to bail her…[12]*

—◦◦◦—

In the *Pall Mall Gazette*'s Maiden Tribute of Modern Babylon
articles, Mr Armstrong had been portrayed as "drunk and
indifferent"[13] but in the witness box he gave the impression of an
illiterate, desperate father, who eventually made his way to France,
in the company of an officer from Scotland Yard, to search for his
child. The fact that Mr Armstrong maintained all along that he
had no idea that his daughter was leaving home or where she was
going and that his permission had not been requested was crucial
to the case against Stead and the others.

Stead was headstrong, but not stupid and certainly not
ignorant of the law. However, he had been quick to buy a child
who would feature at the centre of his series of articles to expose
the sex trade, and had not done his homework properly. The law
clearly stated that a child could only be bought if the purchaser
received the consent of "both parents".[14]

The case at the Old Bailey hinged, therefore, on the fact that, it
appeared, Mr Charles Armstrong knew nothing about the alleged
"sale" of his daughter to Rebecca Jarrett. That made the taking
of Eliza an offence. Even if his wife was fully aware of where her
child was going, and why, it counted as nothing for the defence,
because Charles Armstrong had not given his permission.

One of the Attorney General's main aims when Eliza's father
stood in the witness box at the Old Bailey would be to prove that
not only had he *not* agreed to his daughter's going away, he had
also known nothing about it at all.

—∿∿—

### Tuesday, 27 October, Central Criminal Court: Charles Armstrong (Witness for the Prosecution)

*I struck my wife because she ought to have waited until I came home. I asked who she [Eliza] had gone with. She said Mrs. Broughton recommended her; she did not mention the name. I asked "What is the name of the lady?" My wife could not tell me. I asked the address, and she said "Somewhere in Croydon". I said "It won't take more than two hours to go down in my brother-in-law's trap and see her". Then she told me she did not know the address in Croydon, and it was upon that I struck her. I thought she ought to have stopped until I came home. I did not ask whether there was any talk of wages; I never spoke to her, because she was locked up, and I did not speak to her till the next morning.*

*She told me about the rig-out of new clothes in which my daughter had gone; I thought it was very fancy for a service like that. She had plain and neat clothes, and nailed boots; I gave 6s. 6d. for them. The old clothes came home; they are here, they were in the box when I came from France; I saw some of them. I did not know that she had not taken her clothes with her; I knew nothing at all about them. It was an odd thing that she should leave behind the working clothes and have a new rig out. My wife did not tell me that on 1st August she had been asked to consult me whether I wished my daughter back or not. If she had I would have told her different, because I wanted her home. My wife did not tell me that on 19th July she had been to the Mansion House and was assured that her child was safe and well and in decent service. I did not know that she had been to the Mansion House, and been examined there. It did not come to my*

*knowledge that my neighbours in the street were saying
that Mrs. Broughton had got money for selling the
child. My wife had the blame; it was talked all about the
neighbourhood.*

*The talk began about a month or six weeks afterwards,
when she never wrote to us. It was funny she did not write
for three weeks; the neighbours began to talk then. I did
not go to the Magistrate, nor to the Mansion House, nor
to Mr. Booth; I left the whole mutter [sic] to my wife. I
cannot tell you how the neighbours learnt that she did not
write; I don't know...* [15]

---

Charles Armstrong was adamant that he was completely ignorant
of the whereabouts of his daughter. His evidence to the Old Bailey
jury indicated that his wife had left him completely in the dark
and he thought she might have been too frightened to divulge her
fear that "Lily" might be their own Eliza.

---

*I cannot tell when I first heard anything about the Pall
Mall Gazette; I could not read it. I heard some chaps
reading it at the corner of the street... I could not tell
when it was that I heard my neighbours saying that my
wife had sold the child; it was every day, three weeks
or a month after the child went away, because the child
did not write. She did not have the chance to write, I do
not think. She was supposed to write every month; that
was the agreement. That is what my wife told me when
three weeks had passed, and no letter came, it was in
everybody's mouth that my wife had sold the child, and
they blamed me as well for it, and said I was quite as
bad as my wife. Of course they thought I knew something
about it. I said I was not at home on the day she went*

*away. I did not tell them that I had had words with my wife – I did not tell them my business at all; they had nothing at all to do with it; do you think I tell everybody that I knock my wife about?*

*I never heard the Pall Mall Gazette mentioned… I first heard the reading of the Pall Mall Gazette before I heard anything about the child. I did not study it myself; I cannot read, and I did not know…*

*… I heard that Mrs. Broughton had got a sovereign, which neighbours thought was for taking away my daughter. I never asked my wife whether she knew anything about it; it is not likely. I did not want to ask her… When I found the child did not write I told her to go to the police-court; that was the best place… I felt very cross about it, and it struck me that my girl went away for a bad purpose. People do not give sovereigns away for nothing, I think.*

*I did not think it was my business to go and make a row with Mrs. Broughton; I would not do such a thing… I am in the habit of leaving all these things about my daughter to my wife – she has full power to act for me in these things. I did not ask my wife at any time what explanation Mrs. Broughton had to give about that sovereign. My wife told me that she had heard that her daughter was safe; she said she had a letter from the daughter, but there was no place to write back again.[16]*

---

Obtaining only the consent of Eliza's mother, and failing to get her father's permission was central to the charges against Stead, Booth, Jarrett, Combe, and Jacques. It was a simple misjudgment on Stead's part but later, instead of displaying embarrassment, he decided instead to view the parental permission issue as a legal technicality and would try to turn it to his advantage. Years after the trial, one of his favourite anecdotes was that he could have avoided the charge against him, the trial and prison if he had revealed something that he claimed he could prove – that the Armstrongs were never legally married, or at least not married at the time of their daughter's birth, so Eliza was effectively illegitimate.[17]

So why did Stead decide not to use this information? Was he determined to face a trial even at the risk of embarrassment and imprisonment not just for himself and others? He later revealed that he fixed upon this course of action in order to spare Eliza's feelings and that he refused to embarrass the mother by forcing her to produce her marriage licence in public, even though he would have been perfectly entitled to do so. However, it is more likely that it was Sir Charles Russell who dissuaded him from attempting to prove Eliza's legitimacy, in order to protect the family from more public humiliation.[18]

Had all this been raised in court, there would have been no case to answer. But it was not.

Stead would have his day in court.

## CHAPTER 19

# THE CASE FOR THE PROSECUTION

The case for the prosecution at the trial of William Thomas Stead, Rebecca Jarrett, Elizabeth Combe, Sampson Jacques, and Bramwell Booth ran for a good part of a week. In addition to the evidence from Elizabeth and Charles Armstrong there was a succession of witnesses who all related the finer details of the circumstances of Eliza's departure from Charles Street over and over again.

Even before Mr Charles Armstrong gave his evidence, the court had seen Mrs Ann "Nancy" Broughton on the stand on Monday, 26 October. She began by telling the court how she first met Rebecca Jarrett at Claridge's, how the transaction for a "servant" for her friend had come about, how Eliza had finally been selected, and her part in the negotiations with the girl's mother. During her statement and under cross-examination, she denied that she had ever procured a child and she said she had never "kept a brothel". Even Stead had begun to query this in the weeks after the Maiden Tribute articles were run, so the defence appeared to quietly drop that point.[1] There was also a good deal of complicated discussion about how much money the good natured Mrs Broughton received, and what it was payment for.

As one would expect, the Old Bailey court case was being closely followed by all the newspapers in addition to the *Pall Mall Gazette*. The *Daily Telegraph* commented on Mrs Broughton's evidence, reporting that she "frequently contradicted her own previous statements and those of the Armstrongs on points of detail, and some rather significant admissions were elicited from her; but she adhered as firmly as the previous witnesses to the assertion that Jarrett took Eliza away under the pretence of employing her as a servant in her own house.[2]

—✦—

### Monday, 26 October, Central Criminal Court: Ann Broughton (Witness for the Prosecution)

*I will swear she did not tell me she wanted a girl for a man. So help me God she did not, she never said anything whatever about wanting a girl for a man in my room, and not in my hearing at all... I did not at the police-court or elsewhere say that Jarrett said that she wanted a girl for a man... I did not know that she meant had she been a pure girl, and that no one had been meddling with her; nothing like that ever struck me...[3]*

—✦—

On the crucial point of the monetary transactions which preceded Eliza's departure, Mrs Broughton was adamant that the money she received was certainly not in payment for a child.

—✦—

*... on Wednesday Jarrett gave me a sovereign between 10 and 11 o'clock in the morning. Jane Farrer was in the room at the time. She [Rebecca] called me over, "Nancy", I said "Yes, Becky", She said "I am going to stop to dinner, and you have no money to get it". I said "Yes, I have bacon in the cupboard, potatoes on the fire, and money in the cup". She held her hands out like this and said "Take this, Nancy," and I said "No, Becky". I did not see what it was. "I want nothing to get no dinner, for*

*I have got it here". "Take it," she says; "you have got a
shawl in pawn". I said "No". I told her that I hadn't a
shawl to my back. I told her "What did it matter to her
about my shawl being in pawn?" "Well, Nancy," she
says, "I promised you I should try to pay you some day
for the kind assistance done towards me in and out of
the hospitals". I said I did not expect nothing, and what
I had done was with a good heart. I put out my hand,
and she put it into my hand. I never looked to see what it
was, and I put it behind the boards on the mantel-piece;
it remained there until just between 1 and 2. I did not
say more about it, and we sat and had dinner when my
husband came in at 12 o'clock. The money she had given
me I put behind the vase on the mantel-piece. I looked
at it when she had gone to buy the clothes. Besides that
money she had given me half a sovereign to get some
whisky. She gave me the sovereign between 10 and 11,
the half-sovereign was for a quartern of whisky; I went
out and got the whisky, and got 9s. 6d. change and that
handed back to her.[4]*

---

Mrs Broughton maintained that she did not know Rebecca
Jarrett's previous history as a brothel-keeper and prostitute.
When cross-examined by Stead she stuck to her professions of
innocence of the whole affair, and said she had not been aware of
Rebecca Jarrett's intentions.

---

*I was not asked to get a girl just over 13. She did not say
"I do not want a girl that has been romping about with
boys in the street". I will swear she did not tell me she
wanted a girl for a man, so help me God she did not. She
never said anything whatever about wanting a girl for a*

man in my room, and not in my hearing at all… I did
not at the police-court or elsewhere say that Jarrett said
that she wanted a girl for a man. I never had any doubt
about it. When she asked me if Eliza had ever larked
about with boys and girls I did not know what she meant;
only the same as the rest of the children larking about.
I did not know that she meant had she been a pure girl,
and that no one had been meddling with her; nothing like
that ever struck me.

Mrs. Armstrong on the Tuesday night said "I will not
let my child go after calling me names". She said "You are
a b— cow, I will not let my daughter go". I do not know
why she said that; of course I do excuse a woman when
she has had a drop… I was surprised that she should use
that language, and walked indoors. I thought she blamed
me for the girl going away. The woman had had a drop of
drink, and of course I did not take much notice; I walked
away, I do not know that she called me names which
implied that she thought the place was very bad indeed;
it is very excusable in a person with a drop of drink… I
never told Mrs. Armstrong Rebecca Jarrett was a genuine
woman, or anything of the kind, I suppose she picked it out
of the papers. Eliza was going for a month's trial – Rebecca
Jarrett repeated in my room that it was for a month and
not for a week. I said at the police-court that the child was
going for a week on trial; she was to go for a month, and
that she had to come back the same as she went. Jarrett
did not say anything to me that she was to return the girl
to me if she found she was not a pure girl; such a thing
was never mentioned. When she said "If she did not suit" I
understood by that, of course, if she was not able to do the
work. I did not know what was meant by she would return
her the same as she went no more than the poor mother did.
I attached no bad meaning to it whatever…

*... When Rebecca gave me the sovereign I did not know
how much it was. I said at the police-court it may have
been a French halfpenny for anything I knew, I did not
look to see what shape it was. I took it like this, and put it
on the mantel-shelf – there were not two sovereigns there;
so help me God there were not – what should I do with the
other one? I only found one sovereign behind the mantel-
piece. I am sure and certain there was only one sovereign.
When Rebecca gave me the sovereign, and I did not know
how much it was, I said to her that she could not afford
it... I never thought of looking at it until such time as
they were going to buy the clothes, between 1 and 2. I had
found out what it was after buying the clothes, before she
came back. I will not be sure whether I did say anything
to her then; I will not be sure. I know I told her I fetched
my shawl out of pawn – I was surprised when I found it
was a sovereign; it was a great deal more than I expected.
I believe I thanked her when she came back – I said, "Why,
Becky! Do you know what you have given me?" She said,
"I know, Nancy". I said, "Thank you; that is more than I
expected". I asked her what did she give it me for, and she
said, "I promised it to you, Nancy". I have never said this
before to-day about thanking her. I did not want money for
her staying to dinner. She did not say she gave it for the
trouble I had been at in getting her a girl. The agreement
was not made with the girl then; she asked me to get her a
girl the next day, when she pronounced about the shawl.*[5]

---

From Mrs Broughton the Old Bailey jury also gained an insight
into how she began to be blamed for helping Rebecca Jarrett take
the child away, once the *Pall Mall Gazette* began publishing the
Maiden Tribute articles and Mrs Armstrong began to suspect that
the girl "Lily" was, in fact, her daughter Eliza.

*Mrs Broughton: ... Mrs. Armstrong came round to my
house on July 11th or 10th, or about that time. She came
and read a bit of the Pall Mall Gazette, about some child
of the name of "Lillie" [sic]. She did not ask me any
questions about it.*

*Mr Stead: "And she came and talked to you about it?"*

*Mrs Broughton: Yes – no one else had spoken to me
about it before... The first time she came to me about
her daughter was the time she abused me... She abused
me at the street door... She told me she was going to
the Marylebone Courthouse, and she blamed me for her
going away, and said if it had not been for me the child
would not have gone... I was standing at my own street
door. She had these two letters in her hand, and she said,
"Here is Rebecca Jarrett, she has actually been trying to
take another child away, another girl away". I do not
know what that referred to; I looked at her then, I never
answered, I never spoke a word; I stood at the door all the
time. She called me everything. She called me whore and
prostitute, and said I had been a prostitute all my lifetime;
and I was not married to the man I was living with, and I
was only living with him, and that she would have me up,
the same as she would have Jarrett up; I don't know why,
that is what I looked at her for. I never answered a word,
good, bad, or indifferent. It was in the street – everyone
was there, the place was crammed. I never said a word,
so help me God. I thought I would leave her to say what
she liked, and I went down afterwards to the Marylebone
Courthouse. I thought I would not answer her as she came
and took on so. She said I sold her child for 5l., and I*

*was a drunken brothel-keeper. She has not said anything
abusive to me since...* [6]

*... I never took steps to explain to Mrs. Armstrong that
I could not have been the person referred to in the Pall
Mall Gazette. I never read the article, I only know what I
heard one and the other say is in the Pall Mall Gazette.
I beg your pardon, Mr. Thomas came in one Saturday
morning. He read it to me all through. I very near
dropped to hear such a thing, me being accused of selling
a child for 5l.? That was some time after the mother
accused me. I was very much astonished; for a woman
not guilty of the crime to be charged with it; and then not
only that, to be put down as a prostitute and a brothel-
keeper – there was no truth in it; I never procured a child,
and never kept a brothel!* [7]

—⁓—

Stead had always maintained that before Eliza was selected to be
taken away by Rebecca Jarrett as part of the Maiden Tribute plot,
several other local girls had been considered and passed over,
mostly because they were too old. Nineteen-year-old Jane Farrer,
another Lisson Grove resident who Nancy Broughton said was
the first to be rejected as a potential "servant" for Rebecca Jarrett,
appeared as part of the prosecution case. Jane was accustomed
to spending a good deal of time in the Broughtons' home and
had witnessed much of the goings on around Derby Day. She
seemed to be an independent witness to the exchanges of money
between Rebecca Jarrett, Mrs Broughton, and Mrs Armstrong.
More importantly, she gave the jury a flavour of what happened
in Charles Street, and how it was that Eliza would eventually be
the child selected to go with Rebecca.

—⁓—

### Tuesday, 27 October, Central Criminal Court: Jane Farrer (Witness for the Prosecution)

*... Jarrett asked Mrs. Broughton if she knowed [sic] a girl that would like a place, as she could not kneel. She wanted a girl to clean the oil-cloth. Mrs. Broughton asked me if I would go. I said, "Yes". Jarrett said I was too big. She asked me my age. I told her nineteen. That was after she said I was too big, she said she wanted one younger. Mrs. Broughton said she thought she could get Elizabeth Stevens. Elizabeth was passing down Charles Street. Mrs. Broughton called her over. Lizzie Stevens went with Mrs. Broughton. I went upstairs, I did not hear no agreement between Lizzie Stevens and Mrs. Jarrett. I did not hear anything said... I went upstairs to my sister-in-law by my own wish. When I came down again Lizzie Stevens was going out of the room. About ten minutes afterwards Eliza Armstrong came in... and asked Mrs. Broughton if Jarrett was the woman who wanted the girl. She said, "Yes," and asked Eliza where her mother was. She said, "Upstairs". Mrs. Broughton asked her to go and fetch her mother; and then Eliza said she was gone out... Mrs. Broughton said she would not let her go without her mother's consent, and Rebecca Jarrett likewise said so. That was 11 o'clock, or a little after... the next day I was at Mrs. Broughton's again, about 10 or half-past. Jarrett came again, about half-past 10... I saw her come in – she told Mrs Broughton that she was going to stay to dinner, and Mrs. Broughton says, "Are you," and Jarrett said, "Yes". She said, "You ain't got no money to get no dinner with". Mrs. Broughton said, "Yes, I have". Jarrett said, "No, you ain't". Mrs. Broughton said, "Yes, I have; I have got it in the place". Jarrett said, "Never mind, take this," offering her something. Mrs. Broughton said, "No, thank you, I have got my dinner". Jarrett said, "Never*

*mind, you have got a shawl in pawn". Mrs. Broughton said,
"That don't matter to you". Jarrett said, "Yes, it do," and
then Jarrett put something into Mrs. Broughton's hand, who
put it on the mantel-piece, without seeming to look at it,
behind the image – I did not see what it was.*

*After that, about 11 or half-past, Jarrett asked Mrs.
Broughton if she had a girl for her. She said "No"…
(Jarrett) said "Don't you know of a poor little orphan
girl, that would like a good home?" Mrs. Broughton
said she thought she did, and she would go down to little
Alice West. Then Mrs. Armstrong came back into Mrs.
Broughton's room with Mrs. Broughton, and told Jarrett
that she had let her "Liza go"; then Jarrett asked Mrs.
Armstrong if she was willing to let 'Liza go. She said
"Yes,"… and "Liza went upstairs with her mother and
came back about 2 or half-past 2 – that was all that was
said at that time; when she came back I was still there.
Her mother did not come back with her. Jarrett then took
her out to buy the clothes… they were away about an hour,
and when they came back me and Mrs. Broughton had
gone out. We came back about 3; Jarrett was at the street
door and Liza Armstrong, and whilst having tea Jarrett
trimmed the hat in Mrs. Broughton's room. Mrs. Armstrong
came in, and asked Mrs. Broughton for sixpence; that was
after the clothes were pawned. She said she had not got
sixpence, and then Jarrett took something out of her purse
and gave it to Mrs. Armstrong, saying that would do her
much better. I did not see what it was, but Jarrett said it
was a shilling, and Mrs. Armstrong went out…*[8]

---

Jane, it emerged, also wrote some of the letters which circulated
around that time between Jarrett and others, because Mrs
Broughton could not read or write.[9]

The prosecution witnesses now came thick and fast. Elizabeth "Lizzie Stevens" who at seventeen was also considered "too old" to be Rebecca Jarrett's new servant, was next on the witness stand, followed by Henry William Smith, a cabbie who explained how it was that Sampson Jacques hired him to deliver the child Eliza and Jarrett to Poland Street in his four-wheeled cab.[10]

A couple of the police officers who had been involved in helping to track down Eliza once she had been reported missing by her mother were next to give their account of the saga. A Scotland Yard Inspector, Charles Von Turnow, detailed how, in August 1885, he had accompanied Eliza's father, Charles Armstrong, to France to seek his daughter out,[11] but first up was Inspector Edward Borner who told the court how, at the instruction of the Marylebone Magistrate after Mrs Armstrong had reported her daughter missing, he had made the initial investigation into the child's departure from home. He took the jury through his visit to Winchester to Mrs Butler's House of Rest and his subsequent conversation with that lady which led him, on 16 July, to seek an interview with Bramwell Booth at the headquarters of The Salvation Army in London.

———

### Tuesday, 27 October, Central Criminal Court; Edward Borner (Witness for the Prosecution)

*I said, "I am Inspector Borner; I have come to see you with respect to a case that appeared in Lloyd's Newspaper of last Sunday about a girl named Eliza Armstrong; I have been referred to you by Mrs. Josephine Butler, of Winchester".*
*He said, "Yes, I know something of the case, but I cannot tell you exactly where the child is at present, but if you like I will have inquiries made during the day, and let you know". I thanked him, and asked him if he would send the*

*address to Mr. Munroe. Commissioner of Police, Scotland Yard; he said he would do so, and I left."*[12]

——∿∿——

It was from Inspector Borner that the jury learned a little more of the frustrations faced by the police and the court when Bramwell Booth failed to produce Eliza, even though he had promised to do so. The Inspector's evidence didn't paint the second-in-command of The Salvation Army in a particularly positive light, but even though Borner was a prosecution witness, the court may well have begun to understand Booth's motivations for withholding information on the Armstrong girl. He continued:

——∿∿——

*... Up to my next interview, 31st July, so far as I know, no address had been received. On that 31st July I attended at the Marylebone Police-court before Mr. Cooke, and after receiving his instructions went again to Mr. Booth at 101, Queen Victoria Street, and saw him. He said, "Since I saw you last, my position as regards the girl Armstrong is very much altered; she is now under my control, and in service with a lady on the Continent; she is being well brought up and educated as a Christian" ... He said, "We shall be prepared to make application that the child should become a ward in Chancery rather than return to the same kind of living". I asked him if he would see the mother the following day. He said, "Yes, any time between 11 and 4". He said that he had had inquiries made, and found that the mother was a drunken woman, and the neighbourhood a bad one for the child to go to, or to return to...*

*... Next day, 1st August, about 11 o'clock, after seeing the Magistrate the previous evening, Mrs. Armstrong, Inspector Conquest, and I went again to Mr. Booth's. I said*

*to him, "This is Mrs. Armstrong," and to Mrs. Armstrong,
"This is Mr. Booth, now speak to him". She said, "I have
come to speak to you about my child, I want her back". He
said, "You cannot have her, for she is in the South of France
with a lady, being well brought up and educated". She
said, "Why cannot I have her back?" He said, "Because I
have been put to great expense; have you 100l.?" She said,
"No, Sir, I am only a poor woman". He said, "Well, that
is about what it cost me; why don't you let her remain? I
will pay you her wages monthly, or how you like, and I will
give you her address, and you can communicate with her,
and when she comes to England you can see her; if you
will sign a receipt I will pay you the wages due to her;"
And turning to me he said, "What do you think, two or
three shillings a week?" I said, "That is a question which
I cannot interfere in, it is for the parents". Mrs. Armstrong
said, "No, Sir, I want my child back". I said to Mr. Booth,
"The mother seems to be under the impression that the
child has been tampered with or outraged". He said to
the mother, "I can assure you that when the child was
brought to me she was pure". The mother clasped her hands
together and said, "Thank God for that," and burst out
crying. Mr. Booth said, "She was examined by a medical
gentleman, and I have a certificate, and if Mr. Cooke would
like to see it I will find it". I said, "I do not think that will
be necessary, but I will mention it to Mr. Cooke". He said,
"Why don't you let her remain?". She said, "Because I
want her back to take before a Magistrate to prove that
I never sold her." Mr. Booth said, "She would not know
whether she was sold". The mother said, "Oh, yes, a girl of
13 would know whether she was sold or not". He then got
up from his seat and went to a desk. He said, "Well, if you
are determined to have her back," taking from the desk a
piece of paper, "there, this is her address, that is all I can*

*do for you"… the mother thanked him, and he said, "You
had better consult your husband, and let me know if you
determine to let the child remain" – she said, "Yes, I will,
Sir". We then left.*[13]

———~~~———

As the prosecution case continued on Tuesday, 27 October, Inspector Borner was replaced in the witness box by Dr Heywood Smith, who described himself as a friend, although not a member, of The Salvation Army. Appearing under a court-ordered subpoena, he was a renowned Harley Street physician, an alumnus of Oxford University and, among other things, a Member of the Royal College of Physicians.

For those involved in the Maiden Tribute affair, it was very important that there was medical proof that Eliza Armstrong had not been harmed by her experience in the brothel in Poland Street or through her contact with Mr Stead and Mrs Jarrett, and it was Heywood Smith who had examined the child in the early hours of 4 June 1885, the day after she was removed from home. The examination took place at 27 Nottingham Place, an establishment run by a Miss Hutchinson who had previously taken in patients for the doctor and who, Heywood Smith knew, also had connections with The Salvation Army.

———~~~———

### Tuesday, 27 October, Central Criminal Court: Dr. Heywood Smith (Witness for the Prosecution)

*… I gave Miss Hutchinson some chloroform, which I had
taken with me. I gave her instructions to give it to the
child. I went into the room while Miss Hutchinson was
administering the chloroform; Jarrett was in the room
in bed all the time, in a different bed from the child. She*

*was awake. I spoke to her, I dare say, by her name, Mrs. Sullivan – I think that is most likely, that is the name I put in my notes...*

*The chloroform affected the child, she went off under the influence of it. I examined her just by the touch only; I examined her private parts, to see in fact whether the child was a virgin. That was in the presence of Jarrett... The child did not wake at all during the time... I subsequently wrote out a certificate... I sent that certificate under cover to Mr. Booth; the certificate was to Mr. Stead. I put it in an envelope, which I directed to Mr. Bramwell Booth, 101, Queen Victoria Street, I think. I did not make more than one copy of it.*

*The substance of the certificate was to the effect that I had examined Eliza Armstrong, and found her to be virgo intacta.*[14]

---

A few more minor witnesses followed, and finally one of William Stead's own reporters took the stand. Luke Nunnery, described as a "shorthand writer", had taken notes at St. James's Hall, on Friday, 21 August, and in a short statement to the Old Bailey, described how the editor of the *Pall Mall Gazette* had announced that evening his sole responsibility in the case of the "Lily" of his Maiden Tribute exposé.

With Mr Nunnery's evidence, the case for the prosecution rested.

# CHAPTER 20

# THE DEFENCE BEGINS

Mr Charles Russell QC knew he had something of an uphill struggle when, on Thursday, 29 October 1885, he rose for his opening address in the defence of Rebecca Jarrett, charged with others of abducting Eliza Armstrong. Her appearance, and her previous life and background would certainly make convincing a jury of her innocence a difficult task.

Rebecca limped up to the stand – her bad hip obviously causing her pain in every step. Observers in the packed Old Bailey courtroom might have observed her height – she was taller than most women of her time, somewhat overweight, and no beauty. The jury would have observed, as Florence Booth had done some months earlier, that Rebecca's face showed the effects of a lifetime of alcohol abuse.[1] Her clothing and demeanour were austere and her hair was cut in a fringe which could just be seen under a hat that, according to one newspaper report, looked a little like the "caps" worn by The Salvation Army.[2]

In a long testimony, over two whole days, Rebecca, under questioning from Sir Charles' junior defence counsel, Mr Charles Matthews, told the court her side of the story. After the details of her life as a child growing up in the sex trade, and then her life as a prostitute and brothel-keeper, Rebecca explained how she had finally come to know The Salvation Army, had been "reformed", and come under the influence of Mrs Josephine Butler. Finally, she explained how she eventually became entangled with Mr Stead and his Maiden Tribute scheme, albeit much against her wishes.

The sight of a "fallen" woman in the dock was not an unusual one, but a woman who claimed to be reformed was another matter, and it was likely that not everyone was convinced by Rebecca's story. Whereas previous witnesses – Mrs Armstrong and Mrs Broughton – had denied that they knew why Eliza was being taken away, Rebecca Jarrett was adamant that she had made it perfectly clear why she wanted a girl. She swore, on oath, that she had told Mrs Broughton and Mrs Armstrong that she needed a "pure girl" and if Eliza proved not to be pure then she would be returned. She also insisted that she had paid a total of £5 for Eliza.[3]

By all accounts, Jarrett did well in her first evidence, which included a blow-by-blow account of everything that had happened on Derby Day and thereafter. As the questioning became more difficult, Rebecca seemed to become rather confused and even to contradict herself; it is believed because she had conflicting loyalties. Her new Salvation Army friends – many of them, including Florence Booth, in court to support her – could see that she was struggling. She wanted to please those who had done so much for her in recent months since she had been rescued from her life in the sex trade. But she also still felt some allegiance to her old acquaintances from the streets and had promised some of these former companions that she would not reveal their names.[4]

The cross-examination by the Attorney General Sir Richard Webster was brutal. His very first question to Rebecca cut straight to the core of his argument – that she was a woman not to be trusted, regardless of her so-called "reformation".

"Prior to being employed at Claridges, had you kept gay houses?" he barked across the courtroom.

"Please sir, don't go back on my past life!"[5]

But her request was pointless. Webster persisted and very soon had his witness in tears. By the time she entered a second day of giving evidence, she had become withdrawn and even rude.[6] Stead is reported to have buried his head in his hands as Rebecca's evidence went from bad to worse under cross-examination[7] and Bramwell could only stare in horror and regret. He later documented the unfortunate turn of events, and reported that he felt in some way to blame.

*She had kept a house of ill fame, and certain things were brought forward relating to her past which she had not the courage to admit. It was a cruel ordeal for her, and I repented while I sat in the dock listening to her in the witness-box that I had allowed her to embark on such an adventure. Yet I am satisfied that the evidence we obtained through her was an essential link in the chain, and that without it we should never have enforced the need for raising the age.[8]*

Despite these failings, at the end of the trial the summing up by her defence counsel Charles Russell was a spectacular appeal.[9] Russell argued that Rebecca was in an impossible position. How could she show her reformed character if not by keeping her word that she would not expose the names of former accomplices in vice?[10] His speech was, according to Bramwell Booth, a masterpiece.

*It was one of the most wonderful efforts. He spoke for two hours, and when he sat down, my dear wife sent up a note to me in the dock saying that she did not care how the case ended after that speech! "It is worth it all." Although Rebecca Jarrett in her evidence had produced an unfavourable impression, yet when Russell finished speaking for her there was not a dry eye in the Court. Even the Judge and the Clerk of Arraigns were moved by the appeal on her behalf.[11]*

The defence case moved on. As the team of lawyers defending those in the dock worked their way up to the evidence to be given by the other defendants, there were witnesses who would swear to Eliza Armstrong's good treatment at the hands of The Salvation Army, especially once the child was taken to France, which also showed Rebecca Jarrett in a caring and positive light.

### Monday, 2 November, Central Criminal Court: Blanche Young (Witness for the Defence)

*I am an officer in the Salvation "Army," and live at the headquarters in Paris, in the Avenue Laumiere. I recollect Rebecca Jarrett arriving in company with Mrs. Combe and the child in Paris, on, I think, the 14th of June. I was not told how the child was brought to Paris, or how she had got possession of her, I was simply told briefly that she had been rescued, and that I was to look after the child kindly, and I did so. The child seemed very much attached to Rebecca. I recollect the Friday evening, 5th of June, when Rebecca left, the day after she arrived. I recollect her speaking to the child and giving her kindly advice as she was leaving, and on parting with her she kissed the child and told her to be good. She said, "Your mother did not give you to me for service, but for something worse."[12]*

---

If there had been any doubt that Eliza was in any way mistreated or taken advantage of during her stay with The Salvation Army in France, Miss Young was even able to clarify one point which might have been worrying the jury. In her earlier testimony, Eliza had said that while staying in Paris she had been on the streets "selling" *The War Cry*, the Salvation Army newspaper. Miss Young was questioned on this point by Mr Horne-Payne, one of Bramwell Booth's legal team and explained that Eliza did occasionally go out with the "girls", some of whom did have licences to sell the journal, but that in Eliza's case, she just went for a walk.[13]

Blanche Young was replaced by Professor James Stuart MP, the parliamentary representative for Hackney in London, who had promoted the Criminal Law Amendment Bill when it came to the House of Commons in July. He gave some evidence about his part in the promotion of the law and a journey he took to Paris with Rebecca Jarrett in the September to help confirm some details in her story.[14]

But now it was time for the court to hear from the man who had persuaded Rebecca to undertake her mission to remove Eliza from home to help prove the theory that girls could be bought, and sold, for the sex trade.

There was a hush in the court as the name of the next witness was called out.

"William Thomas Stead."

## CHAPTER 21

# STEAD ON THE STAND

William Thomas Stead, much acclaimed editor of the *Pall Mall Gazette*, finally took the stand at London's Central Criminal Court. Before the questioning started, as one of the legal defence team – he was defending himself – he was permitted to deliver a statement. He started by acknowledging how "strange and almost incomprehensible" it might seem to them that he "an English gentleman and public journalist" should be in the dock at the Old Bailey to answer a criminal charge.[1]

He admitted that his "crimes" would be considered heinous were it not for the fact, in his eyes, that this was not an ordinary crime and that when he "ordered the purchase" of Eliza Armstrong he was doing so in order to expose the Great Social Evil… the trade in young girls for the sex industry.[2]

Having categorically established his guilt the jury were now faced with a series of witness statements, evidence, and cross-examinations which would run over two days, to try to explain Stead's good character and the reasoning for his behaviour.

Once again, the courtroom, which by this time must have been very familiar with the details of the events running up to and following the departure of Eliza from Charles Street, heard the story retold, this time from the perspective of the man who was at the centre of it all. Stead was questioned at length about how he came to devise the idea for the buying of a child, and his motivations and his modus operandi in gathering the facts he needed for his exposé of the sex trade through his Secret Commission. This, he said, had brought him into a world with which he was unaccustomed, and it certainly gave the court, and the jury, a good understanding of how he saw the value of investigative journalism.

———∾∾———

### *Tuesday, 3 November, Central Criminal Court: William Thomas Stead (recalled). (Further cross-examined by the Attorney General)*

*I objected to criminal proceedings being taken against those who had given me information, first because I had obtained the information under the promise of secrecy... to have done so would have made me a common informer, who would have wormed himself into the confidence of persons who were criminal, and then appeared in the witness-box to punish them, and I had not been two or three days in the investigation when I found I could not do that.*

*I will tell you exactly how it occurred to my mind: the first or second day that I was in a brothel, drinking champagne with the mistress of that brothel, and telling her lies about what I wanted, as I had to do, otherwise I would have been summarily ejected, I felt, after getting into her confidence in that way, I could not go and expose her personally; there are a dozen or more persons doing the same as this woman; I cannot find more than this woman (or only two or three more), who has helped me to ascertain what the system is, why should I be the means of punishing the one individual, out of a hundred equally guilty, who have enabled me to expose the system. I have stated that the police were prosecuting me, whilst they were allowing persons whom they could have prosecuted to go unprosecuted, and I think it is true. I have never communicated to the police any information as to any*

*individual; I have said so, and I would not do so. The*
*facts which were communicated to me were communicated*
*under the influence, while I was drinking champagne and*
*giving money pretty freely; that is the only way in which*
*you can obtain any information concerning what goes on,*
*to go to brothels and act as the people there do. I think the*
*information so obtained is perfectly reliable. The police*
*do this kind of thing constantly; as the detective force do*
*assume those disguises, and worm themselves into people's*
*confidence when engaged in dynamite conspiracies and*
*otherwise, I think, in the interest of young girls, and for*
*the exposure of an infernal system like this, they might*
*and ought to worm themselves into the confidence of these*
*people, it is their business.*[3]

---

To another question from the jury as to why he had felt it necessary
to go to such lengths to gather the information he required, and
to protect the identities of those who had given him information
or who, like Eliza and her mother, were implicated in the case, the
editor was clear.

---

*My object was to get at this horrible state of things cost*
*what it might. If I had communicated to the police I*
*should have had to say that such and such a brothel-*
*keeper is in the habit of procuring young girls. The*
*Attorney General has asked if I could possibly expect the*
*police to do that kind of thing. Can you expect me, after*
*worming myself into the confidence of women, one tithe*
*of the women, to select for punishment the only person*
*who unwillingly helped me, while the other ninety-nine*
*persons were all equally guilty? I declared to Jarrett over*
*and over again that I would not expose Mrs. Armstrong or*

*Mrs. Broughton, I had never mentioned Mrs. Armstrong or Mrs. Broughton; not only that, but I have asked Mrs. Butler and Mr. Booth not to say anything to bring Mrs. Armstrong into trouble.*

*I was told by Jarrett that the mother had sold the child. It did not occur to my mind that by pursuing this course I was tempting parents of poor children to commit the most horrible crime conceivable, for this reason, I have stated to the Court repeatedly it was only girls in the market that I wished to buy, and not other girls; for instance, there are many mothers who sell their daughters to be seduced as soon as they come to seducible age. That is my statement, and the statement made to me. I said to Jarrett and to others, "If you know of any such cases from the brothel-keepers, of girls who would be sold if I did not buy, will you buy them and hand them over to me?" I mean to say that Eliza Armstrong was in the market, that was my impression, so I was told, that she had twice over been offered to Mrs. Broughton. I fully believed that if I had not taken Eliza Armstrong somebody else would have ruined her. That is the essence of my case.*[4]

—◈◈◈—

The little man with the red beard had the task not just of answering questions from the court, the prosecution, and the defence teams, but also needed to give a good account of himself and his character before the jury. The court record shows that as part of Stead's examination of himself – although how that worked is anybody's guess – he reiterated the compromising situations in which he had been forced to place himself as part of his Secret Commission, which might have explained how some of his reported evidence in the *Pall Mall Gazette* articles turned out to be contradictory.

—◦◦◦—

**Tuesday, 3 November, Central Criminal Court:**
**William Thomas Stead (The Witness in re-examination**
**by himself)**

*...The Government changed hands, and Mr. Gladstone*
*went out and Lord Salisbury came in. That naturally*
*increased the strain and tension upon me during the time*
*of the crisis. Before and subsequently I was in the habit*
*at nights of going to brothels to meet the brothel-keepers*
*as a customer, and to drink with brothel-keepers. I am*
*a teetotaler, it was difficult for me to drink champagne,*
*and therefore I would like to say that in justice to Jarrett,*
*that drinking and smoking as I was not used to it before*
*I undertook this inquiry, I might have confused some of*
*the details of what Jarrett told me. But, to the best of my*
*belief, when I was writing on the 28th June, the first part*
*of that manuscript was written from what I remembered*
*Jarrett told me, and I had no object or reason to insert a*
*single word beyond what I heard, I have told the story*
*as near as possible as it was told to me as I remembered*
*it. But I took no notes at the time, and three weeks or a*
*month of a Ministerial crisis, to say nothing of what I*
*went through, was enough to confuse one as to details...*[5]

—◦◦◦—

Stead's phenomenal memory, which had always stood him in
good measure – he often undertook an interview and then wrote
it back verbatim, without the need of notes taken at the time –
may have failed him, but through his evidence, clearly stated, he
hoped to get the jury on his side.

If there was any doubt in their minds, Stead now called a series
of witnesses who would bring some legal views on the case of "Lily"
as well as extra detail about the lengths to which Stead, apparently,

had gone in order to ensure the legitimacy of his Maiden Tribute case. First up was William Shaen, a highly experienced solicitor and senior partner in the firm of Shaen, Roscoe, Massey, and Henderson. Mr Shaen had for thirty-seven years been legal adviser to an organization named the Society for the Enforcement of Laws for the Protection of Women and had long taken an interest in the amendment of laws to protect women.

He had, he told the court, been one of the individuals to whom Stead had turned for advice as he prepared The Maiden Tribute series, although he was at pains to point out he had no direct involvement in the case.

—⁓—

### Tuesday, 3 November, Central Criminal Court: William Shaen (Witness for the Defence)

*In my interview with Mr. Stead it was not a question of motives that we discussed; it was a question of how we could procure evidence that what he was about to do was not a criminal act at all, although it appeared so, I mean the procuration of children.*

*A child may be purchased for a boarding school to save it from a brothel. I merely say that the purchase of a child is not a crime by English law, it is simply a nullity. But suppose you took away a child without the father's consent, that is decidedly a crime.*

*That is the case we are trying, but Mr. Stead explained to me what he intended to do, and that it might have the appearance of abduction, and I told him if he took care that there was no criminal act or intent on his part, that facts might be proved against him that might have that appearance, but which he might meet with evidence to show that that which he did was not any step towards crime, but something quite different...*[6]

—⁓—

Ralph Thicknesse was a Lincoln's Inn barrister and Honorary Secretary of the Minor's Protection Society who had got involved after the case of "Lily" had been exposed in the *Pall Mall Gazette*, and after he had attended the demonstration in Hyde Park on 22 August, to raise awareness of the Armstrongs' case, and to raise money for their costs in trying to secure legal redress for their loss of Eliza. He had also been present at St James's Hall the previous day to hear Stead's public announcement of his "guilt" in acquiring the child who had featured in his controversial series.

Mr Thicknesse had started out by trying to get Mr Stead to hand over Eliza, who was still not returned to her parents. He reported to the court that during that conversation he had been persuaded that, perhaps, it would be better if Eliza stayed where she was.

---

### Tuesday, 3 November, Central Criminal Court: Ralph Thicknesse (Witness for the Defence)

*He [Stead] had told me he had bought the child, and did not want to restore her to her mother, who would probably sell her again, but that he could not keep her if her mother asked for her back.*

*I felt, I think, more strongly than he did at the moment that everything should be done to keep her from going back, and I said so. I told him that I thought he was too easy about letting her go back to her mother. I thought everything should be done by persuasion to induce the mother to let her stay where she was, or to find some other place for her home, and then it was agreed that I should go to the mother and be the means of communication between him and the mother, the point being that it was morally wrong to send it back, though legally right… The net result of the conversation was that Stead recognized his legal*

*responsibility to give up the child when her mother formally*
*demanded it, but that it would be so morally wrong to do it*
*that we ought to postpone to the last moment the fulfilment*
*of our legal responsibility…*[7]

———

Ralph Thicknesse had worked with all the parties, including the police, to oversee the return of Eliza to her mother. But his evidence helped to back up Stead and Bramwell Booth's case that they honestly believed, as a result of the evidence they had before them, that to return Eliza to her parents would not be in her best interests. They had convinced themselves that the parents, or at least the mother, who had sold a daughter would do so again given an opportunity.

But finally, as Ralph Thicknesse told the court, he and Sampson Jacques had been instrumental in reuniting Eliza with her mother at William Stead's home in Wimbledon, although the hospitality had been down to Emma Stead as her husband had decided to stay at the office. This piece of evidence from Mr Thicknesse served not only to give the court a picture of the reunion, but also helped to confirm that Mrs Armstrong had been happy that Eliza had been returned unharmed.

———

*… Mr. Jacques went with me to Charles Street on Monday*
*morning. Inspector Borner was in the room. I did not know*
*who he was, but Mrs. Armstrong said might he go with*
*her; he explained who he was, and I said he had better*
*go, when I knew who he was. We all went to Wimbledon*
*together, and the eldest daughter Elizabeth went too.*
*Mrs. Stead met us and put us in the drawing-room. Mrs.*
*Armstrong was with me, and Mr. Jacques went out with her*
*to fetch Eliza, and then came back, and Eliza walked into*
*the room. Mrs. Armstrong was sitting on the chair, and she*

*said "Why, Eliza, where have you been?" and Eliza came*
*up to her and put her arms around her mother's neck, and*
*Mrs. Stead took the mother and two daughters into the*
*dining-room, as we had previously arranged, and they*
*were left alone, so that they might talk about anything.*
*Inspector Borner said his instructions were… not to*
*interfere with her discretion; if she wished to take the child*
*away his instructions were to bring her to Scotland Yard.*
*After lunch I had a talk with Mrs. Armstrong – myself,*
*Mr. Jacques, and Mrs. Armstrong were present, Eliza was*
*not present. I understood from Mrs. Stead that nothing*
*would induce the mother to leave the girl. I gave that up*
*as hopeless. She seemed firm upon that. She said that Mrs.*
*Armstrong said she would take her child home with her,*
*and I told Mrs. Armstrong that it was a great pity, but we*
*accepted it as decided by that time.*

*… I asked her if she was satisfied that her daughter*
*was all right, and had been well looked after, and so*
*on, and whether she had any reason to believe from her*
*conversation with her daughter that she had been subjected*
*to any outrage… I asked her generally if she was satisfied*
*that the daughter was all right before reading the paper,*
*and she said she was, and she appeared so…[8]*

———

At this point in his evidence, Ralph Thickness produced a piece
of paper on which was written a statement from Mrs Armstrong,
signed by her on the day that she was reunited with Eliza. Mr
Thicknesse continued.

———

*… This is the paper I read. I read the whole of it as it is*
*there slowly. I am certain I read these words: "I am quite*
*satisfied that she has been subjected to no outrage or bad*

*usage" I paused for her assent, she nodded her head, or
said "Yes". I offered to have a doctor called that she might
be examined if it was wished, and the mother refused, she
said she was quite satisfied that there was no need for it
from what Eliza had told her. I handed her the paper, and
she took it to the desk. I cannot say whether she read it,
but she had every opportunity, and she put her signature
where it is now at the bottom. It was written at the same
time, the ink is a little bit smudged. Mrs. Stead was
coming in and out. I read it over to her clause by clause
after I had written the whole of it. I am certain that I read
that she [Eliza] had been subjected to no outrage or bad
usage; I laid special stress upon those words, and after I
had read the whole I did not put a pen to paper beyond
signing my name as witness. I swear that most solemnly
I showed the certificate to Inspector Borner as we walked
out of the house towards the station, and handed it to
him… we then came up in the train with the inspector
and the children, and went to the Treasury and made a
statement – that is all I had to do with the case.*[9]

—◦◦◦—

Stead's defence case also included Old Bailey appearances by
Howard Vincent, head of the Metropolitan Police's Criminal
Investigation Department (CID) who recounted how the editor
had been in touch in May and had questioned him about
"procuring girls for houses of ill fame in London". Mr Vincent
stressed that Stead "did not ask me to be, and I was not, in any way
responsible for what he did subsequently" and that he warned the
editor of the "dangerous consequences" of taking action and that
he could get "a stain on his character that might never be wiped
off" and it could end up with him in the dock!

Vincent commented, "That the Archbishop of Canterbury had
given him the same advice, and I said that he had better follow it.

He told me that whatever the risk was, he should put this thing through, or words to that effect. He was exceedingly anxious for the passing of the law..."[10]

The long day of evidence meandered on and now Stead brought out his big guns, starting with Benjamin Scott giving his account of the May through August 1885 period.

———

### *Tuesday, 3 November, Central Criminal Court: Benjamin Scott (Witness for the Defence)*

*I entirely approved of the inquiry; it has lifted from my spirit a weight which has been on it by day as well as night for many years, and I am deeply thankful for what has taken place. The inquiry is called the Commission of the Pall Mall Gazette, and the committee of which I was chairman passed a resolution approving of it. After you had commenced the inquiry I introduced Mr. Jacques to you under the name of Mussabini. I told you I knew nothing about him personally beyond the fact that he made communications to me as chairman of my committee.*

*He came to me in March and made proposals which the committee did not see their way to take up, and I knew nothing further of Mr. Jacques. I simply sent him to you saying that I thought he might be useful in the present inquiry. I knew in March that he had been to several newspaper offices respecting a proposal that he should visit the Continent, where he said he knew where to place his hands on English girls who were detained against their will.[11]*

———

Lord Dalhousie, who had represented the Home Office in the House of Lords in Gladstone's government, was also called to the stand. He had tried to get the Criminal Law Amendment Bill through the House of Lords before the Whitsun break that May, when the bill had been "talked out" by George Cavendish-Bentinck MP. He explained that he had told Stead that there was no need to "abduct" a girl under the age of sixteen in order to help his bill through Parliament.[12] There was also a minor piece of evidence regarding the *Pall Mall Gazette*'s Secret Commission fact gathering on the age of young mothers in "lying-in" London workhouses but the man who delivered that note of clarification would have interested not just the court but also the reporters covering the case. This was another Member of Parliament, George Russell, who was Under Secretary to the Local Government Board in the Gladstone administration, giving evidence on behalf of Stead.

There was a similarly brief appearance by someone who would have attracted popular attention by her presence in the witness stand – Miss Ellice Hopkins who described herself as "the Miss Hopkins whose name is used in relation to the enactments of the Industrial Schools Act which is called sometimes Miss Hopkins's Act". She had been in the public eye for at least nine years, since she decided to devote herself to raising the age of protection for English girls. She told the Old Bailey she had met the editor of the *Pall Mall Gazette* earlier that year and had written to him, asking him to publish an article she had written about the protection of young girls, with a view to securing the amendment of the law. That article was indeed subsequently published in the *Gazette*.

Character and material witnesses of this calibre would, Stead hoped, prove that his scheme to expose the sex trade had not been a spur of the moment decision, but had been long coming, and influenced by some of the most prominent campaigners for raising the age of consent. In his summing up he admitted to making some blunders in his reporting and methods, but he wanted the court to be absolutely aware of his fine intentions.

—◦◦◦—

*My own impression was that the father was a drunken*
*sweep who did not care where his girl was going to. I may*
*be right or wrong, but I am absolutely convinced that so*
*far as the mother and Mrs. Broughton were concerned,*
*the child was handed over to me for an immoral purpose.*
*I acted upon that belief, and that belief governed every*
*subsequent step in the proceedings. What I tried to do was*
*not to abduct a child, but to raise up such a sentiment*
*in the country as to render abduction and all kindred*
*offences more dangerous than they had been...*[13]

—◦◦◦—

Stead then requested to call others with whom he had consulted over the matter and who, he hoped, would suitably impress the court, but this was turned down. Mr Justice Lopes denied permission for their appearance on the basis that the individuals would give the court details on the editor's motives rather than on the facts in the case. So the jury, and the packed courthouse, were denied the opportunity to see the Archbishop of Canterbury, Edward Benson in the witness stand, along with, among others, two Home Secretaries, Sir William Harcourt and Sir Richard Cross, and the philanthropist Dr Thomas Barnardo.

The minds of the men of the jury must have been whirling with the many witnesses being called and all the information and detail being presented, but there were still three defence cases to be heard – Mrs Elizabeth Combe, Mr Sampson Jacques, and the second-in-command of The Salvation Army, Mr William Bramwell Booth.

# CHAPTER 22

# THE DEFENCE WRAPS UP

Tuesday, 3 November 1885, was an extraordinarily busy day for the court, for after Stead ended his defence, with his array of outstanding witnesses from the world of politics, the police, and human rights campaigning, came the final defendants.

Sampson Jacques, it appears from the records, did not give evidence in his own defence. The court had already heard, from many of the witnesses, details of his role in the removal of Eliza from her parents, his part in ensuring her delivery to France and then back to England. He had been present for that reunion at William Stead's house in Wimbledon but perhaps felt that he could offer no more by the way of information to the jury.

Jacques is something of a mystery to this day and even his name remains so. Stead, in his evidence, had said he knew Jacques as "Mussabini" (that was his name) and that "Jacques" had been the pseudonym he had used during his undercover enquiries for the Secret Commission. All the reporters and investigators, Stead admitted, had used false names for some of their enquiries. But just why "Mussabini" was prosecuted under the name "Jacques" – that name appears in all the official Old Bailey records – is as much an enigma as the man himself.

Elizabeth Combe, however, was not such a complicated character. She gave her account simply to the court, recounting how she, a resident of Switzerland and a "member" of The Salvation Army there for the past two and a half years, had become involved with Stead and Eliza. She was one of the early converts to The Salvation Army who came not from the working classes, but from a higher social order. She had first come to know about William and Catherine Booth through her son who had come under their influence a few years before. In her home in Switzerland she had often hosted English members of the organization when they arrived in the country and found themselves "persecuted".[1]

—∿∿—

### Tuesday, 3 November, Central Criminal Court: Elizabeth Combe (Examined by Mr. Horne Payne )

*I am a widow lady of private fortune, generally having residence and house at No. 11, Rue Livrier, Geneva. I have one surviving son – he is called "Lieutenant" Combe in the Salvation "Army".*

*"I have a brother Theodore Berard, who lives at Loriol, France…*

*I first came to England from Switzerland, on the 25th of May, I think, on the Whit Monday…When I arrived in England I went straight to the Clapton Training Home… In the course of the next week I received a message from Mr. Booth… he asked me at that time whether I was disposed to travel, if I was a good sailor; and I said I thought I was. That was all he said; he might require me later on… I had no knowledge whatever of the investigation by the Committee, or any of the matters I have heard spoken to here.*

*On the Wednesday night a gentleman came up to Clapton on the 3rd of June and fetched me down to London, to headquarters in Queen Victoria Street…he fetched me between 8 and 9 o'clock on the 3rd of June. I met Mr. Booth, I believe, at the door of the headquarters, and he took me with him immediately. We stopped a Hansom cab and both got in. My share of the conversation was not very great in the Hansom cab, not with the noise. I*

*did not know where I was going. He took me in the Hansom*
*cab to a house. I did not know who resided in the house at*
*that time, or whether it was a doctor's or any other house.*
*He spoke to me in a general way about the wickedness and*
*bad things going on in London; and I really am not quite*
*sure whether he asked me just at that time to take some*
*little girl over or away with me; that I had to take charge of*
*a young girl... He told me that night that a child had been*
*bought, and that they wanted to prove that a child could*
*be bought for bad purposes and taken over to the Continent.*
*I believe he told me about the Continent at that time, but I*
*could not swear it, but I believe he did.[2]*

Mrs Combe explained how the next day she had gone to a property which she now thought was Dr Heywood Smith's house, where she thought she spoke with Stead. She later went with a Miss Peck to Nottingham Place where she met Rebecca Jarrett and the child she later knew as Eliza, who she reported didn't look that happy. Eventually, after Miss Peck had gone to buy a coat for the little girl, Mrs Combe, Rebecca, and Eliza went to the railway station, where they picked up some tickets to Paris which had already been purchased for them. On arrival in the French capital city they had gone to 3, Avenue Laumiere, which was the home of Miss Catherine "Katie" Booth, the Booths' eldest daughter, who, just a few years previously had established the "L'Armee du Salut" in France.

The Avenue Laumiere house was by 1885 a training home for women who had committed to become leaders of The Salvation Army and there were four or five female "cadets" living there. Later, on advice from Bramwell Booth, Mrs Combe wrote to her brother, who lived in the south of France, asking him to take Eliza and to care for her, or find a comfortable home for her.

With Elizabeth Combe's evidence concluded, the final chief witness in the case stood up. While Mrs Combe had been just a matter of minutes in the witness box, Bramwell Booth was in the dock considerably longer. From Booth the court heard, yet again, the fine details of his involvement in the Eliza Armstrong affair.

In the gallery the Booth family and other Salvationists and friends who had gathered every day to support their man would have leant forward in anticipation, perhaps even silently praying for Bramwell as he began his testimony.

As a high profile and recognized "man of God", Bramwell would have felt bound to tell the truth. Yet his evidence seems to have been rather at odds with some of the facts, although perhaps that is a matter of interpretation. He had denied that he knew anything about the abduction of the child Eliza in advance, but agreed that he had been aware that Stead had planned to prove that young girls could be bought and sold, although he skimmed over that at the start of his evidence, which really picked up the circumstances of Derby Day and beyond.

—*∿∿*—

### Tuesday, 3 November, Central Criminal Court: William Bramwell Booth (The Prisoner)

*[Stead] … told me that Jarrett, "Rebecca" he called her, had purchased a child as though for an immoral purpose from two women, one of them being an old associate, or an old friend of hers, and the other being the child's mother; that Rebecca had paid one of the women 2l.(two pounds) for procuring the child, and the mother 1l., and that 2l. more would be paid to the procuress when the child's purity or virginity, I do not remember the word exactly, had been certified.*

*He also told me that the child had been dressed in new clothes, and that she had seen her father, who knew the purpose for which she was going, and that the child had been taken to the house of a French midwife, whose business it was to certify young girls for immoral men;*

*that from there she had been taken to a brothel. He
also told me that the Frenchwoman had supplied some
chloroform, that she had been to a brothel in some street
off Regent Street, and that there chloroform had been
administered to her after she had been put into bed, and
that then he, Mr. Stead, had gone into the room to the
child, and that she was absolutely at his mercy; that from
there they had come to Dr. Smith's, and that he had now
taken her to some rooms for the night, and that during the
night Dr. Smith was going to examine her.*

*There was some conversation on my part, some
expressions of horror, and so on, and after that he asked me
to go and see Dr. Smith in the morning, just to know from
him if the child was all right, and then allow Madame
Combe, although he did not mention her name, the person
I brought, to accompany her to Paris with Jarrett... then
Mr. Stead went away, and I went to bed – I should think it
was very nearly 2 o'clock... I breakfasted at the same place
next morning, and went round immediately after taking
breakfast to Dr. Heywood Smith's alone. Dr. Heywood
Smith told me he had made an examination. I learnt as
the result of the examination that the child was pure.*

*I went back again and told Madame Combe that
she was to go with Jarrett to Paris in company with the
child... I saw her off at the station. Mr. Stead was there
too. I ought to say I really did not see the child although
I knew she was there. I had told Madame Combe nothing
further, down to the time she left for Paris.*

*She went to Paris, and resided at the Salvation
Training Home there. I said to Madame Combe that I
wished to have the child removed from Paris, and asked
her if she had any friends in France who could receive the
child and train her properly; and Madame Combe said she
had a sister, or a brother, or a sister-in-law who would take*

*the child if she requested it, and would teach her and train her, and bring her up in a virtuous and Christian manner.*

*I do not think I asked Madame Combe where these people resided. I had the fullest confidence in Madame Combe, and with her assurance that the people referred to were of that character, I assented to the child being sent there. Then I asked her to telegraph to Paris to her own son there, as she told me that the child knew her son, and would probably travel with him without demur, and comfortably and happily. I asked her to send a telegram desiring or instructing her son to take the child to this house, which afterwards turned out to be at L'Oriol.[3]*

---

It was clear proof of his involvement in helping to remove Eliza from the country, but regardless of this, Bramwell Booth got off lightly. There were few difficult questions, even under cross-examination. Perhaps it was because Stead had already effectively exonerated The Salvation Army and their representative on trial. In the witness box, Bramwell gave the impression of a man who truly believed that, but for his actions and that of his Salvation Army, Eliza would have been doomed to a life of shame.

---

### Tuesday, 3 November, Central Criminal Court: William Bramwell Booth (The Prisoner) continued

*On the 16th July I had a visit from Inspector Borner. He introduced himself, and as near as I can remember he told me he had been instructed by the Magistrate at Marylebone to call upon me with reference to a child which had been inquired for by her mother, and named Eliza Armstrong, and he asked me if I knew where the child was, or anything about it. I said yes, the child was in our care, and she was in good hands and well cared*

*for. I am not sure whether I volunteered the child's address
to the inspector or not. My impression is that I volunteered
the address. If I did not volunteer it he did not ask for it...*

*The next interview was on 31st July, and I saw him a
third time the 1st August. He at neither of those interviews
asked me for Rebecca Jarrett's address. There was certainly
nothing said about 100l. on the last interview, the third
interview, or the second interview. I was going to say that
nothing was said about 100l. at the interview on the 1st
August, when the mother was present, and I was about to
say that I think the Inspector has confused something that
was said on the previous morning when he called upon me
in speaking to him of the child and in reply I said I was so
desirous for the child's welfare, or something to that effect,
that I would be prepared to make an application to the
Court of Chancery to make her a ward of Court, even if it
cost 100l. I think I did use those words upon that occasion.
I told him that I was really very much concerned for the
child's welfare and that I thought it would be a most terrible
calamity for her to go back to her old associates. At that
same interview he asked me if I would see the mother and
assure her of the child's well-being, and I said "Yes"...* [4]

—◦◦◦—

Once Bramwell eventually met Mrs Armstrong, he told the
court, there was no reasoning with her, even though he believed
it would be better to leave Eliza where she was. The mother had
different ideas.

—◦◦◦—

### Tuesday, 3 November, Central Criminal Court: William Bramwell Booth (The Prisoner) continued

*I then said she might take it from me that no harm
had come to the child; that she had been examined by a*

*medical man; and, speaking to them collectively, I said,*
*if they wished, they could see the certificate. When I had*
*told the mother this, she expressed herself as very thankful*
*that this was so. She may have said "Thank God," or*
*"I am very thankful," or some expression of that kind.*
*I said to her, "Did you not know something of Rebecca*
*Jarrett?" I think I said, "I understood from what you said*
*to Lloyd's reporter," or some words to that effect, "that*
*you knew Rebecca Jarrett before this," to which she said,*
*"Yes, I did". I then said, "Did you know what sort of a*
*woman she was?" and she said "Yes" and I said "What?"*
*and she said a gay woman. I then said, "Was it not a very*
*extraordinary thing that you should let your little child go*
*with such a woman?" She made no answer...* [5]

In his later memoirs, Bramwell Booth would recall his time in the dock at the Old Bailey. He particularly commented on his questioning by the Attorney General, who he had previously noted had treated Rebecca Jarrett ill and who metered out some of the same treatment to himself. For someone unaccustomed to appearing in a court of law, and probably more used to being treated with deference rather than suspicion, Bramwell appears to have felt rather hard done by. His words also give us an insight into how the court case was being perceived outside the court, among supporters of The Salvation Army.

*During his cross-examination, Sir Richard Webster showed*
*some tendency to bully. One of his favourite methods in*
*cross-examining was to repeat the question, "Do I understand*
*you to say...?" At last I said to him in reply to one such*
*repetition, "Sir Richard, I have told you once. Why do you ask*
*me again?"' From that point his manner greatly improved.*
*One small circumstance which I recall with regard to*

> *Webster was our discovery of a bundle of letters on the table*
> *of the apartment assigned to our use, which Webster had*
> *obviously mislaid. I took them up and read them one or two,*
> *thinking they were ours, but finding that they belonged to*
> *the prosecuting counsel, sent them to him. I gathered enough*
> *of their contents to know that they were letters from his*
> *constituents – he had just been elected for Launceston – hotly*
> *criticizing him for appearing against The Salvation Army!*[6]

Bramwell Booth took his seat. His evidence was done. The jury just had to hear one final short statement from Mr E. Tyas Cook, the deputy editor of the *Pall Mall Gazette*, regarding the editing of the Maiden Tribute of Modern Babylon articles, and the case for the defence was concluded.

Summings up followed, including that for Rebecca Jarrett which moved the courtroom to tears. Soon the decision would be in the hands of the jury. Although still confident that he would be acquitted, Bramwell Booth was now philosophical about what might lie ahead for him, as he wrote in a letter to his mother from the Old Bailey:

> *As to the case I have no regrets as to what I did. The mistakes*
> *and accidents all through have only been such as are usually*
> *attached to all human enterprises. I regret them, but I could*
> *not prevent them, glad as I would have been to do so. It is*
> *painful to have all regard for motive shut out of what they*
> *think it well to shut it out from, and yet to imply all sorts of*
> *bad motives in connexion [sic] with the smallest incidents of*
> *the affair. But I do beg you not to be distressed in any way*
> *about me personally. God will take care of me!*
>
> *Then another thing. I do hope that no efforts will be made*
> *on my behalf, if we go to prison, that are not made on behalf*
> *of Stead. Do please let me beg this of you...*[7]

Stead made one final impassioned plea to the jury, reiterating that he had only undertaken the Maiden Tribute scheme for a higher purpose – the changing of the law on consent.[8] However, he was aware that they were bound to bring in a guilty verdict, not least because he had admitted his central role in the plot to take Eliza. But, being a showman, he wasn't going to let an opportunity pass him by and he now took centre stage. As he summed up his case, he once again took the opportunity to pronounce that it was he, and he alone, who was responsible. Of his co-defendant, the reformed prostitute, he spoke protectively: "I believe in Jarrett as I do in the Bible. I honour her, driven and harassed as she was in her evidence here for refusing to answer questions that would incriminate her old friends…"[9]

He finished with a flamboyant flourish: " … if I am found guilty, I shall make no appeal. By your verdict, I shall stand; and, if in the opinion of twelve Englishmen – sons of English mothers, fathers possibly of English girls – if they say I am guilty, I will take my punishment and I shall not flinch."[10]

The courtroom broke into applause.

The leading prosecutor, the Attorney General of England and Wales Sir Richard Webster, had however, already made a good case, and in his final speech merely had to repeat all the evidence which the jury had heard, which proved that Eliza had been taken without the permission of both parents.

The Armstrongs, Sir Richard maintained, were a respectable Christian family, by and large, apart from the mother "being given at times" to drink. They had, he stressed, been libelled by a woman of appalling character who had admitted lying under oath, Rebecca Jarrett who, the Attorney General said, had posed as a "… repentant Magdalen… it is clear she is one of those women who had been led to exaggerate her guilt for the purpose of glorifying herself and exaggerating her merit at the present time… She was introduced to Stead as a woman who had been steeped in iniquity and sin who was now repentant… Such a woman that Stead told her she deserved to be hanged and damned."[11]

Nothing, the Attorney General concluded, justified what had happened to Eliza Armstrong.

When Sir Richard finally resumed his seat, it was the end of a very long day. The judge suspended the case for the night and requested the jury to reconvene at 10 o'clock, when he would begin his summing up.[12]

Saturday, 7 November 1885 – the final day of the case – saw the courtroom at the Old Bailey once again packed to the rafters. Mr Justice Lopes began by reminding the court that this was the first case of any great importance, to be tried under the new Act of Parliament which allowed people to give evidence in their own trial.[13] This new law, ironically, was the same Criminal Law Amendment Act which the accused in the dock before him at the Old Bailey had helped to pass in the summer.[14]

The judge's summing up, as had been some of his questioning of the accused, was unequivocal in its condemnation of those standing before him. He slated Rebecca Jarrett's character, describing her as "that abominable woman"[15] and, although complimenting Stead on the conducting of his own defence,[16] he nevertheless saved most of his criticism for him, denouncing his odious Maiden Tribute of Modern Babylon articles. He reiterated that Stead had "deluged for some months our streets and the whole country with an amount of filth which tainted the minds of the children he was so anxious to protect and which had been, and ever would be, a disgrace to journalism."[17]

But Justice Lopes took his personal condemnation of Mr Stead one step further, accusing him of acting out of pride rather than moral indignation, and he also made a great deal of the damage which he said had been caused to Mr and Mrs Armstrong, and to Eliza. "The child herself has been dragged through the dirt, examined by a woman who has a vile character, subjected to chloroform..."[18]

There was no doubt in some minds, particularly that of Stead, that the judge's final words on the case were biased and that it could only mean a guilty verdict. As Stead recalled years later:

*The Judge had spent the whole day summing up against us. His animus was undisguised. He constructed a series of questions, to which the jury would have to answer yes or no, with such care that it was simply impossible for them to do other than return the verdict of guilty. But so signal had been vindication of the motives and the method of the defendant, that there were many who believed that the jury, despite the charge of the Judge, would persist in returning a verdict of not guilty.*

*I had no such expectations. I knew that I should be convicted. I knew also that I should have to spent two months in gaol. My friends rallied me about the absurdity of my forecast. It was one of the intuitions which enable us sometimes to foresee what is about to happen.*[19]

If Judge Lopes had any worries that, indeed, the jury might be inclined to acquit the accused, he warned them against being influenced by anything other than that which they had heard in court. Even then, in the final moments of an address delivered over about five hours,[20] he could not resist giving one last moral judgment on the whole case.

———————

*I expect you have heard much talk outside the Court regarding the circumstances and matters of this case. I am quite certain that you will not allow anything that you have heard outside to affect your judgment, and that you will be guided only by the evidence you have heard from the witnesses on oath. I would warn you, although I feel it is not necessary, perhaps, to do so, not to be prejudiced against Stead, because in our streets and throughout our provinces some months ago, there were circulated, emanating from the Pall Mall Gazette*

*offices, disgusting and filthy articles – articles so filthy*
*and so disgusting that one cannot help fearing that they*
*may have suggested to innocent women and children the*
*existence of vice and wickedness which had never occurred*
*to their minds before.*[21]

—◈◈◈—

With those words ringing in their ears, the twelve men of the jury
retired to consider their verdict.

# CHAPTER 23

# VERDICT

The moment when Stead and his co-defendants learned their fate in the Maiden Tribute trial was one of high tension. A few years later William Stead wrote of the atmosphere in the courtroom as the jury filed into the room:

> ... *the night of my conviction... remains indelibly impressed upon my memory. The crowded Court, the strained excitement, the hushed suspense, the outburst of feeling when the verdict was announced, all recur to me as if they had occurred but yesterday...*[1]

After several hours of deliberation without a conclusion, the jury had returned to the court seeking further guidance from the judge. The foreman, James Branch, had requested direction on a point of law and the courtroom had burst into spontaneous applause, which infuriated the judge. Mr Justice Lopes' direction to the jury was clear – only *one* point should be their concern. Regardless of the motives of the accused individuals, was Eliza Armstrong taken without her father's permission and against his will?[2]

The defendants and their family, friends, supporters, and legal advisers, as well as the masses of interested onlookers and gentlemen of the press, all poised to note the verdict, awaited the return of the jurors. "The well of the Court was crowded with counsel," Stead wrote later.

> *The leaders of the Bar were there, and, on either side, gathered the friends of the opposing parties. The jury were absent for a considerable time and the crowded Court buzzed with eager conversation as everybody canvassed the possible verdict with his neighbours.*[3]

For the Booth family this was an anxious time. In addition to some of his siblings and other Salvation Army colleagues, friends, and supporters, Bramwell Booth's wife Florence had attended the court every day carrying her four-month-old baby – another "Catherine" (who would become Commissioner Catherine Bramwell Booth).[4]

Stead's memory of the day is that he felt no concern – he knew the inevitable outcome.

> *Suddenly there was a thrilling whisper: "They are coming, they are coming." Everyone hushed his talk. Those who had seats sat down. Those who crowded the corridors craned their necks towards the jury box. The twelve good men and true, headed by their foreman, filed back into the box. Then the Judge, in a silence profound as death, asked if they had agreed upon their verdict.*
>
> *"We have," said the foreman. Everyone held their breath and waited to hear the next fateful words...*[5]

> *Rebecca Jarrett: guilty.*
> *William Thomas Stead: guilty.*
> *Sampson Jacques: not guilty.*
> *Elizabeth Combe: not guilty.*
> *William Bramwell Booth: not guilty.*

But that was not the end of the matter. The jury had asked the judge to take into consideration that Mr Stead had been "deceived by his agents"[6] which even Stead described as an "extraordinary rider" to their verdict, as he later observed: "They recommended me to mercy, and they wished to put on record their high appreciation of the services I had rendered the nation by securing the passage of a much needed law for the protection of young girls."[7]

In fact, Stead later also reported that the foreman of the jury felt so badly about the verdict on the editor that he called upon Mrs Stead in Wimbledon explaining "with tears in his eyes" how, given the judge's instructions, they had had little option but to find her husband guilty. Stead, by this time serving a jail sentence, wrote to Emma instructing her to tell the foreman not to grieve about it and admitting that if he had been in the foreman's position, he "should have done the same as he did".[8]

Bramwell Booth, although acquitted, would have to await his final fate. Before the formalities of his case could be concluded, there was a second trial to come, which would see Stead, Jarrett, Jacques, and the midwife, Louise Mourey, face a charge of indecent assault. This related to the intimate medical examination of Eliza by Madame Mourey. The accused had but a day's reprieve from court before the second trial was to begin on Monday, 9 November.

It was Lord Mayor's Day in London and Stead, knowing that he would soon be incarcerated, went out and about. "I spent hours walking up and down through the streets through the thousands who turned out to see London's annual pageant. I was going to be secluded from my fellow creatures for some months. I wanted to take my fill of the crowd before I returned to my cell."[9]

As Stead was making the most of his last hours of freedom William Booth was quietly observing proceedings from the sidelines. Although delighted that the Criminal Law Amendment Act had been put into law, and that his "Army" had come out of the trial relatively unscathed, General Booth had become increasingly dissatisfied with Mr Stead and his behaviour. Stead, he believed, was "thrusting, eager and headlong", and although he had been happy to use him in a higher cause and appeared grateful for his assistance, he never wholly trusted him.[10]

Some believe this indifference to Stead was the result of pique – Stead, while mentioning Bramwell in the Maiden Tribute articles, made no reference to The Salvation Army as such. While this had, undoubtedly, partly helped in proving his eldest son's innocence in court, Booth the elder continued to distance himself from the editor of the *Pall Mall Gazette*. Later he would refuse to take part in any appeals for a remission of Mr Stead's jail sentence, a campaign led by Mrs Josephine Butler.[11]

William Booth's letter to his wife Catherine as the second trial concluded gives an indication of his conflicted feelings towards Stead, especially following an "apology" which the editor had written to his readers in which he regretted the methods he had employed to raise the issue of the child sex trade.

*Rookwood, Stamford Hill, N.,*
*[Monday] Nov. 9, '85.*

*My dearest Love,*
    *I... must say I am heartily sick of the whole affair.*
    *The enclosed is Stead's account of things, which appears in to-night's Pall Mall Gazette.*
    *It is such a throwing up of the sponge and leaving us all in the lurch that I cannot go any further on in the agitation. To soap anybody down in that fashion is to me disgusting. I understand all the way through that the Attorney General was hard upon our people, and on Sat. all said that the Judge was quite a partisan. And here is Stead, abandons poor Rebecca, and said that the verdict is just, etc., etc., etc., according to the evidence, etc...*
    *We shall see what is done to-morrow. Stead won't be put in prison, in my opinion, but will drop back into his old role of journalist, and leave us smeared with the tar of this affair to fight it out with blackguards and brothel-keepers all over the world.*
    *I am sure the S.A. is the thing, and our lines are all right. We shall see tremendous things. We are deciding for our International Council in June next, and shall have Soldiers from all parts of the world and 2000 Officers. This will wipe out the very memory of Eliza Armstrong.*
    *Bramwell is not quite out of the wood yet. We will wire you to-morrow how things go.*
    ***(William Booth)*** [12]

The second trial was little more than a formality, given that all of the evidence had been heard in the first hearing. Both Stead and Rebecca Jarrett declined to give evidence in the proceedings and they were not legally represented in the trial. Sampson Jacques, who had been quiet during the initial court case, made what was described as a "spirited speech in his own defence". Lawyers acting for Louise Mourey attempted to argue that there was no such thing as an indecent assault by a female on another female, an opinion that was rapidly and firmly squashed by Judge Lopes.[13]

The jury spent less than an hour deliberating this second verdict and the four defendants on trial for the indecent assault on Eliza Armstrong – Stead, Jarrett, Jacques, and Mourey – were all found guilty. Mr Justice Lopes swiftly moved on to the sentences for both trials.

Elizabeth Combe, the judge ruled, had had no knowledge of how Eliza had come to be in her care or how she had been separated from her parents, and was formally discharged. The judge confirmed that Bramwell Booth was acquitted on all charges. Both judge and jury had accepted that he had honestly believed that Eliza's mother had been happy to pass the care of her thirteen-year-old child to the care of The Salvation Army in France.[14]

Now Judge Lopes turned to the four guilty parties, first addressing Stead, who he recognized had had some "good motives" for acting as he did for which, he said, he would give him some credit. He also took into consideration the recommendation for mercy from the jury at the end of the first trial. However, this would not mean the man would go free, Judge Lopes ruled:

—⁓—

*... I cannot forget that you are an educated man, who should have known that the law cannot be broken to promote any supposed good, and that the sanctity of private life cannot be invaded for the furtherance of the views of an individual who, I am inclined to believe,*

*thought the end would sanctity the means. Now, in these*
*circumstances, I need not say that I have given the most*
*intense and anxious consideration to your case, and I have*
*come to the conclusion that I cannot pass anything but a*
*substantial sentence, and that is that you be imprisoned*
*without hard labour for three calendar months.*[15]

——◦◦◦——

Next he asked Rebecca Jarrett who along with Stead had also been found guilty on both charges – abduction and indecent assault – to stand to hear her sentence. She leaned on the railings in front of her to raise herself wearily to her feet.

——◦◦◦——

*… There is no doubt a mitigating circumstance in your*
*case, but there is also an aggravating circumstance. The*
*mitigating circumstance is that you only undertook what*
*you did under extreme pressure, but the aggravating*
*circumstance is that, after a most patient hearing, and*
*having regard to the finding of the jury, I am firmly*
*convinced you mislead your employer, Stead.*[16]

——◦◦◦——

Jarrett was sentenced to six months in prison, without hard labour. The private investigator-cum-reporter Sampson Jacques received a one month sentence on the assault charge, again without hard labour.

Finally Judge Lopes turned his attention to the "midwife" Madame Louise Mourey, for whom he had kept back just a little more vitriol.

——◦◦◦——

*I cannot look at your case in the same light as the others.*
*I have considered it with much anxiety. It has been stated*
*over and over again by those charged with you, that you*

*are a professional abortionist, and that you obtain your living in that way… If I had evidence before me which led me to believe you were a professional abortionist, and gained your livelihood in the way suggested, I would subject you to the highest punishment the law enables me to impose. You have been found guilty of indecent assault – a most serious indecent assault. This child, thirteen years old, late in the afternoon, is brought to you by people of whom you know nothing, you are asked to examine the child, and you examine it in the way described. I fear much that at the time you knew, or had reason to suspect the child was intended for outrage; at any rate, I know you could have been animated by no good motive. I know, too, that you received payment and reward for what you did. In these circumstances, not knowing whether you deserve all the imputations cast upon you, the sentence I pass on you is that you be imprisoned and kept to hard labour for six calendar months.*[17]

---

Following sentencing, the convicted criminals were quickly taken away, through a labyrinth of underground corridors into the nearby Newgate prison. There they spent a dismal hour in a cold cell before being packed into a Black Maria police van – the very kind that had safely transported them and their co-defendants to Bow Street Magistrates' Court when the crowd got ugly. They were then driven through the streets of the city to the prisons where they were destined to see out their sentences.

CHAPTER 24

# PRISON

Coldbath Fields Prison in Clerkenwell, otherwise known as the Middlesex House of Correction, had a reputation for being old fashioned and extraordinarily strict.[1] It was to this place of incarceration that William Thomas Stead and Sampson Jacques were taken shortly after their sentencing. A prison had stood on the Coldbath-in-the-Fields site since the reign of King James I, but it had been rebuilt at the end of the eighteenth century and then extended about thirty years before the editor of the *Pall Mall Gazette* became its latest inmate. It was home to prisoners on short sentences of up to two years and it had a reputation for its uncompromising regime of silence.[2]

Entering the world of the penal institution would not have been an easy experience for W. T. Stead, who, although not from a privileged background, would never have experienced anything quite like Coldbath. On arrival he would have been medically examined and searched. His hair would have been cut short by the prison barber and he would have endured a cold shower.[3] There would have been the inevitable abuse from his fellow "felons", although he did later write that he enjoyed cordial relations with most of those with whom he shared the prison.

At the start of his imprisonment there would have been no privileges, although that would soon change. Although he had been deserted by William Booth, Stead still had friends in high places and, the moment he was sentenced, they started to campaign on his behalf. His sentence and imprisonment had hit the headlines. Many of his colleagues and rivals at newspapers across London had covered his trial in minute detail and now, the sordid facts having all been covered, they turned to their own judgment of the case and the man at the centre of it.

On the morning after sentencing, *The Times* railed against the editor of the *Pall Mall Gazette*: "Nothing less than imprisonment would have been an adequate warning to fanatics of all kinds."[4] Most of the papers supported the Armstrong parents' case and agreed that Stead and the others deserved what they got. The *Morning Post*[5] went so far as to say that the sentences imposed were insufficient: "It would have been more consonant with the principles of justice to have awarded heavier sentences to Stead, Jarrett and Jacques than to Madame Mourey who 'did not do one-hundredth part of the injury to the child that was done by the other defendants.'"[6]

But Stead still had many allies. Appeals for clemency and leniency began immediately, perhaps prompted by a *Pall Mall Gazette* narrative of their editor's initial experiences in Coldbath.

### MR. STEAD IN PRISON

*To-day the Rev. Benjamin Waugh was permitted by the courtesy of the Home Office to hold half an hour's conversation with the prisoner on matters of business. Mr. Waugh was shown into the waiting-room, bare, barren, and forbidding, with a long deal table in the middle of the room, with bench-like seats round it. There the visitor waited for a quarter of an hour, when he was taken upstairs to the visiting room, where the prisoner was already seated. The visiting-room, it is sufficient to say, is similar to the first, but with a better light. A warder sat in the room, and Mr. Waugh sat at the other end of the table, for he was not allowed either to shake hands with or otherwise welcome his friend. Mr. Stead wore a yellow Glengarry-shaped cap, of which he observed that it "was like the cap he wore when a boy, but that it was without the ribbons." He wore a loose-fitting short jacket of rough light yellow material, buttoned at the throat – of course without a collar, showing all the tops of the shirt and waistcoat in irregular line. He appeared to have been "cropped," but the visitor was allowed to ask no questions. His beard and moustache, of course, remained. His trousers were loose, baggy, of yellow linen of the duck type, with the Government arrows stamped with ink in four different places. His boots were large and must have been uncomfortable; one was patched upon the toe, and the other had a thick new yellow leather sole upon it. He wore a round cloth label on his left breast marked R 2/8.*

*Mr. Stead looked very cold, and put his hands inside his baggy sleeves as if for warmth. He was in good spirits, and seemed able to say many things, but the interview was business. Mr. Stead was supplied with a mattress last night. By the regulation of the prison he has a Bible in his cell, but from its situation we have reason to believe that he will not have light to read it. Mr. Stead arrived at Coldbath Fields last night, when he received the regulation supper of skilly and brown bread. He was knocked up at six for a breakfast of skilly and brown bread, after which he saw the doctor. His dinner is suet pudding and brown bread at noon, and supper at 5.30 of skilly and brown bread. He sees no one again till breakfast the next morning. It may be said that a prisoner sentenced to hard labour has to pick three pounds of oakum as his daily task: Mr. Stead, not having been so sentenced, will have to pick one pound.[7]*

According to his daughter Estelle, the response to her father's conditions in Coldbath was immediate.

*... the news of his conviction and sentence struck like setting a match to gunpowder. The effect was instantaneous,*

*explosive, seeming to liberate the pent-up horror that
had gripped the whole country, while the deadly drama
was slowly being unfolded at the Old Bailey, day by day.
Avalanches of telegrams poured in upon Queen Victoria,
the Prime Minister and the Home Office. Protests and
petitions were showered upon the Government.[8]*

Supporters like Josephine Butler rallied around Stead and there
was an immediate response from his home town.

*An urgent petition from Howden-upon-Tyne, "praying
for a reduction in the sentence," sped on its way to the
Home Secretary by the night mail, on the very day of his
conviction. The news had reached Newcastle at five o'clock
in the afternoon, and the good people of the village of his
boyhood lost no time in voicing their sentiments...[9]*

From leading church figures there was a similar show of support.
Just the day after Stead's conviction, the Roman Catholic
Archbishop of Westminster, Cardinal Henry Manning, wrote
personally to Stead in prison. The letter is dated 11 November:

*My dear Mr Stead,
    "All things work together for good to them that love God."
You have served Him with a single eye. And "The work has
been done," as you wrote on the sentence. No sentence can
undo it... You have now the crown upon your work – that
is, to suffer for errors of judgement and a literal reach of the
law which left the moral life of England almost without
defence... I believe what has now befallen you will work
some unforeseen and great good for your consolation.[10]*

As a result of the pressure upon them, within days of the sentence
being handed down at the Old Bailey, the Home Secretary

announced that Stead had been granted the privileges of a "first-class prisoner".[11] He was transferred to Holloway prison – a more recent addition to the English prison system having been opened in the early 1850s as a mixed prison. The governor is believed to have been among those who felt Stead had been hard done by, especially since those who traded in girls still roamed free.[12]

At Holloway, Stead was given a pleasant room of his own and he even had his family around for Christmas 1885,[13] at which time he also wrote to his sister, assuring her of his comfort. In keeping with his journalistic background, he gave the letter a title – "Christmas Letter to be read to the family".

> *If any of you imagine that I, being a prisoner, am needing consolation and that you ought to address me at the X-mas-tide in accents of crape, don't… "Weep not for me though you know I am here" – a free rendering of an old hymn – is my admonition to you. But rather rejoice, yea, exceedingly rejoice. For I am here in the pleasantest little room imaginable, with a snug arm-chair and a blazing fire, and the walls all gay with Christmas cards and evergreens, and the cupboard full of Christmas cheer; and what is far more, my heart full of joy and peace and good-will to all men, including Mr Justice Lopes and all the rest.[14]*

Estelle's narrative, written after her father's death, also included his description of Boxing Day in Holloway: "… there was a 'merry Christmas party' in my cell; the children, then five in number, were there with their mother. What romps we had! Blindman's buff, puss-in-the-corner, and all other merry Christmas games. Never was the grim old prison a scene of a happier festival."[15]

Stead was free to wear his own clothes, buy his own food and was even allowed to employ a 'servant' – a poorer inmate who did his chores, including making up the fire in his room.[16] And, in a rather bizarre twist given the name he had bestowed on Eliza Armstrong for the purposes of his Maiden Tribute of Modern Babylon articles, it was said he had in his room a posy of lilies sent to him by an admirer which had been "forced into premature bloom".[17]

But while Stead's time in jail was undoubtedly much more comfortable than the experience of the majority of inmates of English prisons of the time – the penal system was well known for some harsh conditions – perhaps the worst effect for a man used to going where he wanted, at will, would have been the enforced confinement. Despite the fact that later in life he would look back on his time spent in Holloway as among the "happiest" in his life, he was still separate from the world – he reported that he was only able to see his wife, children, and a couple of colleagues.[18]

During his time in prison, however, Stead took the opportunity to keep in touch with political life. He wrote numerous letters to the government and to others, including the former Prime Minister William Gladstone who, not long hence, would take up the reins of power once again. Stead was allowed to carry on his work as editor of the *Pall Mall Gazette,* as indicated by references in that same Christmas letter to his sister.

> *I have indeed had a very happy and joyous time. I am sorry about Jarrett and Heywood Smith, and I also sometimes get bothered about money... With that exception, I have great serenity of soul. I spend my time in working. I have written all the leaders but one since I came here, and several of the reviews. I have written an article on "Government by Journalism".[19]*

He also corresponded with his co-defendant Bramwell Booth, writing letters from his Holloway cell, in which he urged him not to be "down in the dumps".

*I tell you, my imprisonment is a great blessing and will be a greater. It would be a thousand pities to get me out. Don't be savage or indignant or contemptuous or anything, but joyful and grateful and willing to do God's will.*[20]

Stead's time inside was a period of spiritual reflection and at one point, it appears, he even toyed with the idea of joining the ranks of The Salvation Army, as he confided in Bramwell.

*… Altho' I am as ever strongly drawn to the Army and more than ever penetrated by the thought that I am not fit to tie the shoe-laces of the humblest of your cadets, I am not going to join the Army. My work lies otherwhere. A great idea and luminous has dawned upon me in the solitude here that my work, that is to say the work God wants me for, is to raise up a band of men and women who will labour to save England and collective humanity and the kingdom of this world with – say – a tenth part of the zeal and devotion that you Army people show in saving individuals.*

*We want a revival of civic virtue, of patriotic religion, of the Salvation of the State and its political and collective action. You look after the individual. It is right, it is the root of all. But I look after the composite and collective individuals. I want to organise a Salvation Army of the secular sort with a religious spirit in it, and if God wants it done and He thinks that I am the man for the job "I'm game" as the saying is.*[21]

Stead's Christian faith had always been central to his conviction and his actions, and his time in Holloway was giving him ample opportunity to contemplate what he thought God might have in store for the next stage of his life. But, even so, some of his aspirations appeared somewhat exaggerated, if not delusional, especially when it came to political ambition.

At one point while in prison he came to believe himself "the most important man in the world"[22] and in one of his most famous articles, the "Government by Journalism" which he referred to in the Christmas 1885 letter and was later published in the *Contemporary Review* journal in May 1886, he argued that the press might be considered more important than government in the life of the nation, especially since it didn't take time off for recesses. Stead maintained that journalists were to be the "watchmen" of society and that "... Parliament is merely a part of the machinery of government. The newspaper is that, and more besides. It has become a necessity of life."[23]

In that article too, he referred to another concept he believed would make for the betterment of society, which he had shared with Bramwell Booth, and in correspondence with his sister.

*I think I wrote you, did I not? About my idea of founding a Secular Salvation Army that will consist of all who are willing to bestir themselves and take trouble for England's sake, with my newspaper as its War Cry and myself as its General. It is a great idea. It links both the church idea on to the journal and combines both for saving the world on its secular side.[24]*

In January 1886 William Thomas Stead was released from his captivity. Although he later reported that his time as an inmate had left him nervous in crowds – he claimed he was particularly fearful about jumping on a moving train during the morning rush hour and was not so confident when arranging news interviews[25] – none of this initially manifested itself.

For Rebecca Jarrett and Louise Mourey the experience of prison was very different. After the verdict at the Old Bailey on 10 November 1885, the women were dispatched to Millbank Prison in Pimlico, a London penal institution which had started life in 1816 as the National Penitentiary, with a rather grim reputation. For many years it had housed convicts destined for transportation to Australia and, after large-scale transportation had ended in 1853, Millbank gradually became a local prison. By the time Rebecca Jarrett and Louise Mourey were incarcerated there, the jail had less than a year left in the main prison system – in 1870 it was re-designated as a military prison.[26] However, it still may have accommodated more than 1,000 prisoners in cramped conditions.[27]

Louise Mourey had been sentenced to six months with hard labour and, unfortunately, she died while in prison. Although she had spent a good deal of her life in a trade which exploited others, some newspapers reckoned she was the hard done by party in the whole Armstrong affair. However, no regret at Madame Mourey's passing was expressed by any of those who were, ultimately, responsible for the situation in which she died.

Although more than a hundred petitions had been received for Rebecca Jarrett's early release from prison, she served out her time in the austere Millbank environment[28] where there was precious little comfort and a round of mundane daily tasks. However, she wasn't badly treated, according to her own accounts, and she was certainly not abandoned. Her new friends in The Salvation Army visited her regularly. The "Army Mother" Catherine Booth, who had been one of those who petitioned the Home Secretary against Rebecca's sentence, was among the visitors. She reported her fury on finding Rebecca "in a stone cell with only a mat to lie on".[29]

Catherine Booth came out of the whole Maiden Tribute affair much better than her husband, who was still determined to distance himself from Stead.[30] Indeed, in a letter to his wife written the day after the sentencing, he downplayed the periods of imprisonment imposed, and appeared to remain determined not to involve his Salvation Army, although he seemed conflicted about whether he, his wife and family, and his organization should advocate on behalf of the editor of the *Pall Mall Gazette*.

*Rockwood Road,*
*[Wednesday] Nov. 11, '85.*

*My dearest Love,*
*... To begin with, Stead has innumerable friends who worship him, and who will agitate the country, and do so far better without us mixed up in it, than with us. Indeed, it is a far great relief to them, I have no doubt, for us to be out of it, so that they can ask for a favour to Stead, or justice, if you like to call it, without having to ask for us at the same time. We shall therefore embarrass them by mixing ourselves up with it, so that on his account it will be better for us to remain separate.*

*... The jury have absolved us from blame, and all the Judge could rake up to say was, "that we ought to have given up the child," which had we known what he knows now we would have done. If we could help Stead, we ought to do so, and we will help him by petitioning or holding meetings on our own lines.*

*Then as to Jarrett, the sentence is not a heavy one; she has no hard labour, her disease will get her all manner of attention; it is possible that she will be treated as a first-class misdemeanant, and on the whole it may really be better for her to be in than out.*

*Then again, she has behaved badly in some respects, perhaps we could not expect anything else from her; still when we remember what she was, and the notice that has been taken of her, she was under a very great obligation to us. It may do her soul good; she says it will, and that she will come out and spend the rest of her days working for God..."*

**(William Booth)** [31]

When their son Bramwell was acquitted on all charges both William and Catherine saw this as a complete vindication of the role of The

Salvation Army in the matter. Yet that a man who had given his life over to the salvation of humanity could be quite so insensitive, even in private, is extraordinary. While Catherine displayed righteous indignation at the sentences of those who had stood alongside her eldest son in the Old Bailey dock, William Booth remained watchful and annoyed. He had had to be persuaded to get involved in the Purity Campaign to which his wife was committed, and he remained sceptical about its outcome.[32]

As William Booth grew older he did become more cantankerous, and certainly he and his wife became increasingly overpowering and domineering as leaders, but perhaps it was just General Booth's over-riding concern for the safety of his life-long mission which was only now coming into its own, and made him appear so unfeeling at the time of the Maiden Tribute trial. To protect the work to which God had called him so many years before in his home town of Nottingham, perhaps he occasionally lost sight of some important values. It is known that he never allowed even his family and personal attachments to come before his Army, and he was aware that the Armstrong case and resulting trial had the potential to destroy the movement he and Catherine had spent their lives creating.[33]

Mrs Booth, however, was not her husband. She picked up her pen once again and petitioned the Home Secretary on behalf of those who had been found guilty at the Old Bailey.[34] Later Rebecca reflected on the improvements in her situation which resulted from that intervention.

*My sentence was 6 months in Millbank Prison. I must say I was treated by all the officers with the greatest kindness and care and respect. The dear old Army Mother walked with 90 ladies with many more names to get me out, but the Home Secretary came to see me, asked me how I was in my health. I said pretty fair but I felt the cold. Through the petition I got a warmer cell. I had indoor exercise... Xmas Day... I spent in my prison cell... a tin cup of gruel was my Xmas breakfast with a dry small loaf. The dear old Commissioner Railton wrote me such a lovely letter to cheer me up. He wished he could take my place but the Chaplin [sic] Mr. Merrick told me they could not for if they let me free they would have to do for others who really got like [sic] poor children for the immoral purpose...*[35]

Surrounded by prisoners who swore and cursed constantly, and were forever maintaining their innocence, Rebecca reported that although she endured a miserable Christmas, she was pleased to receive gifts from the outside, including a warm vest and four shawls made by friends. This included one shawl on which the old lady who had made it had stitched the words "With Loving Kindness".

Rebecca had entered jail not a particularly well woman and towards the end of her time in Millbank, Prisoner No. 4, as she was known, became ill and the doctor was called.

*I asked to let me die but He (the doctor) looked so kindly at me – "no No 4 ,you have to get better and do more work yet." His kind face and the officer's care got me up again. I then had a nice hot dinner and a knife and fork to eat them with. I then was taken into the ward. I had been in a small room by myself. I got tea up there it was all right even those poor things who had done some to get there was nice and kind to me and treated me with the greatest of respect.*

*As I looked in there [sic] poor faces I felt a great big lump of gratitude raise up in my heart. Only for God's children I might have been worse than them...*[36]

Throughout her time in Millbank, it appears Rebecca developed further in her Christian faith, despite being surrounded by female villains of the sort she had spent most of her life with. She was known to many of the other women as "Jarrett of the Armstrong case" and met others who were in prison for a lot longer for similar crimes.

Soon, with spring in the air, Rebecca was set for release, when she was scooped up by The Salvation Army who took her under their wing once again. She spent the next forty years in their ranks, working for them mostly among the disadvantaged and street women, people who were living the life from which she had been "rescued". She was determined to serve Jesus Christ to the end of her days as a totally reformed character and in her memoir written towards the end of her life she remembered her release day and what it meant for her future life.

*I left Millbank prison on April 10, tried to open my home again but I could not it was too trying just coming myself out off [sic] prison.*

*Letters I had sent to me by people who said I was in the wrong place I ought to be shielded from outside life all together off [sic] course from outside. They did not understand my life. They felt I ought to be shut up in a box and never let out again… I should have lost my reason but my Precious Friend Mrs. Gen. Booth held on to me.*

*Here I am 40 years since I first entered the Salvation Army Home in Hanbury St., a poor drunken broken up woman. Mrs. Gen. and Mrs. Bramwell Booth did not look at that side. I was degraded sunken down low by drink. Their work was to try and raise me up…*

*Today I have defeated the devil drink 39 years. Here I am living amongst those who like myself once are fighting the drink. I pray each day for God to help me. I am now nearing my other Home, I am near 79 years in age but I am closing my earthly life with sincere gratitude to the Salvation Army and the precious officers for their care and devotion to me.*[37]

# EPILOGUE

After his release from prison, even while his professional reputation appeared unaffected by his trial, conviction, and incarceration, W. T. Stead's relationship with The Salvation Army, and particularly its founder William Booth, appeared to be at rock bottom.

Booth had distanced himself from the *Pall Mall Gazette* editor. No senior representative of The Salvation Army attended a rally the day after Stead's release from prison. This event at the Exeter Hall in London saw him heralded as a hero by among others the Young Men's Christian Association, who presented him with a Bible. However, despite the disappointing turn out from his Salvation Army friends, he took to the stage for more than an hour, committing himself to continuing the work of helping to throw a light on the darkness of the sex trade and the hypocrisy of the times.

Magnanimously, Mr Stead also thanked The Salvation Army "from the Chief of the Staff down to the humblest private" for their help over the previous trying months. It is interesting to note here that he failed to mention or offer any thanks to the General of the movement, William Booth.[1]

Stead returned to his family in Wimbledon and to his office in Northumberland Street and his campaigning journalism. Rather than trying to forget his time in the dock, he was determined to make a virtue of it. He wrote a pamphlet about his time in prison and when he walked free from Holloway he carried with him his prison uniform, having received permission from the friendly governor to do so. Each year, on the anniversary of his conviction – 10 November – he wore that uniform to work, with pride.

Although his influence declined over the years, Stead's time in the dock at the Old Bailey and period of imprisonment had made him more notorious as a person of passion and belief, prepared to go even to jail for his journalism, religious motivation, and worthy causes.

In succeeding years he would continue to fight for the cause of the "disinherited of the world"[2] and to expose privileged men whom he claimed "ruined" women, including in 1887, a Mrs Mildred Langworthy. According to Stead, this unfortunate woman had been the victim of a "fraudulent marriage" to millionaire Edward Langworthy, who had fathered her child but then fled the country after filing for bankruptcy.[3] The *Pall Mall Gazette* was among those that campaigned on her behalf and eventually Mrs Langworthy took the matter to court. Although it was proved that she had not been legally married, she received a judgment for "alimony" and a payout for breach of promise, although she never received the funds because her "husband", with whom she did eventually reunite, was bankrupt.[4]

Stead also continued his dabbling in foreign affairs and his interest in Russia remained. At one point during a visit there he met Tsar Alexander III and published a book called *The Truth About Russia*. In the years after leaving prison, his international travels also included a trip to Rome, after which he wrote his account of the Vatican in *The Pope and the New Era*.[5] Latterly, he became increasingly involved in the developing global Peace Movement.

As the years progressed, Stead also became increasingly interested in spiritualism – the belief that the spirits of dead people are able and want to communicate with the living, which is invariably facilitated through "mediums"[6] and it is perhaps this that also helped to alienate him from William Booth. Stead's growing fascination in the supernatural certainly helped to gradually destroy his political reputation and gave him a name for being something of an increasingly crazy zealot.[7]

Although he continued to maintain that his Christian faith was sincere, Stead's interest in spiritualism had begun early, towards the end of his time at the *Northern Echo* in Newcastle, and his arrival in London had seen him renew his interest.

He had attended his first séance in 1881 and over the years dipped in and out of the world of spiritualism, increasingly reporting premonitions and psychic episodes. Throughout his trial at the Old Bailey he put his calmness down to the fact that he "knew" he would be convicted and imprisoned. Indeed, when he finally heard the sentence against him from Mr Justice Lopes – three months – he had been taken aback.

As he wrote many years later,

> *I was so certain that I was going to prison for two months that I with difficulty restrained myself from saying: 'My Lord, have you not made a mistake? It ought to be two months.' I fortunately restrained myself. When I got into my cell I found that the sentence ran from the opening of the Session, and that the precise period of detention I had to undergo was two months and seven days. The Judge had come as near verifying my prediction as it was possible for him to do.*[8]

Apart from his journalism, Stead also resumed an interest in fiction writing, including in 1886, a story called "How the Mail Steamer went down in Mid Atlantic". He followed this up some years later, in 1892, with another tale entitled "From the Old World to the New". In years to come these stories were scrutinized closely as "premonitions" of his death.[9] By 1891 he was writing "real" ghost stories and in 1893 he created a quarterly magazine on spiritualism called *Borderland*, with him in the editor's chair, a short-lived venture but one which cast him increasingly as a strange and deluded character who was losing touch with reality. He reckoned to have contact with dead people, and he wrote up their stories via what was known as "automatic" writing, including one of his most famous works, "Letters from Julia" – based on "conversations" he claimed he had had with a dead American journalist called Julia Amis.[10]

Perhaps it was his increasingly peculiar behaviour which William Booth would have viewed with suspicion, as well as their falling out over the Maiden Tribute affair, that kept Stead and the General apart for a period. However, they did not remain alienated. Just a few years after the court case, Stead helped General Booth to write his landmark book on poverty, social justice, and Christian faith – *In Darkest England and the Way Out* – which was published just two weeks after the death of Booth's dear wife, Catherine.

When she had first felt a lump in her breast, Catherine had turned to their old friend Dr Heywood Smith. After the trial and the disclosure that he had been the physician who had "validated" Eliza Armstrong's virginity before she was taken away to France by The Salvation Army, the doctor had been severely reprimanded by the Royal College of Physicians. The British Lying-in Hospital, where he was part of the medical team, removed him from the staff and he had resigned his position as the Secretary of the British Medical Association.[11] But he had remained in practice and so it was he who first examined Catherine and referred her to an expert in the field, Sir James Paget at St Bartholomew's Hospital, who diagnosed cancer. Catherine Booth would be "promoted to Glory" – The Salvation Army's term for death – in October 1890.[12]

Whatever animosity there had been between William Stead and William Booth was long gone by 1912 – the year in which both died. Early in the year, just before Stead was due to once again travel to the USA, he wrote a tribute to the leader of The Salvation Army which would eventually be published in a journal called *The Fortnightly Review* in December 1912. In it, Stead recognized Booth's overwhelming motivations in life, and the depths of his spiritual nature.

*The great secret of his success is to be found in the
concentration of all the forces of a very strong personality
upon the achievement of a great end. He was from his
boyhood consumed by a passion for souls, a passion which
extended itself in later years to a great desire for the welfare
of their bodies, that is, on the human side. General Booth
himself would maintain that all his enthusiasm for humanity
would have profited him nothing had he not been sustained
and directed by the constant practice of earnest prayer.[13]*

As Stead's popularity had declined, he feared obscurity and had taken to touring the world when finances allowed, in the guise of an international peace keeper[14] advocating and preaching against war and conflict. This brought some invitations to conferences and on 17 March 1912 he had received a cable from New York inviting him to address "... the Great Men and Religious Congress in Carnegie Hall, April 22nd, with President Taft... We pay expenses. Subject World Peace".[15]

On Wednesday, 10 April, Stead boarded the ship which was to transport him across the Atlantic – the RMS *Titanic*. He and the majority of the 2,200 plus passengers and crew left the port of Southampton on the southern coast of England that day and after stopping briefly in Cherbourg, France and Queenstown (now Cobh), Ireland were due in New York on Wednesday morning, 17 April.

William Thomas Stead was one of the more than 1,500 people who died on 15 April 1912, when the *Titanic* – the largest ship in the world at the time and described as "unsinkable" – hit an iceberg and sunk south-west of Newfoundland.

It is said that when he heard that the ship was foundering, the "old" newspaper editor – although he was only sixty-two when he died – was unconcerned and retired to his cabin to read. He was later seen doing the same in the First Class Smoking Room, but there were also reports of him on deck, helping the last remaining women and children into life boats and giving up his own life jacket to another.[16] All kinds of apocryphal stories abound as to Stead's final hours – claims that he was the person to ask the orchestra to play several well-known songs, including "Nearer my God to Thee" as the ship sank, and that he stood praying at the rail as the vessel finally sank. Other accounts have Mr Stead clinging to a life raft and trying to help others to do the same, before finally succumbing to the icy water and slipping silently to the bottom of the ocean.[17] Whatever the details of the last moments of Stead's life, his passing was mourned across the world. Although his journalistic influence had declined in the years before his death, he had made an impact on his world. Two memorials were erected to him – one in London, on Victoria Embankment opposite Temple underground station and quite near to Fleet Street, and another in Central Park in New York.[18]

Just a few months after Stead's death, on 20 August 1912, the "General" of The Salvation Army William Booth also finally "laid down his sword" and died, aged eighty-three, to be succeeded, as planned, by his eldest son Bramwell Booth.

The Old Bailey trial had, in the end, not greatly affected the Booths, but it had raised the Army's profile considerably. And the Army continued to flourish. By the time of William Booth's death in 1912, it was thriving across the world, was in fifty-three countries and boasted nearly 16,000 officers or leaders and "cadets" in training. The worldwide membership of Salvationist "soldiers" was in the millions and the movement's reputation as a global church and charity organization was firmly established. It continued to grow under General Bramwell Booth, who was international leader almost up until his own death, at the age of seventy-three, in June 1929.

Rebecca Jarrett lived to the ripe old age of eighty-seven and died in 1928, having spent more than four decades within the ranks of The Salvation Army, working to rescue street girls. A month before her death she was a guest at a gathering of the Congress Hall Salvation Army in Clapton in London, a reunion of people from around Great Britain who were involved in the creation and growth of the organization's Women's Social Work. The meeting brought together around a thousand associates from across the country as well as General Bramwell Booth, his wife Florence, and other officer leaders. The hostess of the event was Commissioner Catherine Bramwell Booth, then head of The Salvation Army's burgeoning Women's Social Work, which had grown out of those small beginnings and the hospitality of Mrs Elizabeth Cotterill in Hanbury Street in the East End of London.[19] This was the same Catherine who was a babe in arms and being nursed by her mother Florence during the Old Bailey trial.

Rebecca Jarrett had been part of similar reunions across the years and she would not miss this one, despite her age. Her story had been penned some years earlier and she referred to it when, at the Clapton Congress Hall gathering, she reviewed her life, her own salvation, and what it meant for subsequent generations of vulnerable girls and young women.

*You know, I have often told you in the meetings – forty one years ago there was not a home in London to help women to get over the drink; they said it was no good, they never could.*

*Yes they can! I am one.*

*They said that after the age of twenty-five it was no use – women could never be made to give up lives of immorality.*

*Yes, they do, and turn out bright, beautiful women.*

*At seventeen years of age a poor girl could not be taken into any home with her baby. The only thing she could do was to go into the workhouse with it, and even there she was insulted by the rough men at the gate.*

*Today they have opened homes for the drunkard, and homes where they take in the lost girl, and homes for the mother with her dear little baby.*

*I am closing my life; I do earnestly ask that these doors be kept open for them.*[20]

A month later Rebecca Jarrett was "promoted to glory" and was buried with the Bible she took with her into Millbank Prison in 1885, which had been her companion during her six months of imprisonment.[21]

And what of Eliza Armstrong?

After the trial, the girl was returned to her parents. The newspapers continued to follow the Armstrongs, with *The Times* in particular running letters from various people involved in the case, including Mr Edward Thomas, the man who allegedly encouraged Mr and Mrs Armstrong to press charges against Stead.[22] At first, there were rumours that the Armstrongs might try to sue those involved in the case, but after taking advice, that idea was dropped. Perhaps, after all, they just wanted the fuss over the case to die down, so they could return to something resembling a normal life. However, thanks to a public subscription fund organized for them by Mr Poland, the junior prosecution counsel, the family were able to move away from their home in Charles Street.[23]

There are various ideas about what happened to Eliza Armstrong.

*The Times* reported soon after the trial that she had gone to The Princess Louise Home in Essex, also known as "The National Society for the Protection of Young Girls," where she would receive two years of education, after which she would enter service.[24] Some accounts, however, have her adopted by The Salvation Army; Bramwell Booth wrote that after the trial The Salvation Army assisted Eliza "more or less".[25] We know little more of Eliza except one hint that her life after the Old Bailey wasn't unhappy – she apparently once wrote a letter of thanks to Mr Stead, telling him that she had married a good man and was mother to six children.[26]

Like most ordinary individuals who live unremarkable lives, Eliza herself has faded with time. However, her contribution to the future and in particular, the protection of young girls in British society, should not be forgotten.

The newspaper campaign in which she figured so centrally helped to define the journalism of the future and the man who orchestrated it, William Thomas Stead, has gone down in history as the forerunner of the twenty-first-century UK tabloid media, with its focus on celebrity and scandal. Without Eliza, it could be said, The Salvation Army might have struggled to grow its reputation quite so quickly as the nineteenth century concluded.

Most importantly, Eliza's story helped to shine a spotlight on the facts of sex trafficking in Victorian London. This brought about a change in a law which, for the most part, has served to protect young people from sexual predators and exploitation right through to modern times. As some now call for the age of consent in the UK to be dropped back to fifteen and with the problem of sexual exploitation and trafficking still high on the agenda for many secular and Christian groups, including The Salvation Army, it is worth considering the case of a thirteen-year-old girl "bought" for the sex trade in 1885.

Unfortunately, there are still "Elizas" around the world – millions of young girls and other vulnerable men, women, and children, who find themselves at the mercy of others for whom they are a mere economic commodity ripe for exploitation. They are the victims of human trafficking – "the modern day slavery". If we take a moment to look up from our history books we may conclude that unfortunately, nothing much has changed and, perhaps, there is little we might do to change the status quo. But there are lessons to be learned from the Armstrong case. It shows us that, if we are to see an end, once and for all, to human trafficking – for sex or illegal labour purposes – it may not just be down to governments, charities, and even the media, to highlight and solve the problem.

As in Eliza Armstrong's time, society may wish to turn a blind eye to the issue or try to pretend that what they may see around them is just a part of life about which they can do nothing.

But for some, a reminder of a child bought for £5 and the court case which captured the imagination of the world in 1885 will be the impetus for courage. Because if there are to be no more Elizas, we may need to follow in the footsteps of those who have gone before, to make a noise against the pervading culture of the day; to shout loud that exploitation is simply unacceptable; to challenge complacency and a "not my problem" attitude which may prevail in living rooms, clubs, and even churches across our world. We may even be called upon to expose those who perpetuate the exploitation of others for their own personal and economic benefit, even if such action is to the detriment of our personal safety, reputation, and even our freedom.

If that is the final outcome of The Maiden Tribute of Modern Babylon articles then the legacy of the Armstrong Girl will have, at last, been fulfilled.

# A NOTE FROM THE AUTHOR

The idea for this title came about when I was writing my first book for Lion Hudson publishers: *William and Catherine – the love story of the founders of The Salvation Army, told through their letters* (Monarch Books 2013).

I was aware of The Maiden Tribute of Modern Babylon articles printed in a leading London newspaper in the 1880s that was followed by a high-profile court case in which The Salvation Army were involved. But until I began delving into the lives of William and Catherine Booth, who created this international Christian movement, I was really unaware of the finer details of the case, the reasons why it was so important at the time, and the fascinating individuals involved.

What I have discovered as I have looked back in history is intriguing. The sex trafficking of young girls was a real problem in mid to late Victorian England. I discovered a superficially respectable culture, and a government which appeared to turn a blind eye to the issue, at a time when the age of consent was just thirteen. This led me to ask the very difficult question – why on earth would anyone want to perpetuate a law which allowed sex with children whom we now regard as "minors"? Girls like the Armstrong Girl – the child Eliza who was at the centre of the court case – without whom we would not have this story at all.

I also discovered an inspiring campaigning newspaper editor, William Thomas (W. T.) Stead, described as "the first tabloid journalist". Stead's methods were extraordinary and undoubtedly self-serving, but also motivated by deep concern for the victims of the sex trade. He pushed the boundaries of journalism and made as many friends as enemies.

As I researched, it occurred to me that many of these themes are not stuck in the past but are incredibly modern. We unfortunately live at a time when exploitation and human trafficking, including for sexual purposes, are still commonplace and today there are people who would wish to see the age of consent reduced. Journalistic practices which shock and result in high profile court cases have again made the British headlines in recent years. And people still fight for the rights of others who have no voice of their own, sometimes to their own detriment.

Although the stories of W. T. Stead and the Maiden Tribute trial, and that of The Salvation Army's involvement in one of the great scandals of 1885 have been told before, in this book my aim is to bring many strands together and to present them to a new generation.

The materials I have drawn on for this re-telling of the Maiden Tribute story include some of the excellent books which have been written on the subject of W. T. Stead and other narratives about the early days of The Salvation Army and those campaigning for the rights of women in the mid to late Victorian era. Among the sources are contemporaneous newspaper articles, memoirs, and letters, and I have inter-connected these with extracts from some of the evidence given at the Maiden Tribute trial at the Old Bailey in October and November 1885.

The bibliography will give you details of the sources I've used to research this subject. I want to say a special thanks to the team at the University of Sheffield and their Old Bailey Online website for the use of these transcripts from the trial. I've been also greatly helped in my research by a fantastic website dedicated to the life and works of William Thomas Stead – www.attackingthedevil. co.uk – the W. T. Stead Resources site put together by the historian, writer, and web designer Owen Mulpetre (BA, MPhil). From this site I was able to source the articles contained in the "Maiden Tribute of Modern Babylon" series which also feature in this book.

Thanks to the team at The Salvation Army's International Heritage Centre in London for their help in sourcing so much of the fascinating Salvation Army side of the story. And thanks to the

British Library in London, where the personal letters of William and Catherine Booth are held in trust for the Booth family. Once again, as I did in my first book on the Booths, I have turned to some of their personal letters for inspiration about this particular period in Salvation Army history and, most particularly, for William Booth's take on Stead and his antics. I'm grateful to the Booth family for making the letters available through the British Library, which allowed me once again to hear the distinct voice of the founders of The Salvation Army speaking across more than a century since the Old Bailey trial.

Final thanks must also go to Lion Hudson for once again believing in me and to my editor, Alison Hull, for her attention to detail and endurance with this enthusiast and passionate author.

# ENDNOTES

## Chapter 1

1. *Old Bailey Proceedings Online* (t18851019–1031), trial of REBECCA JARRETT, WILLIAM THOMAS STEAD, SAMPSON JACQUES, WILLIAM BRAMWELL BOOTH, and ELIZABETH COMBE, Unlawfully taking Eliza Armstrong, aged 13, out of the possession and against the will of her father. *Other Counts* charging the taking from the possession of the mother. Eliza Armstrong evidence Oct. 23 1885. (www.oldbaileyonline. org, version 7.0, accessed 24 Feb. 2015).

2. W. T. Stead, "Notice to our Readers: A Frank Warning", The *Pall Mall Gazette*, July 4, 1885 [Online] Available at The W. T. Stead Resource Site. http://www.attackingthedevil.co.uk/pmg/tribute/notice.php (Date accessed 24 Feb. 2015)

3. Alison Plowden, *The Case of Eliza Armstrong: "a child of 13 bought for £5"*, London: British Broadcasting Corporation, 1974. p. 53.

4. *Ibid.*

5. Richard Collier, *The General Next to God: The Story of William Booth and The Salvation Army*, Collins, 1965, p. 127.

6. *Old Bailey Proceedings Online* (t18851019–1031), Unlawfully taking Eliza Armstrong: Eliza Armstrong evidence Oct. 23 1885. (www.oldbaileyonline. org, version 7.0, accessed 24 Feb. 2015).

7. *Ibid.*

## Chapter 2

1. Michael Pearson, *The Age of Consent: Victorian Prostitution and Its Enemies*, Newton Abbot: David and Charles, 1972, p. 23.

2. Pearson, *The Age of Consent*, p. 25.

3. Evangeline Holland, The Amorous Life of Edward VII: http://www. edwardianpromenade.com/royalty/the-amorous-life-of-edward-vii/ (last accessed 24 Feb. 2015).

4. Roger J. Green, *The Life and Ministry of William Booth, Founder of The Salvation Army*, Nashville: Abingdon Press, 2005, p. 151.

5. Pearson, *The Age of Consent*, p. 25.

6. Roy Hattersley, *Blood and Fire: William and Catherine Booth and the Salvation Army*, Little, Brown and Company, 1999, p. 307.

7. Pearson, *The Age of Consent*, p. 25.

8. William Acton, *Prostitution, Considered in its Moral, Social, and Sanitary Aspect, in London and other large cities and Garrison Towns, with Proposals*

*for the Control and Prevention of Attendant Evils*, 1857. Found on *The Great Social Evil: "The Hurlot's House" and Prostitutes in Victorian London*, Rhianna Shaw. http://www.victorianweb.org/authors/wilde/shaw.html

9. Pearson, *The Age of Consent*, p. 25.

10. *Ibid.*

11. Hattersley, *Blood and Fire*, p. 305.

## Chapter 3

1. *Rebecca Jarrett's Narrative*, original papers c. 1928, written in her own hand and held in The Salvation Army Heritage Centre, London.

2. Madge Unsworth, *Maiden Tribute: A study in Voluntary Social Service*, Salvationist Publishing and Supplies,1954, p. 22.

3. *Ibid.*

4. Jenty Fairbanks, *Booth's Boots: Social Service Beginnings in The Salvation Army*, The Salvation Army, 1983, p. 18.

5. Unsworth, *Maiden Tribute*, p. 22.

6. *Ibid.*

7. Lee Jackson, *Daily Life in Victorian London: An Extraordinary Anthology, Edmund Yates, His Recollections and Experiences 1885 Victorian London*, Ebooks No 4, 2011, Kindle edition.

8. Unsworth, *Maiden Tribute*, p. 23.

9. *Ibid.*

10. *Ibid.*

11. *Ibid.*

12. *Old Bailey Proceedings Online* (t18851019–1031), Unlawfully taking Eliza Armstrong: Rebecca Jarrett evidence Oct. 29 1885. (www.oldbaileyonline.org, version 7.0, accessed 24 Feb. 2015).

13. Unsworth, *Maiden Tribute*, pp. 23–24.

## Chapter 4

1. Unsworth, *Maiden Tribute*, p. 24.

2. http://en.wikipedia.org/wiki/Elijah_Cadman (last accessed 24 Feb. 2015).

3. *Ibid.*

4. Unsworth, *Maiden Tribute*, p. 24.

5. *Ibid.*

6. Unsworth, *Maiden Tribute*, p. 21.

7. Robert Sandall, *The History of The Salvation Army Volume III, Social Reform and Welfare Work*, Thomas Nelson and Sons Ltd: The Salvation Army, 1955, p. 27.

8. Unsworth, *Maiden Tribute*, p. 24.

9. *The War Cry*, 25 Oct. 1884, found in Unsworth, *Maiden Tribute*, p. 20.

10. Unsworth, *Maiden Tribute*, p. 25.

11. Bramwell Booth, *Echoes and Memories: The Salvation Army*, 1925, reprinted Hodder and Stoughton, 1977, p. 124.
12. Fairbanks, *Booth's Boots*, pp. 13–14.
13. *Sunday Circle*, 25 March 1933, found in Unsworth, *Maiden Tribute*, p. 25.
14. Florence Booth memoir, found in Unsworth, *Maiden Tribute*, p. 26.
15. *Ibid.*

## Chapter 5

1. *Old Bailey Proceedings Online* (t18851019–1031), Unlawfully taking Eliza Armstrong: Josephine Butler evidence November 2, 1885. (www.oldbaileyonline.org, version 7.0, accessed 24 Feb. 2015).
2. http://en.wikipedia.org/wiki/Contagious_Diseases_Acts (last accessed 24 Feb. 2015).
3. Hattersley, *Blood and Fire*, p. 309.
4. *Ibid.*
5. Green, *Life and Ministry of William Booth*, p. 153.
6. Green, *Life and Ministry of William Booth*, p. 152.
7. Booth, *Echoes and Memories*, pp. 125–126.

## Chapter 6

1. Victor Pierce Jones, *Saint or Sensationalist? The Story of WT Stead*: Gooday Publishers, 1988, p. 11.
2. W. Sydney Robinson, *Muckraker: the Scandalous Life and Times of W. T. Stead, Britain's First Investigative Journalist*, The Robson Press, 2013, p. 46.
3. Plowden, *Case of Eliza Armstrong*, p.120.
4. Robinson, *Muckraker*, pp. 47–48.
5. Pierce Jones, *Saint or Sensationalist?* p. 1.
6. Pierce Jones, *Saint or Sensationalist?* p. 2.
7. Pierce Jones, *Saint or Sensationalist?* p. 3.
8. W. T. Stead, Reminiscences of the Maiden Tribute Campaign (undated), quoted in Estelle W. Stead, *My Father*, pp. 19–20.
9. Robinson, *Muckraker*, pp. 2–3.
10. Robinson, *Muckraker*, p. 3.
11. *Ibid.*
12. Robinson, *Muckraker*, p. 11.
13. Pierce Jones, *Saint or Sensationalist?* p. 3.
14. Pierce Jones, *Saint or Sensationalist?* p. 4.
15. *Ibid.*
16. Robinson, *Muckraker*, p.16.
17. Robinson, *Muckraker*, p.15.
18. Robinson, *Muckraker*, p.14.
19. Robinson, *Muckraker*, p.17.

20. J. O. Baylen, "New Journalism in Late Victorian Britain", *The Australian Journal of Politics and History*, XVIII (1972) pp. 368–69 found in Robinson, *Muckraker*, p. 19.

## Chapter 7

1. *Old Bailey Proceedings Online* (t18851019–1031), Unlawfully taking Eliza Armstrong: William Thomas Stead evidence November 2, 1885. (www. oldbaileyonline.org, version 7.0, 24 Feb. 2015).
2. W. T. Stead, Reminiscences, quoted in Estelle W. Stead, *My Father*, pp. 125–126.
3. Bramwell Booth, *Echoes and Memories*, p. 128.
4. Estelle W. Stead, *My Father*, pp. 82–83.
5. Robinson, *Muckraker*, p. 24.
6. Robinson, *Muckraker*, p. 28.
7. Robinson, *Muckraker*, pp. 3–4.
8. Robinson, *Muckraker*, p. 35.
9. Robinson, *Muckraker*, p. 36.
10. Robinson, *Muckraker*, pp. 28–29.
11. http://en.wikipedia.org/wiki/List_of_Prime_Ministers_of_the_United_Kingdom#19th_century (last accessed 24 Feb. 2015).
12. Robinson, *Muckraker*, p. 41.
13. Robinson, *Muckraker*, p. 49.
14. Robinson, *Muckraker*, p. 54.
15. Robinson, *Muckraker*, p. 57.
16. Robinson, *Muckraker*, p. 58.
17. *Ibid.*
18. Pierce Jones, *Saint or Sensationalist?* p. 18.
19. Robinson, *Muckraker*, p. 58.
20. http://en.wikipedia.org/wiki/Charles_George_Gordon (last accessed 24 Feb. 2015).
21. Pierce Jones, *Saint or Sensationalist?* pp. 17–19.
22. Robinson, *Muckraker*, p. 59.
23. Robinson, *Muckraker*, p. 62.
24. Pierce Jones, *Saint or Sensationalist?* p. 20.
25. Robinson, *Muckraker*, p. 61.
26. Pierce Jones, *Saint or Sensationalist?* p. 21.
27. Robinson, *Muckraker*, p. 61.
28. http://en.wikipedia.org/wiki/1885_in_the_United_Kingdom (last accessed 24 Feb. 2015).
29. Robinson, *Muckraker*, p. 61.
30. Pierce Jones, *Saint or Sensationalist?* p. 17.

## Chapter 8

1. W. T. Stead, "We bid you be of Hope", *The Pall Mall Gazette*, July 4, 1885 [Online] Available: The W. T. Stead Resource Site. http://www.attackingthedevil.co.uk/pmg/tribute/hope.php (Date accessed 24 Feb. 2015).

2. Roger J. Green, *The Life and Ministry of William Booth*, Founder of The Salvation Army, Nashville: Abingdon Press, 2005, pp.151–152.

3. Hattersley, *Blood and Fire*, p. 311.

4. Hattersley, *Blood and Fire*, p. 312.

5. *Ibid.*

6. F. Booth-Tucker, *The Life of Catherine Booth*, Vol. 1, Salvation Army, 1892, found in Hattersley, p. 312.

7. Hattersley, *Blood and Fire*, pp. 312–313.

8. Pierce Jones, *Saint or Sensationalist?* p. 26.

9. *Old Bailey Proceedings Online* (t18851019–1031), Unlawfully taking Eliza Armstrong: William Thomas Stead evidence November 2, 1885. (www.oldbaileyonline.org, version 7.0, 24 Feb. 2015).

10. *Ibid.*

## Chapter 9

1. W. T. Stead, "The Maiden Tribute of Modern Babylon I: the Report of our Secret Commission", *The Pall Mall Gazette*, July 6, 1885. [Online] Available: The W. T. Stead Resource Site.
http://www.attackingthedevil.co.uk/pmg/tribute/mt1.php/ (last accessed 24 Feb. 2015).

2. *Ibid.*

3. W. T. Stead, "The Truth about our Secret Commission", *The Pall Mall Gazette*, July 9, 1885). [Online] Available: The W. T. Stead Resource Site. http://www.attackingthedevil.co.uk/pmg/tribute/truth.php (last accessed 24 Feb. 2015).

4. Booth, *Echoes and Memories*, p. 128.

5. W. T. Stead, "The Truth about our Secret Commission", *The Pall Mall Gazette*, July 9, 1885. [Online] Available: The W. T. Stead Resource Site. http://www.attackingthedevil.co.uk/pmg/tribute/truth.php (last accessed 24 Feb. 2015).

6. *Ibid.*

7. W. T. Stead, "The Maiden Tribute of Modern Babylon I: the Report of our Secret Commission", *The Pall Mall Gazette*, July 6, 1885. [Online] Available: The W. T. Stead Resource Site. http://www.attackingthedevil.co.uk/pmg/tribute/mt1.php (last accessed 24 Feb. 2015)

8. W. T. Stead, "We bid you be of Hope", *The Pall Mall Gazette*, July 4, 1885 [Online] Available: The W. T. Stead Resource Site. http://www.attackingthedevil.co.uk/pmg/tribute/hope.php (last accessed 24 Feb. 2015)

9. *Ibid.*
10. W. T. Stead, "The Maiden Tribute of Modern Babylon I: the Report of our Secret Commission", *The Pall Mall Gazette*, July 6, 1885. [Online] Available: The W.T. Stead Resource Site.
http://www.attackingthedevil.co.uk/pmg/tribute/mt1.php (last accessed 24 Feb. 2015).

### Chapter 10
1. W. T. Stead, "The Maiden Tribute of Modern Babylon I: the Report of our Secret Commission", *The Pall Mall Gazette*, July 6, 1885. [Online] Available: The W.T. Stead Resource Site.
http://www.attackingthedevil.co.uk/pmg/tribute/mt1.php (last accessed 24 Feb. 2015).
2. *Ibid.*
3. *Old Bailey Proceedings Online* (t18851019–1031), Unlawfully taking Eliza Armstrong: Eliza Armstrong evidence Oct. 23 1885. (www.oldbaileyonline. org, version 7.0, accessed 25 Feb. 2015).

### Chapter 11
1. Pearson, *Age of Consent*, p. 156.
2. Pierce Jones, *Saint or Sensationalist?* pp. 26–27.
3. *Ibid.*
4. *Ibid.*
5. W. T. Stead, "The Maiden Tribute of Modern Babylon II: the Report of our Secret Commission", *The Pall Mall Gazette*, July 6, 1885. [Online] Available: The W. T. Stead Resource Site.
http://www.attackingthedevil.co.uk/pmg/tribute/mt2.php (last accessed 24 Feb. 2015)
6. *Ibid.*
7. *Ibid.*
8. *Ibid.*
9. *Ibid.*
10. *Ibid.*
11. *Ibid.*
12. *Ibid.*
13. *Ibid.*

### Chapter 12
1. http://en.wikipedia.org/wiki/Eliza_Armstrong_case (last accessed 25 Feb. 2015).
2. Pearson, *Age of Consent*, p. 156.
3. Sandall, *History of The Salvation Army Volume III,* p 32.
4. Pierce Jones, *Saint or Sensationalist?* p. 27.

5. Pierce Jones, *Saint or Sensationalist?* p. 23.

6. Robinson, *Muckraker*, p. 74.

7. Robinson, *Muckraker*, p. 75.

8. http://en.wikipedia.org/wiki/George_Cavendish-Bentinck (last accessed 25 Feb. 2015).

9. http://en.wikipedia.org/wiki/Judge_Advocate_General_of_the_Armed_Forces (last accessed 25 Feb. 2015).

10. http://en.wikipedia.org/wiki/Cleveland_Street_scandal (last accessed 25 Feb. 2015).

11. Morris B. Kaplan, *Sodom on The Thames: Sex, Love, and Scandal in Wilde Times,* Cornell University, 2005. Part 3, West End Scandals, p. 201 (accessed through https://books.google.co.uk/books).

12. Plowden, *Case of Eliza Armstrong*, p.124.

13. W. T. Stead, "The Truth about our Secret Commission", *The Pall Mall Gazette,* July 9, 1885. [Online] Available: The W. T. Stead Resource Site. http://www.attackingthedevil.co.uk/pmg/tribute/truth.php (last accessed 24 Feb. 2015).

14. http://en.wikipedia.org/wiki/Mary_Jeffries (last accessed 25 Feb. 2015).

15. Pearson, *Age of Consent*, p. 99.

16. http://en.wikipedia.org/wiki/Mary_Jeffries (last accessed 25 Feb. 2015).

17. Julia Laite, *Common Prostitutes and Ordinary Citizens: Commercial Sex in London, 1885–1960*, Palgrave Macmillan, 2011, p. 54 (accessed online via http://books.google.co.uk/books).

18. http://en.wikipedia.org/wiki/Mary_Jeffries (last accessed 25 Feb. 2015).

19. Tom Cockburn, *Rethinking Children's Citizenship*, Palgrave Macmillan, 2012, p.104 (accessed online via http://books.google.co.uk/books).

20. http://en.wikipedia.org/wiki/Mary_Jeffries (last accessed 25 Feb. 2015).

21. *Ibid.*

22. Laite, *Common Prostitutes and Ordinary Citizens*, p. 55 (accessed online on http://books.google.co.uk/books).

23. *Ibid.*

24. W. T. Stead, "The Truth about our Secret Commission", *The Pall Mall Gazette,* July 9, 1885. [Online] Available: The W. T. Stead Resource Site. http://www.attackingthedevil.co.uk/pmg/tribute/truth.php (last accessed 24 Feb. 2015).

25. http://everything2.com/title/The+Maiden+Tribute+of+Modern+Babylon (last accessed 25 Feb. 2015).

26. W. T. Stead , "To Our Censors", *The Pall Mall Gazette,* July 13, 1885. [Online] Available: The W. T. Stead Resource Site. http://www.attackingthedevil.co.uk/pmg/tribute/censors.php (last accessed 24 Feb. 2015).

27. *Ibid.*
28. Booth, *Echoes and Memories*, pp. 130 –131.
29. http://en.wikipedia.org/wiki/1885_in_the_United_Kingdom (last accessed 25 Feb. 2015).
30. http://en.wikipedia.org/wiki/List_of_Prime_Ministers_of_the_United_Kingdom#19th_century (last accessed 25 Feb. 2015).
31. Booth, *Echoes and Memories*, p. 131.
32. Pearson, *Age of Consent*, p. 157.
33. *Ibid.*
34. *Ibid.*
35. Pearson, *Age of Consent*, p. 158.

## Chapter 13

1. W. T. Stead, "The Maiden Tribute of Modern Babylon III: the Report of our Secret Commission", *The Pall Mall Gazette*, July 8, 1885. [Online] Available: The W. T. Stead Resource Site.
http://www.attackingthedevil.co.uk/pmg/tribute/mt3.php (last accessed 24 Feb. 2015)
2. W. T. Stead, "To Our Friends the Enemy", *The Pall Mall Gazette*, July 9, 1885. [Online] Available: The W. T. Stead Resource Site.
http://www.attackingthedevil.co.uk/pmg/tribute/enemy.php (last accessed 24 Feb. 2015).
3. *Ibid.*
4. Pearson, *The Age of Consent*, p. 158.
5. W. T. Stead, "To Our Friends the Enemy", *The Pall Mall Gazette*, July 9, 1885. [Online] Available: The W. T. Stead Resource Site.
http://www.attackingthedevil.co.uk/pmg/tribute/enemy.php (last accessed 24 Feb. 2015).
6. Pearson, *The Age of Consent*, p. 159.

## Chapter 14

1. Sandall, *The History of The Salvation Army Volume III*, p. 37.
2. Hattersley, *Blood and Fire*, p. 317.
3. http://en.wikipedia.org/wiki/William_Vernon_Harcourt_(politician) (last accessed 26 Feb. 2015).
4. Booth, *Echoes and Memories*, p. 131.
5. Sandall, *The History of The Salvation Army Volume III*, pp. 35–36.
6. David Bennett, *William Booth and The Salvation Army: Up and Down the City Road*, Marshall Pickering, 1987, p. 119.
7. *Ibid.*
8. Sandall, *The History of The Salvation Army Volume III*, pp. 34–35.
9. Sandall, *The History of The Salvation Army Volume III*, p. 34.

10. *Ibid.*
11. Sandall, *The History of The Salvation Army Volume III*, p. 33.
12. Frederick Booth-Tucker, *The Life of Catherine Booth*, Vol 2, p. 353, Salvation Army 1892, found in Hattersley, p. 316.
13. *Ibid.*
14. Hattersley, *Blood and Fire*, p. 317.
15. Sandall, *History of The Salvation Army Volume III*, p. 34.
16. Sandall, *History of The Salvation Army Volume III*, p. 35.
17. Hattersley, *Blood and Fire*, p. 317.
18. Sandall, *History of The Salvation Army Volume III*, p. 36.
19. *Ibid.*
20. Hattersley, *Blood and Fire*, p. 317.
21. *Ibid.*
22. Sandall, *History of The Salvation Army Volume III*, p. 37.
23. Hattersley, *Blood and Fire*, p. 318.
24. The Salvation Army War Cry, August 15 1885, from Sandall, *History of The Salvation Army Volume III*, p. 37.
25. Hattersley, *Blood and Fire*, p. 318.
26. The Salvation Army War Cry, August 15 1885, from Sandall, *History of The Salvation Army Volume III*, p. 37.

## Chapter 15

1. Pearson, *The Age of Consent*, p. 170.
2. *Ibid.*
3. Pearson, *The Age of Consent*, p. 172.
4. Plowden, *The Case of Eliza Armstrong*, p. 9.
5. *Ibid.*
6. *Ibid.*
7. *Ibid.*
8. *Ibid.*
9. Pearson, *The Age of Consent*, p. 179.
10. Plowden, *The Case of Eliza Armstrong*, p. 10.
11. *Ibid.*
12. Pearson, *The Age of Consent*, p. 180.
13. Pearson, *The Age of Consent*, p. 186.
14. Pearson, *The Age of Consent*, p. 180.
15. Hattersley, *Blood and Fire*, p. 319.
16. Plowden, *The Case of Eliza Armstrong*, p. 10.
17. *Ibid.*
18. *Ibid.*
19. Robinson, *Muckraker*, p. 103.

20. *Ibid.*

21 "The Eliza Armstrong Case: Being a Verbatim Report of the Proceedings at Bow Street", *Pall Mall Gazette Supplement*, Oct. 3, 1885. [Online] Available: W. T. Stead Resource Site. http://www.attackingthedevil.co.uk/pmg/tribute/armstrong/bow/bowintro.php (last accessed 24 Feb. 2015).

22. Pearson, *The Age of Consent*, p. 187.

23. *Ibid.*

24. "The Eliza Armstrong Case: Being a Verbatim Report of the Proceedings at Bow Street", *Pall Mall Gazette Supplement*, Oct. 3, 1885. [Online] Available: W. T. Stead Resource Site. http://www.attackingthedevil.co.uk/pmg/tribute/armstrong/bow/bowintro.php (last accessed 24 Feb. 2015).

25. Plowden, *The Case of Eliza Armstrong*, p. 47.

26. Hattersley, *Blood and Fire*, p. 320.

27. Plowden, *The Case of Eliza Armstrong*, p. 37.

28. *The Freethinker*, 13 Sept. 1885: original copy found in The Salvation Army International Heritage Centre.

## Chapter 16

1. Booth Papers: Correspondence of William and Catherine Booth (British Library MS64799–64806) found in David Malcolm Bennett, *The Letters of William and Catherine Booth,* Camp Hill Publications, Brisbane, Australia. No. W.B. 164, letter dated September 13, 1885.

2. Booth, *Echoes and Memories,* p. 136.

3. *Ibid.*

4. Robinson, *Muckraker,* p. 104.

5. *Ibid.*

6. *Ibid.*

7. Collier, *The General Next to God,* p. 141.

8. Robinson, *Muckraker,* p. 105.

9. *Ibid.*

10. Plowden, *The Case of Eliza Armstrong,* p. 47.

11. Plowden, *The Case of Eliza Armstrong,* p. 51.

12. Booth Papers. Correspondence of William and Catherine Booth (British Library MS64799–64806) found in Bennett, *The Letters of William and Catherine Booth.* No. W.B. 164, letter dated September 13, 1885.

13. *Ibid.*

14. Pearson, *The Age of Consent,* pp. 188–189.

15. *Ibid.*

16. *Ibid.*

17. *Ibid.*

## Chapter 17

1. Plowden, *The Case of Eliza Armstrong*, p. 53.
2. http://www.cityoflondon.gov.uk/about-the-city/about-us/buildings-we-manage/Pages/old-bailey-history.aspx
3. *Old Bailey Proceedings Online* (t18851019–1031), Unlawfully taking Eliza Armstrong: Oct. 1885, indicted charges. (www.oldbaileyonline.org, version 7.0, accessed 26 Feb. 2015).
4. http://en.wikipedia.org/wiki/Henry_Lopes,_1st_Baron_Ludlow (last accessed 26 Feb. 2015).
5. Pearson, *The Age of Consent*, p. 191.
6. http://en.wikipedia.org/wiki/Harry_Bodkin_Poland (last accessed 26 Feb. 2015).
7. http://en.wikipedia.org/wiki/Henry_Matthews,_1st_Viscount_Llandaff (last accessed 26 Feb. 2015).
8. Booth, *Echoes and Memories*, p. 136.
9. *Ibid.*
10. *Ibid.*
11. Sandall, *History of The Salvation Army Volume III*, pp. 41–42.
12. Plowden, *The Case of Eliza Armstrong*, p. 54.
13. Booth, *Echoes and Memories*, p. 136.
14. Pearson, *The Age of Consent*, p. 192.
15. *Old Bailey Proceedings Online* (t18851019–1031), Unlawfully taking Eliza Armstrong: Eliza Armstrong evidence Oct. 23 1885. (www.oldbaileyonline.org, version 7.0, accessed 26 Feb. 2015).

## Chapter 18

1. *Old Bailey Proceedings Online* (t18851019–1031), Unlawfully taking Eliza Armstrong: Elizabeth Armstrong evidence starting Oct. 23 1885. (www.oldbaileyonline.org, version 7.0, accessed 26 Feb. 2015).
2. Pearson, *The Age of Consent*, p. 193.
3. *Old Bailey Proceedings Online* (t18851019–1031), Unlawfully taking Eliza Armstrong: Elizabeth Armstrong evidence Oct. 24 1885. (www.oldbaileyonline.org, version 7.0, accessed 26 Feb. 2015).
4. Pearson, *The Age of Consent*, pp. 194–195.
5. *Old Bailey Proceedings Online* (t18851019–1031), Unlawfully taking Eliza Armstrong: Elizabeth Armstrong evidence Oct. 24 1885. (www.oldbaileyonline.org, version 7.0, accessed 26 Feb. 2015).
6. *Ibid.*
7. Plowden, *The Case of Eliza Armstrong*, pp. 65–66.
8. *Old Bailey Proceedings Online* (t18851019–1031), Unlawfully taking Eliza Armstrong: Elizabeth Armstrong evidence Oct. 24 1885. (www.oldbaileyonline.org, version 7.0, accessed 26 Feb. 2015).

9. Plowden, *The Case of Eliza Armstrong*, p. 65.

10. *Pearson, The Age of Consent*, p. 200.

11. Plowden, *The Case of Eliza Armstrong*, p. 75.

12. *Old Bailey Proceedings Online* (t18851019–1031), Unlawfully taking Eliza Armstrong: Charles Armstrong evidence Oct. 27 1885. (www.oldbaileyonline.org, version 7.0, 26 Feb. 2015)

13. Pearson, *The Age of Consent*, p. 155

14. Hattersley, *Blood and Fire,* pp. 320–321.

15. *Old Bailey Proceedings Online* (t18851019–1031), Unlawfully taking Eliza Armstrong: Charles Armstrong evidence Oct. 27 1885. (www.oldbaileyonline.org, version 7.0, accessed 26 Feb. 2015).

16. *Ibid.*

17. Robinson, *Muckraker,* p. 107.

18. Robinson, *Muckraker,* p. 108.

## Chapter 19

1. Plowden, *The Case of Eliza Armstrong*, p. 72.

2. *Ibid.*

3. *Old Bailey Proceedings Online* (t18851019–1031), Unlawfully taking Eliza Armstrong: Ann Broughton evidence Oct. 26 1885. (www.oldbaileyonline.org, version 7.0, accessed 26 Feb. 2015).

4. *Ibid.*

5. *Ibid.*

6. *Ibid.*

7. *Ibid.*

8. *Old Bailey Proceedings Online* (t18851019–1031), Unlawfully taking Eliza Armstrong: Jane Farrer evidence Oct. 27 1885. (www.oldbaileyonline.org, version 7.0, accessed 26 Feb. 2015).

9. *Old Bailey Proceedings Online* (t18851019–1031), Unlawfully taking Eliza Armstrong: Ann Broughton evidence Oct. 26 1885. (www.oldbaileyonline.org, version 7.0, accessed 26 Feb. 2015).

10. *Old Bailey Proceedings Online* (t18851019–1031), Unlawfully taking Eliza Armstrong: Henry Smith evidence, Oct. 27 1885. (www.oldbaileyonline.org, version 7.0, accessed 26 Feb. 2015).

11. *Old Bailey Proceedings Online* (t18851019–1031), Unlawfully taking Eliza Armstrong: Charles Von Turnow evidence Oct. 28 1885. (www.oldbaileyonline.org, version 7.0, accessed 26 Feb. 2015).

12. *Old Bailey Proceedings Online* (t18851019–1031), Unlawfully taking Eliza Armstrong: Edward Borner evidence Oct. 27 1885. (www.oldbaileyonline.org, version 7.0, accessed 26 Feb. 2015).

13. *Ibid.*

14. *Old Bailey Proceedings Online* (t18851019–1031), Unlawfully taking Eliza Armstrong: Dr Heywood Smith evidence Oct. 27 1885. (www. oldbaileyonline.org, version 7.0, accessed 26 Feb. 2015).

## Chapter 20

1. *Sunday Circle,* 25 March 1933 in Unsworth, *Maiden Tribute,* p. 25.
2. Pearson, *The Age of Consent,* p. 202.
3. Pearson, *The Age of Consent,* pp. 202–203.
4. Unsworth, *Maiden Tribute,* pp. 33–34.
5. Collier, *The General Next to God,* pp. 142–143.
6. *Ibid.*
7. *Ibid.*
8. Booth, *Echoes and Memories,* p. 137.
9. Unsworth, *Maiden Tribute,* p. 34.
10. Collier, *The General Next to God,* p. 143.
11. Booth, *Echoes and Memories,* p. 138.
12. *Old Bailey Proceedings Online* (t18851019–1031), Unlawfully taking Eliza Armstrong: Oct. 1885, Blanche Young evidence Nov. 2 1885. (www. oldbaileyonline.org, version 7.0, accessed 26 Feb. 2015)
13. *Ibid.*
14. *Old Bailey Proceedings Online* (t18851019–1031), Unlawfully taking Eliza Armstrong: Oct. 1885, Professor James Stuart MP evidence Nov. 2 1885. (www.oldbaileyonline.org, version 7.0, accessed 26 Feb. 2015).

## Chapter 21

1. Plowden, *The Case of Eliza Armstrong,* p. 103.
2. *Ibid.*
3. *Old Bailey Proceedings Online* (t18851019–1031), Unlawfully taking Eliza Armstrong: William Thomas Stead re-examination Nov. 3 1885. (www. oldbaileyonline.org, version 7.0, accessed 26 Feb. 2015).
4. *Ibid.*
5. *Ibid.*
6. *Old Bailey Proceedings Online* (t18851019–1031), Unlawfully taking Eliza Armstrong: William Shaen evidence Nov. 3 1885. (www.oldbaileyonline. org, version 7.0, accessed 26 Feb. 2015).
7. *Old Bailey Proceedings Online* (t18851019–1031), Unlawfully taking Eliza Armstrong: Oct. 1885, Ralph Thicknesse evidence Nov. 3 1885. (www. oldbaileyonline.org, version 7.0, accessed 26 Feb. 2015).
8. *Ibid.*
9. *Ibid.*
10. *Old Bailey Proceedings Online* (t18851019–1031), Unlawfully taking Eliza Armstrong: Oct. 1885, Howard Vincent evidence Nov. 3 1885. (www. oldbaileyonline.org, version 7.0, accessed 26 Feb. 2015).

11. *Old Bailey Proceedings Online* (t18851019–1031), Unlawfully taking Eliza Armstrong: Oct. 1885, Benjamin Scott evidence Nov. 3 1885. (www.oldbaileyonline.org, version 7.0, accessed 26 Feb. 2015).

12. *Old Bailey Proceedings Online* (t18851019–1031), Unlawfully taking Eliza Armstrong: Oct. 1885, Lord Dalhousie evidence Nov. 3 1885. (www.oldbaileyonline.org, version 7.0, accessed 26 Feb. 2015).

13. Plowden, *The Case of Eliza Armstrong*, p. 119.

## Chapter 22

1. *Old Bailey Proceedings Online* (t18851019–1031), Unlawfully taking Eliza Armstrong: Oct. 1885, Elizabeth Combe evidence Nov. 3 1885. (www.oldbaileyonline.org, version 7.0, accessed 26 Feb. 2015).

2. *Ibid.*

3. *Old Bailey Proceedings Online* (t18851019–1031), Unlawfully taking Eliza Armstrong: Oct. 1885, William Bramwell Booth evidence Nov. 3 1885. (www.oldbaileyonline.org, version 7.0, accessed 26 Feb. 2015).

4. *Ibid.*

5. *Ibid.*

6. Booth, *Echoes and Memories*, p. 138.

7. Booth, *Echoes and Memories*, p. 137.

8. Robinson, *Muckraker*, p. 107.

9. Pearson, *The Age of Consent,* p. 209.

10. *Ibid.*

11. Pearson, *The Age of Consent,* pp. 209–210.

12. Plowden, *The Case of Eliza Armstrong*, p. 121.

13. Plowden, *The Case of Eliza Armstrong*, p. 122.

14. David Bentley, *English Criminal Justice in the Nineteenth Century,* The Hambledon Press 1998, p. 185, accessed through https://books.google.co.uk

15. Pearson, *The Age of Consent,* p. 210.

16. Plowden, *The Case of Eliza Armstrong*, p. 123.

17. *The Times* 11 Nov. 1885, found in Hattersley, *Blood and Fire,* pp. 321–322.

18. *Ibid.*

19. W. T. Stead, Reminiscences, Quoted in Estelle W. Stead, *My Father,* p. 130.

20. Collier, *The General Next to God,* p. 143.

21. Plowden, *The Case of Eliza Armstrong*, p. 123.

## Chapter 23

1. W. T. Stead, Reminiscences, Quoted in Estelle W. Stead, *My Father*, p. 123.

2. Collier, *The General Next to God,* p. 143.

3. W. T. Stead, Reminiscences, Quoted in Estelle W. Stead, *My Father,* p. 132.

4. Collier, *The General Next to God,* p. 143.

5. W. T. Stead, Reminiscences, Quoted in Estelle W. Stead, *My Father,* pp. 132–133.

6. Pearson, *The Age of Consent*, p. 210.
7. W. T. Stead, Reminiscences, Quoted in Estelle W. Stead, *My Father*, p. 133.
8. W. T. Stead, Reminiscences, Quoted in Estelle W. Stead, *My Father*, pp. 133–134.
9. W. T. Stead, Reminiscences, Quoted in Estelle W. Stead, *My Father*, pp. 134.
10. Harold Begbie, *Life of William Booth: Founder and First General of The Salvation Army. Vol. 2,* The Macmillan Company, 1920. (Kindle edition) Ch. 4.
11. Hattersley, *Blood and Fire*, p. 323.
12. Booth Papers: Correspondence of William and Catherine Booth (British Library MS64799-64806), found in Bennett, *The Letters of William and Catherine Booth*, No. WB165, letter dated November 9, 1885.
13. Plowden, *The Case of Eliza Armstrong*, p.133.
14. Hattersley, *Blood and Fire*, pp. 322–323.
15. Plowden, *The Case of Eliza Armstrong*, p.135.
16. *Ibid.*
17. *Ibid.*

## Chapter 24

1. http://en.wikipedia.org/wiki/Coldbath_Fields_Prison (last accessed 26 Feb. 2015).
2. *Ibid.*
3. Robinson, *Muckraker*, p.110.
4. Pearson, *The Age of Consent*, p. 212.
5. http://en.wikipedia.org/wiki/The_Morning_Post (last accessed 26 Feb. 2015).
6. Pearson, *The Age of Consent*, p. 212.
7. Benjamin Waugh, *William T. Stead: a Life for the People*, London: Vickers, 1885. [Online] Available: W. T. Stead Resource Site. http://www.attackingthedevil.co.uk/worksabout/waughbook.php (last accessed 26 Feb. 2015).
8. Estelle W. Stead, *My Father*, p. 136.
9. *Ibid.*
10. Estelle W. Stead, *My Father*, p. 137.
11. Hattersley, *Blood and Fire*, p. 323.
12. Pierce Jones, *Saint or Sensationalist?* p. 31.
13. *Ibid.*
14. Letter from W. T. Stead to his sister, in Estelle W. Stead, *My Father*, p. 139.
15. Estelle W. Stead, *My Father*, p. 147.
16. Robinson, *Muckraker*, p. 112.
17. S. Koss, *The Rise and Fall of the Political Press in Britain*, London: Fontana, 1990, pp. 262–263, quoted in Robinson, *Muckraker*, p. 112.

18. W. T. Stead letter to Bramwell Booth Nov. 19 1885 (written from Holloway prison), found in Begbie, *Life of William Booth*, Ch. 4.

19. Letter from W. T. Stead to his sister, in Estelle W. Stead, *My Father*, pp. 141–142.

20. W. T. Stead letter to Bramwell Booth Nov. 19, 1885 (written from Holloway prison), found in Begbie, *Life of William Booth*, Ch. 4.

21. W. T. Stead letter to Bramwell Booth Dec. 13 1885 (written from Holloway prison), found in Begbie, *Life of William Booth*, Ch 4.

22. Robinson, *Muckraker*, p. 113.

23. W. T. Stead, "Government by Journalism", *The Contemporary Review*, vol. 49, 1886. [Online] Available: W. T. Stead Resource Site. http://www.attackingthedevil.co.uk/steadworks/gov.php (Date accessed 26 Feb. 2015).

24. Letter from W. T. Stead to his sister, in Estelle W. Stead, *My Father*, p.142.

25. Pierce Jones, *Saint or Sensationalist?* p. 31.

26. http://en.wikipedia.org/wiki/Millbank_Prison (last accessed 26 Feb. 2015).

27. http://www.victorianlondon.org/prisons/millbank.htm (last accessed 26 Feb. 2015).

28. Unsworth, *Maiden Tribute*, p. 36.

29. Catherine Bramwell Booth, *Catherine Booth: the story of her loves*, Hodder and Stoughton, 1970, p. 397.

30. Hattersley, *Blood and Fire*, p. 323.

31. Booth Papers: Correspondence of William and Catherine Booth (British Library MS64799–64806) found in Bennett, *The Letters of William and Catherine Booth*. No. WB168, letter dated November 11 1885.

32. Begbie, *Life of William Booth*, Ch. 4.

33. *Ibid.*

34. Hattersley, *Blood and Fire*, p. 323.

35. *Rebecca Jarrett's Narrative*: original papers c. 1928.

36. *Ibid.*

37. *Ibid.*

## Epilogue

1. Hattersley, *Blood and Fire*, p. 323.

2. Robinson, *Muckraker*, p.133.

3. Judith R. Walkowitz, *City of Dreadful Delight: Narratives of Sexual Danger in Late-Victorian London*: University of Chicago Press, 1992, p. 126 (accessed on https://books.google.co.uk/books).

4. http://www.edwardianpromenade.com/scandal/sin-and-scandal-the-langworthy-case-of-1887/ (last accessed 26 Feb. 2015).

5. W. T. Stead Timeline. [Online] Available: The W. T. Stead Resource Site. http://www.attackingthedevil.co.uk/timeline.php (last accessed 26 Feb. 2015).

6. http://en.wikipedia.org/wiki/Spiritualism (last accessed 26 Feb. 2015).

7. W. T. Stead & Spiritualism. [Online] Available: The W. T. Stead Resource Site. http://www.attackingthedevil.co.uk/spiritualism (last accessed 26 Feb. 2015).

8. W. T. Stead, Reminiscences, quoted in Estelle W. Stead, *My Father,* p. 134.

9. W. T. Stead & Spiritualism. [Online] Available: The W.T. Stead Resource Site. http://www.attackingthedevil.co.uk/spiritualism (last accessed 26 Feb. 2015).

10. *Ibid.*

11. Hattersley, *Blood and Fire,* p. 324.

12. Booth, *Catherine Booth,* p. 417.

13. William T. Stead, "A Great Heart", published in *Fortnightly Review,* December 1912, pp. 1042–50, included in R.G. Moyles (ed) *I Knew William Booth: an Album of Remembrance,* Crest Books, 2007, p. 89.

14. Robinson, *Muckraker,* p. 249.

15. Pierce Jones, *Saint or Sensationalist?* p. 78.

16. Robinson, *Muckraker,* p. 251.

17. Pierce Jones, *Saint or Sensationalist?* p. 81.

18. Pierce Jones, *Saint or Sensationalist?* p. 83.

19. Unsworth, *Maiden Tribute,* p. 163.

20. Unsworth, *Maiden Tribute,* pp. 163–164.

21. Unsworth, *Maiden Tribute,* p. 163.

22. Hattersley, *Blood and Fire,* p. 324.

23. Plowden, *The Case of Eliza Armstrong,* p.141.

24. Hattersley, *Blood and Fire,* p. 324.

25. Booth, *Echoes and Memories,* p. 139.

26. Plowden, *The Case of Eliza Armstrong,* p. 141.

# BIBLIOGRAPHY

## ORIGINAL SOURCE MATERIAL

*Old Bailey Proceedings Online* (t18851019-1031). Trial of REBECCA JARRETT WILLIAM THOMAS STEAD SAMPSON JACQUES WILLIAM BRAMWELL BOOTH ELIZABETH COMBE, October 1885, Unlawfully taking Eliza Armstrong, aged 13, out of the possession and against the will of her father. *Other Counts* charging the taking from the possession of the mother. (www. oldbaileyonline.org, version 7.0, accessed 26 Feb 2015)

*The Letters of William and Catherine Booth*: originals held in the British Library are part of the Booth family papers, presented by Miss Catherine Bramwell-Booth, O.B.E., O.F., granddaughter of William and Catherine Booth, 22 June 1987.

BOOTH PAPERS Vols I–IV. Correspondence of William and Catherine Booth; 1852–1861. Four volumes. MS 64799–64802.

BOOTH PAPERS Vols V–VIII. Including letters and papers of Catherine Booth, the letters chiefly addressed to her parents John and Sarah Mumford; [1847]–[late 1870s?]. Four volumes. MS 64803-64806.

David Malcolm Bennett, *The Letters of William and Catherine Booth* – reproduced with permission and edited by David Malcolm Bennett, ©2003 The Salvation Army (The letters): © 2003 & 2011 David Malcolm Bennett (Introductory material and footnotes). Published by Camp Hill Publications (Brisbane, Australia).

*Rebecca Jarrett's Narrative*: original papers c. 1928, written in her own hand and held in The Salvation Army International Heritage Centre, London.

*The Freethinker,* Sept. 13 1885: original copy found in The Salvation Army International Heritage Centre, London.

## BOOKS

Cyril Barnes, *Booth's England,* Baldock: Egon Publishers Ltd, 2000.

Cyril Barnes, *God's Army*, Lion Publishing, 1978.

Cyril Barnes, *Words of Catherine Booth,* London: Salvationist Publishing and Supplies, 1981.

Harold Begbie, *Life of William Booth, Founder and First General of The Salvation Army* Vol 2, The Macmillan Company, 1920 (Kindle edition).

David Bennett, *William Booth and The Salvation Army: Up and Down the City Road*, Marshall Pickering, 1987.

David Malcolm Bennett, *The General: William Booth* Vol 2: Xulon Press, 2003.

David Bentley, *English Criminal Justice in the Nineteenth Century*, The Hambledon Press, 1998, p. 185 – excerpts accessed through https://books.google.co.uk

Bramwell Booth, *Echoes and Memories*, The Salvation Army, 1925, reprinted Hodder and Stoughton, 1977.

Catherine Bramwell Booth, *Catherine Booth: the story of her loves*, Hodder and Stoughton, 1970.

Minnie Lindsay Carpenter, *William Booth, Founder of The Salvation Army*, London: The Epworth Press (Edgar C. Barton).

Tom Cockburn, *Rethinking Children's Citizenship*, Palgrave Macmillan, 2012 – excerpts accessed via http://books.google.co.uk/books

Richard Collier, *The General Next to God: The Story of William Booth and The Salvation Army*, Collins, 1965.

Derek Elvin, *Catherine Booth 1829–1890*, France, The Salvation Army Éditions du Signe, 2010.

Jenty Fairbanks, *Booth's Boots: The beginnings of Salvation Army Social Work*, The Salvation Army, 1983.

Christine Garwood, *Mid-Victorian Britain 1850–1889*, Oxford: Shire Living Histories, Shire Publications Ltd., 2011.

Roger J. Green, *The Life and Ministry of William Booth, Founder of The Salvation Army*, Nashville: Abingdon Press, 2005.

Stephen Grinsted, *A Short History of The Salvation Army*, London: edited by Major Stephen Grinsted with assistance of Salvation Army International Heritage Staff and The Salvation Army Schools and Colleges Unit UK, The Salvation Army Shield Books, 2012.

Roy Hattersley, *Blood and Fire: William and Catherine Booth and Their Salvation Army*, London: Little, Brown and Company, 1999.

Glenn K. Horridge, *The Salvation Army Origins and Early Days, 1865–1900*, Godalming Surrey: Ammonite Books, 1993.

Lee Jackson, *Daily Life in Victorian London: An Extraordinary Anthology*, Victorian London Ebooks No 4, 2011.

Morris B. Kaplan, *Sodom on the Thames: Sex, Love, and Scandal in Wilde Times*, Cornell University, 2005, Part 3 West End Scandals – excerpt accessed through https://books.google.co.uk/books

Julia Laite, *Common Prostitutes and Ordinary Citizens: Commercial Sex in London, 1885–1960*, Palgrave Macmillan, 2011 – accessed online via http://books.google.co.uk/books

Cathy Le Feuvre, *William and Catherine: the love story of the founders of The Salvation Army told through their letters*, Monarch Books, 2013.

R. G. Moyles (ed), *I Knew William Booth: an Album of Remembrance*, USA: Crest Books, 2007.

Michael Pearson, *The Age of Consent: Victorian Prostitution and its Enemies*, Newton Abbot: David and Charles, 1972.

Victor Pierce Jones, *Saint or Sensationalist? The Story of W.T. Stead*, Gooday Publishers, 1988.

Alison Plowden, *The Case of Eliza Armstrong: a child of 13 bought for £5*, the British Broadcasting Corporation, 1974.

W. Sydney Robinson, *Muckraker: the Scandalous Life and Times of W.T. Stead, Britain's First Investigative Journalist*, The Robson Press, 2013.

Robert Sandall, *The History of The Salvation Army Volume III: Social Reform and Welfare Work*, Thomas Nelson and Sons Ltd, 1955.

Estelle W. Stead, *My Father, Personal & Spiritual Reminiscences*, New York: George H. Doran Company, 1913 – accessed on catalog.hathitrust.org/Record/006606665.

Madge Unsworth, *Maiden Tribute: A study in Voluntary Social Service*, Salvationist Publishing and Supplies, 1954.

Judith R. Walkowitz, *City of Dreadful Delight: Narratives of Sexual Danger in Late-Victorian London*, University of Chicago Press, 1992 – excerpt accessed on https://books.google.co.uk/books

# INTERNET SOURCES

**The W. T. Stead Resource Site** <http://www.attackingthedevil.co.uk> and sub sites as below. Copyright ©2012 Owen Mulpetre (BA, MPhil). All rights reserved.

http://www.attackingthedevil.co.uk/pmg/tribute/censors.php

http://www.attackingthedevil.co.uk/pmg/tribute/enemy.php

http://www.attackingthedevil.co.uk/pmg/tribute/hope.php

http://www.attackingthedevil.co.uk/pmg/tribute/mt1.php

http://www.attackingthedevil.co.uk/spiritualism

http://www.attackingthedevil.co.uk/steadworks/sally.php

http://www.attackingthedevil.co.uk/steadworks/tribute.php

http://www.attackingthedevil.co.uk/timeline.php

Benjamin Waugh: William T. Stead: a Life for the People (1885) from http://www.attackingthedevil.co.uk/worksabout/waughbook.php

**Salvation Army Sources**

www.salvationarmy.org/ihq

www.salvationarmy.org.uk

www.salvationarmy.org.uk/uki/heritage

www.salvos.org.au

## *Other Internet Sources*

http://www.edwardianpromenade.com/royalty/the-amorous-life-of-edward-vii

http://www.edwardianpromenade.com/scandal/sin-and-scandal-the-langworthy-case-of-1887/Evangeline Holland

http://www.victorianweb.org/authors/wilde/shaw.html – "The Great Social Evil: 'The Harlot's House' and Prostitutes in Victorian London" by Rhianna Shaw

http://en.wikipedia.org/wiki/Cleveland_Street_scandal

http://en.wikipedia.org/wiki/Spiritualism

http://everything2.com/title/The+Maiden+Tribute+of+Modern+Babylon

http://en.wikipedia.org/wiki/1885_in_the_United_Kingdom

http://en.wikipedia.org/wiki/List_of_Prime_Ministers_of_the_United_Kingdom#19th_century

http://en.wikipedia.org/wiki/Victorian_era#Prostitution

http://en.wikipedia.org/wiki/Sexual_Offences_Act_1967

# BIBLIOGRAPHY

http://en.wikipedia.org/wiki/Marriage_Act_1753

http://www.workhouses.org.uk/StMarylebone

The Builder, May 1868 found on http://www.workhouses.org.uk/StMarylebone

http://logicmgmt.com/1876/overview/medicine/hospitals.htm

http://en.wikipedia.org/wiki/Coldbath_Fields_Prison

http://en.wikipedia.org/wiki/Millbank_Prison

http://www.victorianlondon.org/prisons/millbank.htm

http://en.wikipedia.org/wiki/Common-law_marriage

http://www.cityoflondon.gov.uk/about-the-city/about-us/buildings-we-manage/Pages/old-bailey-history.aspx

http://en.wikipedia.org/wiki/Florence_Nightingale

http://en.wikipedia.org/wiki/Elijah_Cadman

http://en.wikipedia.org/wiki/Florence_Eleanor_Soper

http://en.wikipedia.org/wiki/Charles_George_Gordon

http://en.wikipedia.org/wiki/William_Vernon_Harcourt_(politician)

http://en.wikipedia.org/wiki/George_Cavendish-Bentinck

http://en.wikipedia.org/wiki/Mary_Jeffries

http://en.wikipedia.org/wiki/Harry_Bodkin_Poland

http://en.wikipedia.org/wiki/Henry_Matthews,_1st_Viscount_Llandaff

http://en.wikipedia.org/wiki/The_Morning_Post

# William and Catherine

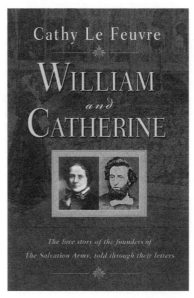

*The love story of the founders of The Salvation Army, told through their letters*

### Cathy Le Feuvre

*"A brilliant new take on the story of William and Catherine Booth in which their personalities, love for each other and achievements come alive in an unprecedented way. A gem of a book."*

**GENERAL JOHN LARSSON (RTD)**

When William Booth met Catherine Mumford in 1852, it was the start of a story that would change the lives of millions of people across the world. Out of their love sprang a new and radical international Christian movement – The Salvation Army.

Throughout their life William and Catherine, when apart, exchanged letters and notes expressing not only their deep love but also a lasting friendship and mutual respect which would survive the challenges of separation, ill health, the struggle of raising a large family, opposition, disappointment and professional uncertainty. The letters, spanning nearly 40 years, reveal both the everyday minutiae of life in Victorian times, and the challenges of being revolutionary Christian thinkers in the second half of the 19th century.

ISBN 978 0 85721 312 9 | £9.99 | $14.99